Richards

WITHDRAWN

MODERN GREAT AMERICANS

ALEXANDER GRAHAM BELL

Modern Great Americans

TWENTY SHORT BIOGRAPHIES OF GREAT AMERICANS
OF MODERN TIMES WHO WON WIDE RECOGNITION
FOR ACHIEVEMENTS IN VARIOUS TYPES
OF ACTIVITY

By

Frederick Houk Law

EDITOR OF "MODERN SHORT STORIES," "MODERN ESSAYS AND STORIES,"
"MODERN PLAYS: SHORT AND LONG," ETC., ETC.

The Century Co.
NEW YORK   LONDON

PREFACE

In this book I have told the biographies of twenty great Americans of modern times, who won fame both within the United States and also in other lands. I have included in this company of great Americans those who performed notable constructive services for the good of mankind, in invention, construction, or science; in literature, nature study, or art; in exploration, or military leadership; in medicine, philanthropy, or statesmanship. In the stories of such men as those named here, all of whom, whether born to poverty or to wealth, worked with their whole hearts in their tasks, tirelessly, and persistently faced all obstacles with a courage that would not admit defeat; and at last won for the generations yet to come, benefits beyond all price,—in the stories of such men I find a kind of heroism greater than the heroism of romance; a kind of wisdom worthy of imitation; and a definite inspiration to the carrying on of the daily task, whatever that task may be.

FREDERICK HOUK LAW.

1926.

CONTENTS

ILLUSTRATIONS

Modern Great Americans

MODERN GREAT AMERICANS

THE CIRCUMSTANCES THAT LEAD TO GREATNESS

Who can read the biography of any great person without wondering about the circumstances that lead to greatness? Why is it that a few most fortunate people lift themselves in achievement so far above all their fellows? Are they of different clay? Had others had equal opportunities, could they have lifted themselves equally high? Does greatness spring principally from forces within a man's own nature, or does it come more from external influences? Is greatness a spark of divine fire, or merely the result of the ceaseless play of circumstance? Do great men's lives set for us examples that we may hope to follow, or do they show us only the happy results of the workings of blind fate?

Here in this volume, gathered together, in a few hundred pages, are the dramatic stories of twenty lives. Here, as on a printed roll of fame, are gathered together the moving life stories that twenty different Americans worked out slowly and patiently through the years, none of them knowing at the time how their stories would develop, nor how they would end. Here are romances more thrilling and more amazing than any that writers of fiction produce: the story of Alexander Bell, the teacher of the deaf and dumb, who finally enabled people to talk across hills and valleys; of John Burroughs, the farm boy, who at last led thousands to take interest in his outdoor world; of Luther Burbank, the gardener who made nature perform his bidding and create new flowers and fruits for the benefit of man; of Andrew Carnegie, once an unknown poverty-stricken operative in a factory, who

3

became the most generous and princely of idealists; of Alexis Carrel, the young surgeon who found new ways to save human life; of Samuel L. Clemens, in early manhood an uneducated pilot on a Mississippi steam-boat, and in mature life the most popular of writers; of Thomas A. Edison, once newsboy on a train, who became the maker of a thousand wonders; of George W. Goethals, a soldier who made the Panama Canal; of William C. Gorgas, an army surgeon apparently destined to obscurity, who freed the world from yellow fever; of Albert A. Michelson, an immigrant boy who became a scientist able to measure the stars; of Robert A. Millikan, the earnest student who went into the world beyond the microscope; of Robert E. Peary, a rural surveyor who ended by planting the American flag upon the North Pole; of John J. Pershing, the quiet persistent soldier who finally led an army of millions of men; of Theodore Richards, the patient chemist who weighed atoms; of Theodore Roosevelt, once a sickly boy, who led a life so strenuous that it glowed with romance from beginning to end; of Elihu Root, the lawyer, who put before the world his great ideals of peace; of John S. Sargent, the artist; of Henry van Dyke, the preacher and teacher who became an artist in words; of Woodrow Wilson, who studied government all his life, and at last led the United States through the greatest of its wars; and finally, of the marvelous Wright brothers, bicycle makers, who invented the means of perfecting human flight.

In some way or another, every one of these life stories is strange beyond mention; for every one of the men, in some way, accomplished what men before had thought impossible.

"There were great men in the days of old," people say, indicating thereby that the days of great men have passed. In the face of what these twenty great Americans did, people may well say, "There are great men in the present." They may even add, "The great men of modern times not only equal the men of the past; they excel them, for they work with as noble ideals and as lofty purposes, but they follow more complicated processes and achieve infinitely farther-reaching results. In the presence of such a company as the twenty whose life stories are told here, we may well feel proud of the times in which we live.

These twenty modern great men are all Americans, not all by birth, nor by citizenship, but by living in the United States, feeling the influence of the great forces of American life, and setting forth the aims, the ideals, the methods, and the spirit of the progressive, forward-looking America in which we live. In their presence we feel a satisfying pride in a land that gives opportunity for such lives, that stimulates such worthy efforts, and that gives both money and fame to those who do great things for the world.

Heredity played a strong part in making all these men great. Strong, hearty forbears; God-fearing, energetic people; educated people; people with high ideals, paved the way toward descendants who at last could accomplish what they themselves perhaps had visioned dimly and hoped for in vain.

Environment, too, affected every man. Unparalleled physical opportunities and the apparently chance determination of a thousand circumstances aided these great ones of the earth to do what none of their people before them had been able to do. A world full of gifts offered itself to them and helped to make them what they became.

Then, also, the provision of materials, of tools and of methods, by generations of people, from the days when the first unknown savages hollowed logs or made rude wheels down to the days when scientists prepared the more immediate way, aided these men. The storing away of knowledge in books, the teachings of schools and colleges, all the groping work of generations that went before them entered into the making of their own lives and helped them to become great. The race that produced them is great; not they alone. Through them speak the ages.

Even then they could have done little if they had not come into the world in a fortunate time. It was the development of the use of iron and steel, as well as the character of Andrew Carnegie, that gave the great ironmaster his greatness; it was the necessity to construct the Panama Canal, as well as the personality of George W. Goethals, that helped the man to become famous. It was the World War, as well as the unconquerable spirit of Woodrow Wilson and of General Pershing, that made those two men noted. So it was with all the others, and so it is with every person who does anything, whether it be good or bad—circumstances always help to make the man.

Two facts, however, stand out in no uncertain light, and give to the men themselves the glory that people commonly ascribe to them. The first is, that one and all greatly desired to learn and to do. Whether or not they inherited tendencies that led them to be inquirers and doers, builders and makers, leaders and stimulators, it is wholly certain that they did, every one of them, work most earnestly to gain knowledge, and try most diligently to work with it. As one reads life after life of these twenty great men he wonders at the intensity of the effort that every man gave to gain information in the field that interested him most. He wonders all the more when he sees that most of these great ones did not find it easy to gain the information that they sought; that many of them, in fact, educated themselves; broke down all barriers to gain knowledge or ability; that many of them risked health, and even life itself, in the quest for knowledge; set themselves lessons to learn, and learned them, whatever the cost.

The second fact that stands out as a determining factor is that every man worked with the most astonishing persistence, putting his whole heart into what he had set himself to perform, permitting nothing to stand in his way. One and all, these men succeeded because they had iron determination, persistent and utterly resistless will power. They would not admit defeat. Baffled, turned back, temporarily laughed at or maligned, they still went on, in some cases succeeding quickly, in others, after long hard years.

We call these men great, first and perhaps most of all, because every one of them did incalculable service for the world.

adding to its store of information, its material advantage or its social and spiritual welfare. Every man of them gave to the world some gift that will have value for centuries to come. In addition to all this they had personal qualities that draw us to them; subtle, human touches of personality; the spirit of pleasing companionship that we feel when we read the stories of their lives, or when we come into the presence of their work. Thus we call these men great because we find that every man, through the whole combination of his life, his work, his personality and his stimulating force exerted good influence on the world.

In some ways, at least, we find greatness allied to divinity, and great men worthy of admiration and emulation. Then, because the study of biography aids one to understand human life a little better, and to value it a little higher, we find it at once a pleasure and a stimulus to new effort. What some men have done, others can do. If some gained education in spite of every obstacle, if some persisted in spite of every defeat, if some gave to the world benefits that make earth a happier place in which to live, then others, also, even in what are perhaps more limited lives and with more limited opportunities, may take new hope, set their faces more sternly toward accomplishment, and likewise, in some measure, become doers, makers, builders, savers, creators and men who will deserve something of the praise that goes with the word "great."

I

ALEXANDER GRAHAM BELL

Inventor of the Telephone

At the Centennial Exposition in Philadelphia, in June, 1876, a tall, slender man whose intensely dark eyes and black hair and black side-whiskers emphasized his pallor, paused with the judges before a small table on which there were several forms of an invention that he had made, something not known before to the public, a device that made possible the electric transmission of speech, the telephone. Eagerly, with pardonable pride, he looked at the glittering new intruments, the first well-finished telephone that had ever been made. In spite of the fact that many people who had come to the Centennial to see the marvels of the day passed by his invention without giving it a thought, and in spite of the fact that the great official catalogue described it in only eighteen words, the young inventor, for he was only twenty-nine, believed that what he had made would bring great benefit to mankind. He felt sure that the telephone was much more than what some people called it, a mere fascinating toy.

Those were remarkable men who saw this first public exhibition of the telephone. There was Sir William Thompson, the great British scientist, and there was Joseph Henry, too, the distinguished American who had experimented so much with electricity; and with these there were others who were striving to find means of applying science to the needs of life. When these men put the instrument to their ears and heard speech that had been transmitted over a wire, they were surprised and immensely pleased. They realized at once the

8

marvel that had been brought about. Sir William Thompson said, "It is the most wonderful thing I have seen in America!"

Among the visitors at the Centennial was the Emperor Dom Pedro of Brazil, then a man fifty-one years of age, noted for his encouragement of art and science. A short time before the first public exhibition of the telephone, the emperor had visited a school in Boston where he had been much interested in watching the young inventor, Alexander Graham Bell, teach the deaf how to speak. His lively interest in science and his personal interest in the inventor led the emperor to curiosity concerning what Bell had made.

Following directions, the distinguished visitor put the receiver to his ear. With a start of surprise he exclaimed, "My God! it talks!"

The telephone did indeed come to the world like a miracle. There was something like magic in its power to transmit speech from a distant place. Even the people of today, who use the telephone constantly, look upon it with unusual respect when they talk with others in far-away cities. With how much greater respect did the people of the past regard the wonderful instrument!

In 1877, Professor Bell exhibited the telephone as a kind of curiosity, much to the amazement of many audiences. One of his announcements said:

"Prof. A. Graham Bell, assisted by Mr. Frederic A. Gower, will give an exhibition of his wonderful and miraculous discovery THE TELEPHONE, before the people of Lawrence as above, when Boston and Lawrence will be connected via the Western Union Telegraph and vocal and instrumental music and conversation will be transmitted a distance of 27 miles and received by the audience in the City Hall.
Prof. Bell will give an explanatory lecture with this marvellous exhibition.

> Cards of Admission, 35 cents
> Reserved Seats, 50 cents."

In this way Alexander Graham Bell, the inventor, intro-duced to the public one of the most useful of modern inventions.

For years the young teacher of the deaf had tried to find how to transmit speech by means of electricity. Only a few months before the opening of the Centennial he had succeeded. In fact, he had patented the invention on March 7, 1876. Even he, with all his high hopes for the invention, could not realize to the full the value of that patent. Some one has said that the three most valuable papers in the world are the Magna Charta, the document that gave freedom to England; the Declaration of Independence, the paper that gave liberty to the United States, and the Bell Telephone Patent, the guarantee to the world of a new method of speech. Certainly in terms of money those three papers may well be called priceless. To the inventor, and to those who helped him, the telephone brought great wealth.

For his work in life, Alexander Graham Bell had chosen to teach the deaf. Born in Edinburgh, Scotland, March 3, 1847, he had lived in Scotland and in England until he was twenty-three. Then, in 1870, he had come with his father to America. Alexander Melville Bell, father of the inventor of the telephone, had come to the new world at the age of fifty-one. For twenty-two years he had lectured on elocution in the University of Edinburgh, and for five years in the University of London. At the time when he came to America he had written five important books on speech, including *Visible Speech*, a system for the writer of all languages in one physiological alphabet, and he had also written a number of less important works. He was an authority on physiological phonetics, as was his father before him, Alexander Bell, grandfather of the inventor. Eliza Symonds Bell, Alexander Graham Bell's mother, the daughter of a doctor in the service of the British Royal Navy, had great skill as a musician and as a painter of portraits.

Alexander Graham Bell, it is to be noted, was born a member of a cultured family, a family especially interested in teaching the art of speech. To that work Professor Bell's father, his grandfather, his uncle, and two of his brothers, had devoted themselves. By carrying on the work that his people had begun, Alexander Graham Bell made himself able to contribute more than all others before him to aiding the speech of the world.

Naturally, in such a family, the boy learned much at home. He studied also at the Royal High School of Edinburgh, and in the University of Edinburgh. When he was twenty-one he became a student in University College, and he also entered the University of London, where his father taught elocution. He began to teach when he was only sixteen. In addition to his own work he frequently assisted his father, and thus he became unusually expert in elocution, in music, and in speech correction. His studies along these lines led him to interest himself in transmitting sound by electricity. He came close to foreseeing his great work in life, for even before he came to America the youth thought that there would come a time when people would "speak by telegraph."

In the midst of his study and his earnest teaching the young man had the sorrow of losing two brothers.

"Alexander will go, too," said the physician, "unless you take him to a better climate."

That was enough for his father, who would make any sacrifices to save his son. The distinguished professor of elocution left his well recognized work in London, and, with his family, crossed the Atlantic and settled in Brantford, Ontario, in Canada, among the pines of the north. As lecturer on philology in Queen's College, Kingston, Ontario, the father continued the work that he had carried on in Edinburgh and in London. The son continued to study speech and electric transmission of messages, and also to teach the deaf.

When the father lectured in Boston, Miss Sarah Fuller, a teacher of the deaf, asked him to teach "visible speech" in her school. Through that request, and because of the remarkable success that Alexander Graham Bell had had when teaching in London in a school for the deaf, it came about that the Board of Education of Boston offered the young man, then twenty-four years old, five hundred dollars to teach deaf-mutes in that city. On April 1, 1871, Alexander Graham Bell entered the United States.

All his life he remained a teacher of the deaf. Whatever his enthusiasms, whatever his success or his failure, his wealth or his fame, he never lost his wish to help the unfortunate.

Like his father and his grandfather, young Bell had natural inventive ability. From his early days he had combined the romantic and the practical. In spite of his love for science he read novels industriously, especially enjoying reading anything whatever that concerned the ancient heroes of Scotland. To those who judged him only by his reading, and by his study of music and song, he appeared likely to lead anything except a practical life. On the other hand, influenced by his own natural inclinations as well as his father's directions, he made interesting studies in speech, in the anatomy of the speech organs, and in the transmission of sound by electricity, a subject that then greatly interested the scientific world. As a mere boy he had made a grotesque head of gutta-percha, had fitted it with an ingenious apparatus representing the organs of speech, had blown into it with a bellows and so manipulated it that he made it produce uncanny sounds that seemed like words.

The investigator was only eighteen when he proved by experiment that "vowel quality was produced by the resonance tones of the mouth cavities mingling faintly with the tones of the voice." He was nineteen when he understood from remarks made by Alexander J. Ellis, a celebrated philologist and writer on phonetics, to whom his father had introduced him, that Hermann Helmholtz, the German scientist, had transmitted vowel sounds through the use of electricity. Actually, Helmholtz had succeeded merely in producing vowel sounds by electricity and tuning forks, but he had not been able to transmit such sounds.

Young Bell's mistake led him to renewed interest in his

own experiments. He thought: "If Helmholtz can transmit vowel sounds by electricity, it is certainly possible to transmit consonant sounds; and if it is possible to transmit vowel sounds and consonant sounds, then it is possible to transmit speech. Perhaps I can find the way to do it!"

Thus the boy of nineteen was looking into the mist of the future, dimly seeing the means by which he was to do an immeasurable service for the world.

It is evident then that the young man of twenty-four who went to Boston in 1871 to teach in the School for the Deaf at 11 Pemberton Square, was much more than an ordinary teacher. He was an expert phonetician, an experimenter with electricity, and a dreaming inventor.

In those early days of his American teaching young Bell made two most important friendships. One was with Gardiner G. Hubbard, a public spirited man whom Miss Fuller had induced to aid in bringing Alexander Graham Bell to Boston. Because his own little daughter had been made deaf by scarlet fever Mr. Hubbard felt especial interest in doing anything to help deaf children.

The other friendship was with Thomas Sanders, a rich man whose oldest child had been born deaf. When this man learned that there was in Boston a young man who, by "visible speech," could teach the deaf to read the lips of others, and also to speak, he took the little boy, then five years old, to the grandmother's home in Salem, and brought it about that Bell should live in the Sanders home in Salem and there teach the child how to speak.

Mr. Hubbard and Mr. Sanders became Alexander Graham Bell's chief supporters. Though influence and through money they enabled Bell to carry to completion his ambitions as an inventor. Mr. Sanders provided $110,000 for work in connection with the telephone before he received the return of a single dollar. So, to the misfortune of two children the telephone owes much of its beginning.

Professor Bell, for the young teacher had become Professor of Vocal Physiology in Boston University, made a great success as a teacher of the deaf. Through the remarkable results of his kindly work he made himself known far and wide in the United States. Nevertheless, Bell continued his experiments to transmit speech by electricity. Up in the attic of the Sanders' house in Salem he worked night after night for three years. In that city where people had once accused old women of witchcraft he proposed to work the magic of sending his voice along a wire, a feat for which the people of superstitious times would certainly have mobbed any one.

Other men before Bell had experimented in transmitting sound. In 1831, Sir Charles Wheatstone showed that a wooden rod, set between two sounding-boards and touching both, will carry music. In 1854, Charles Bourseul, a Frenchman, suggested that it might be possible to send speech by an electric wire, provided a flexible plate received vibrations and opened and closed an electric circuit, and another plate at the farther end of the wire received and transmitted the vibrations. In 1861, Philipp Reis, of Friedrichsdorf, Germany, made a device that carried certain sounds by means of electricity. According to the *Encyclopædia Britannica*, it was Reis who, in a lecture in 1861, first used the word "telephony."

Various scientists tried to invent what we now call the telephone, but no one could make a device that would carry intelligibly the complicated series of vibrations that make human speech. With the exception of Bell, all the experimenters stressed the use of electricity instead of the production of sound.

"If I can make a deaf-mute talk, I can make iron talk!" said he.

At this time Bell was giving thought to three inventions, the phonautograph, an instrument that would make records of the vibrations of speech, and that would thus enable the deaf to make improvement in their own speech; the multiple harmonic telegraph, an apparatus by which one could send several Morse messages on a single wire at the same time; and the telephone, an instrument to transmit speech by means of electricity.

In his experiments in connection with the phonautograph Bell procured from a surgeon a complete human ear, and studied more carefully than ever the reception of sound. He saw how the thin membrane we call the ear-drum responds to vibrations. Placing a straw against it, with the other end of the straw touching and moving on a smoked plate, he saw how the vibrations of air, moving the ear-drum, were constantly transmitted still farther. This suggested the diaphragm for the telephone receiver.

The experiments with the multiple harmonic telegraph appeared to promise the most certain results, and to those experiments Bell gave himself devotedly. Night after night he worked, far beyond midnight, caring nothing for sleep or rest, and never doubting that he could accomplish what he set out to do. The work in the attic became too great for him alone, and so he called in the help of an ingenious man, Thomas A. Watson. Then the experiments demanded more room and more equipment than the attic could give, and so the two men moved to a shop in Boston. One day Bell said to his assistant, "If I could make a current of electricity vary in intensity, precisely as the air varies in density during the production of a sound, I should be able to transmit speech telegraphically."

Like the phonautograph, the multiple telegraph contributed to the telephone. On June 2, 1875, the two men were working on the telegraph, Bell being in one room and Watson in another. Noticing that a transmitter spring had stopped vibrating, Watson plucked it again and again, thus turning down the contact screw so far that the circuit remained unbroken. The resulting undulatory current carried the vibrations to the receiver in the next room, where Bell was working. He heard a faint buzz, the sound of the snapping spring at the other end of the wire. Excitedly he rushed into Watson's room, saying, "What did you do then? Don't change anything! Let me see!'' In a sense, that moment was the birth of the telephone.

Having found that he could make an instrument that would transmit a full sound, Bell resolved to continue until he could make the apparatus transmit the human voice, but for many months the best he could do was to make the instrument give faint sounds such as he had first heard. Patiently the inventor and his assistant continued their experiments, with the result that nine months later, on March 10, 1876, Watson heard the first complete sentence that was ever transmitted by telephone, ''Mr. Watson, please come here; I want you.'' On March 7, 1876, Bell was granted patent number 174,465, a patent that later involved hundreds of millions of dollars.

At first, when the invention was announced, people looked upon the telephone as a kind of interesting toy, but they failed to see that it would change business and increase comfort and safety. In 1877 *The Operator*, a technical publication, said, ''Nobody would care to trust important messages, sometimes involving life and death, or thousands of dollars, to being sent in such a manner.'' In these days, when the telephone upholds business, adds to our pleasures, and moves the daily lives of millions of men and women, it seems strange that the world did not at once rush to Bell for permission to use his great invention. The inventor, with the eyes of a prophet, looked into the future and saw what was to be. In 1878 he wrote ''I believe in the future wires will unite the head offices of the Telephone Company in different cities, and a man in one part of the country may communicate by word of mouth with another in a different place.''

So far from gaining immediate recognition, Bell met with numerous difficulties. Mr. Watson, Bell's assistant, said in 1913: ''Professor Bell's financial problems had begun to press hard for solution. We were very much disappointed because the president of the Western Union Telegraph Company had refused, somewhat contemptuously, Mr. Hubbard's offer to sell him all the Bell patents for the exorbitant sum of

$100,000. . . . Two years later the Western Union would gladly have bought those patents for $25,000,000!''

On October 9, 1876, Bell and Watson had carried on the first long-distance conversation by telephone, Bell being in Boston and Watson in Cambridge, a distance of only two miles, but a distance that in that time made the talking seem a miracle. In spite of such successful experiments it was a full year after the gaining of the patent before any money was paid for the use of the telephone, and even then the sum was only twenty dollars. By the end of two years not one thousand instruments were in use. In fact, in these early days of the telephone the London *Times* spoke of it as "an American humbug." Nevertheless, in four years, that is, in 1880, there were in actual use in the United States 30,872 telephones.

From that time progress went by leaps and bounds. Instead of being limited to talking a distance of two miles, people in 1921 talked over a distance of five thousand five hundred miles. Instead of two telephones there were, in 1925, in the Bell System alone, nearly seventeen million! With the success of the telephone there came a series of legal difficulties. In eleven years the owners of the patents were obliged to fight about six hundred lawsuits. In all of these Bell was declared the inventor.

It must not be forgotten that it was largely through his kindly teaching of the deaf that Bell won to his aid his two powerful associates, Gardiner G. Hubbard and Thomas Sanders. Those two men were towers of strength. Mr. Hubbard was a lawyer, a shrewd, clear-headed thinker, and a man of the greatest public spirit. He had led in introducing illuminating gas in Cambridge; in organizing water works; in opening the first street railway between Cambridge and Boston; in securing a charter for an institution for the education of the deaf, and in many other public works. Mr. Sanders was a successful leather merchant who, out of personal interest in Bell, had been willing to supply him with the money to carry on experiments. While he had expected to advance comparatively small sums only, he had such faith in the inventor that he finally put into the work of making the telephone not only all the money that he had on hand but also all that he could borrow by mortgaging his property. Alexander Graham Bell's capacity to win such strong friends is proof of his greatness of character. His kindly nature, as well as his scientific knowledge and inventive ability, led to his success.

In 1877 Professor Bell married the daughter of Gardiner Hubbard, a young woman whom he had first met when she came to his school to obtain lessons in voice culture. At the time of the wedding he gave her one of the most valuable gifts that any lover ever presented to a sweetheart, for he made over to her, with her father as trustee, practically his entire financial interest in the telephone.

There were many amusing incidents in the early days when Bell was at work trying to improve the telephone. At first people had to talk so loudly in order to be heard over the telephone that it was said that they frightened horses that were out in the street. On the night after Bell and Watson had talked for that first time over the marvelous distance of two miles, the two young men, in their boarding house, talked so joyfully and danced so wildly that the landlady said, "You two will have to leave the house if you can't be quiet at night!" On one occasion an insane man came and said, "Your telephone is a back number. I can show you how to telephone without any wires at all." "How?" they asked him. "Just take off the top of my head and look at my brain!" he answered.

Once, in a Canadian village, where Bell had gone to experiment, he bought from the local stores all the stovepipe wire he could find. Then he tacked the wire along the crooked lines of the rail fence, and utterly amazed the farmers by talking, as they said, "along the fence!"

Then, too, in those first days of the telephone, foreigners who talked over it were amazed to hear it speak in their own languages. They seemed to think that since the invention had been made by an American it could speak nothing except English.

The first telephone booth was made when Watson, remembering his landlady's scolding for the noise that he and Bell had made at night, rigged up a shelter of bed-blankets and crawled under them in order to talk without waking the house. That gave the idea that led to the modern booths.

As for the familiar "Hello!" so closely associated with the telephone, neither Bell nor Watson had thought of using the word. They always said, "Ahoy!" as if they were signaling a ship!

When he had ended his years of struggle, and when the telephone had brought him both honor and wealth, Bell went on in the same spirit that had moved him before. He had two deep desires in life, one being to do all that he could for the welfare of the deaf, and the other being to apply scientific truth to the advantage of mankind. Until the day of his death, August 2, 1922, at the age of seventy-five, Bell continued to work along these two lines of interest. In 1887 he founded and liberally endowed the Volta Bureau for the Increase of Knowledge Relating to the Deaf. He founded, and at one time presided over, the American Association to Promote the Teaching of Speech to the Deaf. For many years he was President of the Board of Clarke School for the Deaf, in Northampton, Mass. In 1900 he materially aided in making the United States Census report concerning the deaf in the United States. In addition to all this he wrote *The Education of Deaf Children*, and various other works relating to the deaf.

His invention of the "telephone probe," a means of enabling surgeons to detect the presence of bullets or other pieces of metal in the human body, a device first used in endeavoring to save the life of President Garfield, brought him, from the University of Heidelberg, the honorary degree of Doctor of Medicine.

In 1880 he wrote, "I have heard a ray of the sun laugh and cough and sing! . . . I have been able to hear a shadow!"

By this he meant to say that he had invented the photophone, an apparatus by which every variation of light is made to produce a sound. The practical scientific uses of the photophone are many in number.

In 1891, over ten years before the invention of the airplane, he provided five thousand dollars to aid in advancing the study of flight. To that study he gave great attention, investigating especially the tetrahedral principle in kite structure, and continuing his experiments until he had made a kite that could lift more than three hundred pounds in addition to its own weight. His contributions to the study of flight were most valuable.

Professor Bell gained patents for many other inventions, such as the spectrophone, by which, through sound, he investigated the invisible colors of the spectrum; the audiometer, by which he measured the power of hearing; the graphophone, by which he reproduced speech, and he continued to find great pleasure, even to the very last, in investigating scientific problems.

All his life he maintained that he could do his best work at night. In his early days his work as teaching of the deaf left him no time except the night for experimenting. In those days he cultivated habits that became lasting. Usually at about ten o'clock he began intensive study, which he continued through the quiet of the night until three or four o'clock in the morning. In those night hours he felt freedom from the interruptions of the day, and a strengthening of his eager spirit of investigation.

Naturally honors crowded upon him. The Republic of France gave him the Volta Prize for the invention of the telephone; the President of the French Republic decorated him with the Cross of the Legion of Honor; Harvard, Amherst, Dartmouth, the University of Edinburgh, Oxford University, and many other colleges and universities gave him degrees; and a long list of learned societies bestowed upon him various awards.

In the United States, in addition to his work for the deaf,

Professor Bell gave $50,000 to establish a weekly scientific publication called *Science*. He served as regent of the Smithsonian Institution, and president of the National Geographic Society. In the city of Washington, where he made his home, he became one of the most respected citizens. In his later days especially, tall, white-haired, white-bearded, and exceedingly kindly and genial, he was a distinguished figure. In the last twenty years of his life he spent the summers on his estate at Baddeck, Cape Breton, Nova Scotia, but even there, in that region of serene peace and beauty, he continued to make scientific experiments.

In an address at the twenty-fifth anniversary of the Horace Mann School for the Deaf in Boston, Professor Bell said, in reference to his attempts to make a device that would render visible to the deaf the vibrations of air that affect the ears as sound, "I did not succeed in making an apparatus into which a deaf child could look and see the vibrations of speech so recorded as to enable him to understand what was said. . . . It was a failure; but that apparatus, in process of time, became the telephone of today." Out of his kindly work came one of the greatest of inventions. "I am proud to think," said he, "that I have been a teacher of the deaf. . . ."

II

LUTHER BURBANK

EXPERIMENTER WITH PLANT LIFE

FROM his earliest days Luther Burbank saw his mother caring for flowers that she had planted around their country home, three miles from the village of Lancaster, in Massachusetts. He saw the delight with which she watched new beauty unfold. He learned to share her pleasure in setting out plants and in aiding them to develop.

Even as a baby he had smiled when his mother had placed a flower in his hands. As soon as he had learned to walk he toddled in the garden beside his mother, making efforts to help her. When he was a little older he made the garden his playground, and the flowers and plants his associates.

Lancaster lay in a region of natural beauty. The farm landscape looked like a serene Arcadia. Numerous elm trees, some of them standing in long rows, added an indescribable gentleness and softness. Through the fields the Nashua river wound its slow way. Everywhere there was quiet.

Perhaps because Luther Burbank did not have robust strength he turned especially to the study of outdoor life. Through inherited instincts, surroundings, and his own physical make-up, he became an enthusiastic lover of flowers, plants, and trees. He made himself a student of nature and a scientific worker, and because he developed more new types of plant life than any other person had ever done, he earned the title of "plant wizard."

At times, in the Lancaster home with the Burbank family there lived a cousin, Professor Levi Sumner Burbank, a friend of Louis Agassiz, the great Swiss-American naturalist. The cousin talked of Agassiz and his work, and thus unconsciously did much to develop Luther Burbank's love for flowers into a burning ambition to know more about them and to do more with them, to become, in fact, a naturalist like Agassiz.

Much later in life Luther Burbank wrote a book that he called *Training the Human Plant,* a book concerning the need of sympathetic and understanding education. As he wrote it he must have thought lovingly of the influence that had surrounded him in his boyhood days.

That good mother of his, as she moved about among the flowers in her garden, had little thought that by her kindly example she trained one who would become the greatest of all workers with plants. Happily for her, she lived to the good age of ninety-six, saw the wonders that her son brought about, and died in content at his home in Santa Rosa, California. All her life she had lived in a garden. Through her gentle influence she had led her son to become a master gardener.

It is odd that a great man's success should begin in his home garden. It is still more odd that it should turn definitely upon a hill of potatoes! Luther Burbank made his first great success because he noticed a seed-ball growing on one of the many potato vines in a Massachusetts lot. Knowing that while seed-balls on potato vines are not rare, they are at least unusual, he noted the place and resolved to investigate. When he looked again he met disappointment. He could not find the seed ball! The youth did not know how much depended upon his curiosity. He might have changed the whole current of his life if he had said, "Oh, the thing is gone! Let it go!" Instead, he searched until he found it. In the ball, as if he had opened a sort of Arabian Night's gift, he saw his future, twenty-three potato seeds!

Some accident of nature, a chance wind, a buzzing bee, perhaps only a common potato bug, had brought about a form of cross-pollination. Pollen from another plant had given new strength. Nature showed evidence of bringing about something new. The happy accident, a mere accident and nothing more, might have amounted to little if it had escaped the eyes of the young gardener.

"Let's see what will happen," thought young Burbank.

He planted the seeds, and watched the growth. When at last he dug the potatoes he noticed that of all the plants that had grown from those seeds, two were especially productive. He selected from those two hills the best potatoes, and planted them. From that seed-ball that he had noticed so accidentally, and from the selected growth that sprang from it, the investigator grew what he called the "Burbank Potato," a large valuable type of potato.

Later, by selling seed potatoes, young Burbank earned the first money that he ever gained through plant creation, one hundred and fifty dollars. By developing the Burbank Potato he made it possible for farmers in the United States to increase their annual earnings by many millions of dollars.

In this early experiment Luther Burbank followed a process that he followed all his life. He observed, developed, selected, and continued to experiment until he had aided nature to do what she had never done before. He accomplished with vegetables, with flowers, with fruits, with trees, what people call "miracles." He aided and directed nature, and developed plant strength, or beauty, or usefulness.

He developed a cactus without thorns; a dozen varieties of prunes; many new kinds of apples, peaches and cherries; varieties of nuts, and berries; hundreds of beautiful flowers; grasses, grains and vegetables of kinds never seen before. He gave to the world entirely new kinds of fruits, such as no man before him had ever tasted. And all this he brought about through the process that he had employed in early life!

This expert gardener made observation the basis of all his work. As a young man, trained by his early garden work and made observant by his deep interest in every growing thing, he had noticed the seed-ball. Slowly, year by year, because he loved his work, he unconsciously trained his eyes to see minute differences that would escape the notice of most men.

He gained the ability to look at thousands of plants and to see the essential, hidden, perhaps, in a single one of them.

Once, when he passed a bed of flowers, he noticed a faint unusual fragrance. Patiently he examined every flower until he found the one that gave forth the new and pleasing odor. He had found another accident of nature, a flower whose perfume especially pleased man. Having found the flower, the gardener carried on intelligent investigations, produced more flowers like the original, and thus added to the world's stock of beauty. He had seen Nature in one of her generous moods, had welcomed her gift, and induced her to give even more.

To develop new plants, Burbank depended upon cross-pollination, the crossing of two kinds of plant life. In the case of the Burbank Potato he had found cross-pollination the result of accident. In his later work, instead of relying upon accident, he instituted a series of experiments that called for the utmost care and delicacy. He crossed thousands and thousands of plants, and observed his results minutely until he succeeded in aiding Nature to develop something new.

At all times he worked with patience. He knew that a plant does not grow over night. He waited weeks, months, and sometimes years, even then often to meet disappointment. He learned through hard experience what every gardener or fruit-grower knows, that a thousand causes may upset the best laid plans.

Luther Burbank dared not make experiments upon a limited scale. In the beginning he had twenty-three chances, the twenty-three potato seeds that gave birth to the Burbank Potato. From twenty-three possibilities, through great good fortune, he had gained two successful results! He knew that he owed those two results to great good luck. For scientific investigation, instead of twenty-three chances, he must have hundreds or even thousands. He must expend an amount of labor and of patience remarkably great.

Whatever natural gifts he possessed, he still had to cultivate power of selection, and ability to see the practical. He could produce freak growths, but what would be the use? He must see the one chance in a thousand to produce what would be of real use to man. However much he loved plants, he could permit no sentimentality. He must summon to a sort of judgment day all that he grew. To the fit he could say, "Grow, develop, increase a thousand fold"; to the unfit, "Depart ye into the fire." Relentlessly he burned plants that did not fulfil the demands of beauty, or strength, or usefulness.

All that Luther Burbank became as a man he foreshadowed by his life in boyhood. To him the old proverb applies remarkably well: "As the twig is bent, so is the tree inclined."

Luther's father, Samuel Walton Burbank, a Massachusetts farmer, succeeded just a little better than his neighbors. He conducted a farm from which he made a good living, and he also had the enterprise to make use of the clay found upon his land, and manufactured pottery and brick. Belonging to the sturdy English stock that had made early New England, he believed in hard work, penny-saving thrift, and simple ambitions. Luther's mother, Olive Ross Burbank, was of Scotch descent. She owed her love of beauty to the same race that produced not only Allan Ramsay and Robert Burns, but also that Gawain Douglas who wrote of Scottish gardens rich with "purple, azure, gold, and gules."

The boy Luther saw his father at work upon his farm and his mother pleasantly occupied in the home and the garden. When he was old enough to take charge of a garden of his own, even though still only a small boy, he took pride in raising corn for the table a full two weeks ahead of his neighbors. He made his corn mature earliest, because he planted seeds in boxes in the house, gave them the proper attention, and then planted the new corn outdoors at the earliest moment. Almost by instinct, even at the start, he made his gardening scientific.

In his ambition to excel in the work that he saw around him, he began to study soils and fertilizers as well as seeds and plants. He questioned his mother, his father, and any of the neighbors who happened to gain marked success. When he wished to learn more than these good friends of his could teach, he turned to books. Thus he read Darwin's *Animals and Plants Under Domestication,* a book that broadened his views and made a lasting effect upon him. He learned that the scope of such work as that in which he was interested extended far beyond the simple surroundings of the farm, and of Massachusetts.

Before Luther Burbank had passed the age when most boys devote their time to games and unproductive amusements, he had made many really valuable experiments in plant development, in the selection of seeds, in cross-pollination, and even in the difficult art of grafting, of which most farmers' sons know little. In such experiments he found a game he could play with living matter, chasing Nature to her secret hiding place, and claiming the forfeit of a new plant. In such contests he found need for skill and persistent effort that not even baseball or football demand. In winning, that is, in making the result of his own planting successful, or of his own selection of seed, or of his own grafting, he gained a pleasure that other boys did not know.

Far from being an only child who turned to solitary pursuits because he lacked companionship, Luther Burbank was his father's thirteenth child! In the little two-story, red brick house where he was born he had every temptation to play. About the brick and pottery works he saw all the people of the little community. Whether he wished it or not, he had to associate with children and with all kinds of adults.

The school that the boy first attended was the country school, in all truth, "a little red schoolhouse," a kind of educational institution that did much for the United States in the days before secondary education became popular. The building, like many buildings in that community, was of substantial red brick, solid and permanent, a fit emblem of the solid hard-working people who made it the shrine of their learning.

When Luther Burbank sat in class in that red brick country school, he appeared the least likely of all the pupils to make himself famous. He was so delicate and slender in figure that he looked as if he lacked physical strength to meet even the ordinary battles of life. He had a pleasing, sensitive face, and blue eyes that looked too gentle to guide him on his way toward fame. He was a quiet boy who said little, and when he did say anything, he spoke in a low voice. He neither looked nor acted like one who would master fate.

How could any teacher in the little, old-fashioned schoolroom, looking at the shy, delicate, sensitive country boy before him, believe that in the future a learned man would say: "His contributions to human comfort are greater in value than all the gold taken from the mines of California!" Dean Brink, of the Kansas State Agricultural College, who made that remark, mentioned "the mines of California" because Luther Burbank, early in life, made himself a citizen of California, and there carried on his great work.

For various reasons Burbank determined to go from one coast of the American continent to California, on the extreme opposite coast. At first he had no thought of leaving the East. He knew that he did not have physical strength sufficient to enable him to do such hard work as his father had carried on. At the same time, being interested in scientific pursuits, he planned to study medicine, become a physician, and settle down to medical practice in the East. Then his father died, the family moved from the pleasant red house with its shading elm trees, to Groton, and the young man had to get work. He found a position with a nurseryman! If he had known all that was to follow, he would have said that fate had taken a hand in his development.

In 1875, in his twenty-sixth year, after he had suffered from a partial sunstroke, he resolved to set out for California, whither many people from his neighborhood had gone. He had worked for a time in a factory in Worcester, Massachusetts, and his success there might have tempted him to remain in mechanical work. He developed considerable skill with machinery, and actually made an invention of real worth. But in spite of all that, he had set his heart on other things.

When Luther Burbank went to California he did not find the journey the easy one that people enjoy to-day. He traveled on slow and uncomfortable trains that made such bad connections that he had long waits. Added to all that, the young man had practically no money. Instead, he had youth, high hopes, and a bag of ten potatoes! What a strange offering to fortune! In Greek mythology, one reads of dragon's teeth; and in fairy stories, of magic cloaks, or golden spears, or seven-league boots, but not of potatoes!

Those ten potatoes, grown from the seed-ball that he had accidentally observed, and kept by permission of the man who had bought the Burbank Potato, were all the fortune that the young traveler took with him! As a matter of fact, in the end, those ten potatoes became of more value to him than they would have been if each had been a nugget of solid gold!

The youth had too little money to pay for a sleeping car ticket and so he curled up on the seats and slept as well as he could, but always most uncomfortably. In the poorly lighted, badly ventilated cars he was bumped and jostled along, night and day over poor roadbeds, moving slowly west.

When at last Luther Burbank reached the land of his dreams, he found a state very different from the California of to-day. He had not expected to find the camp and cabin conditions of the "Forty-Niners," of whom Brete Harte tells, but he found a California still very young. Where we now see southern cities, he saw small semi-Mexican towns. Where we delight in fruit-orchards and in plantations of walnuts, he saw only arid expanses.

Instead of going to any of the more important places, Burbank went some fifty miles north of San Francisco to Santa Rosa, a place then possessed of fewer than five thousand inhabitants. There, in a wide valley, he found especially fertile soil and a climate well adapted to the work he wished to carry on. There he remained and there he worked, until, without his intending to do so, he made the place famous.

The almost penniless adventurer did not find it easy to

secure a place, even in that land of opportunities. He was willing to do anything to earn a living, but he found positions difficult to obtain. Once, when he heard of work that seemed promising he learned that the applicant must own a hatchet. Promptly he invested his scanty fund in buying the implement, only to find that he applied too late, and that he had a hatchet, little money, and no work.

After various applications, the immigrant obtained the disagreeable job of cleaning out hen houses, for which he gained the reward of sleeping in a coop! When he wished meat to eat he bought the cheaper parts such as some people gave to dogs. Nevertheless he was in California, ready and willing to take his chance with the rest of mankind.

When he left his home in the chicken coop he found an even more uncomfortable sleeping place over a hothouse. He had delighted in obtaining work at one of the nurseries in Santa Rosa, but he delighted less when he tried to sleep in his close, hot room. He stifled in the heat and the heavy odors. However successful he became in later life, he did not find it easy to climb the hard ladder that led to success.

Luther Burbank, once again in his favorite work, now busied himself industriously with plants and flowers, did his best for his employer, saved money, and looked ahead to the future. When the proper time came, and he made it come soon, he established a nursery business of his own. In 1877 he succeeded so magnificently that he made exactly fifteen dollars and twenty cents! Nevertheless, willing to work night and day, he determined to go on in the nursery work. Seven years later, from his nursery business, he made more than ten thousand dollars a year. Best of all, he saw orders pouring in upon him at an increasing rate, and knew that he could anticipate greatly increased returns. He had brought this about through hard work and through almost unexampled ingenuity.

One day, in this early period of his success, he received an order for 20,000 young trees. He felt overjoyed at such an order, until he learned that the would-be purchaser would cancel it if he could not have the trees at once. As a practical nurseryman, Burbank knew that the slow growing prune trees would take nearly three years to develop to the size desired. He wished to fill the order. What was he to do? How could he make prune trees grow more rapidly.

"Why didn't the man ask for almond trees?" Burbank thought. "I can grow them over night."

Then immediately he thought, "Why not grow prunes on almond trees?"

At once he planted no less than a hundred thousand of the rapidly growing almond trees, and rejoiced to see them spring up quickly, in accordance with their nature. From these he then selected the strongest and the best, to the number of 20,000, following apparently the Bible saying, "For many are called but few are chosen." On the best of the strong, vigorous, quick-growing almond trees he grafted prune cuttings. In nine months, much less than half the time required by nature, he sent word to the man who had given the order: "Here are your 20,000 prune trees." The plant magician had made his almond trees, because of their grafts, bear, not almonds, but prunes!

Luther Burbank no more changed the ways of nature than did James Watt in harnessing steam and making it work for man. He simply guided the willing forces of nature. To the ordinary observer the growing of prunes on almond trees appeared a miracle. The fact that Burbank had accomplished such an amazing thing advertised him more than anything else he could have done. Then, for almost the first time, people called Luther Burbank a wizard, a magician who bent nature to his course in ways as wonderful as those Shakespeare ascribed to Prospero on the island of *The Tempest*. People looked on the Burbank nurseries with as much respect and awe as the wrecked sailors looked upon the "still-vexed Bermoothes." New patrons piled order upon order; visitors made long pilgrimages to see the wonder-worker, and people at great distance wrote eager letters of inquiry.

Because he saw a new and greater work before him, Luther

Burbank abandoned the success of his nurseries, as well as the excellent income that it brought him, in order to strike out boldly into a new field, that of developing new growths. That entry into a new career he made in 1884 when he was thirty-five years old. About Christmas time, 1885, he bought a farm at Sebastopol, California. From that time to his death, he conducted experimental work on a great scale. In his quiet gardens he accomplished results almost beyond belief.

Burbank, interested in all plant life, saw around him on the desert expanses, the cactus, so common in the arid regions of the Southwest. He saw the plant, a menace to every form of life, thorny, unfriendly, forbidding, keeping cattle and men alike at a distance. Then he experimented until he produced a variety of cactus that forgot to grow the thorns that had characterized its kind for centuries!

Burbank found the cactus of the desert practically useless, even without its thorns, for it contained a hard fibre harmful to cattle. He grew a cactus that had neither thorns nor dangerous fibre! He aided nature, trained the savage species, civilized and softened it, and led to the growth of a cactus that provided food valuable for cattle. He made what once menaced men and animals alike, become a blessing.

In the same way Burbank trained other plants to put aside their weapons. He led walnut trees to grow nuts with thin shells; blackberry vines to throw aside the thorns that prick and scratch; and plums to grow without pits. He induced strawberries to forget the seasons, and to grow throughout the year under his protecting hand. He led the white calla lily to develop a perfume that matched its beauty of appearance. He changed the disagreeable odor of the dahlia to an inviting fragrance.

The wizard apparently found no end to the wonders that he could perform. He heard people laugh at the saying, "The blackberry is red when it is green," and then upset the very name of the berry by producing a plant that grew

Photo from Brown Bros., N. Y.

LUTHER BURBANK

a ripe blackberry that is white! From the seed of a single apple, like a master-magician, he grew thirty-six entirely distinct kinds of apples! Did he upset all the laws of heredity? As a matter of fact, he observed the ways of nature and adapted those ways to the needs or the wishes of man.

Burbank heard fruit-growers complain of the danger of frost, whose sudden coming, they said, destroyed thousands upon thousands of dollars' worth of fruit. He studied both the trees and the conditions, and then brought about the growth of fruit trees that could endure the most sudden changes of temperature. He had taken the trees as if they had been children, and had taught them how to take care of themselves.

Sometimes he brought about wonders that made it seem that he led nature into becoming a humorist. Once he grew an apple that was half a sweet apple and half a sour apple! He grew a daisy that was pink in color, and a poppy that was blue! He made a daisy grow until it was seven inches across, and an amaryllis until it was ten inches in diameter. He grew what he called a pomato, a combination of potato and tomato, a white fruit that makes excellent eating.

As if he wished to see how rapidly he could make nature work, he brought about the development of a walnut tree that grows more quickly than does any other tree in the entire temperate zone, a tree that in thirteen years grows six times the size that the average walnut tree can grow in over twice that time. As if he wished to see how tempting a fruit he could produce, he led to the growth of what the world never before had seen, the plumcot, a combination of the luscious Japanese plum, the American wild plum, and the apricot.

In ancient times people would have called such a man a wizard, in league with the powers of evil, and would have put him to death. In these days of science men look upon Luther Burbank's work as helpful in the extreme, as a contribution to a scientific study of that force that led Lowell to say:

"Every clod feels a stir of might,
An instinct within it that reaches and towers,
And, groping blindly above it for light,
Climbs to a soul in grass and flowers."

Even in Luther Burbank's time some men took the view of the Dark Ages and regarded the "plant wizard" as a wizard in all reality. A clergyman in Santa Rosa invited him to his church, and there, before him, preached a sermon in which he accused the plant-grower of upsetting the laws of God, and therefore of being an enemy of all good men.

"How do you do such wonderful things?" visitors asked Luther Burbank. He replied: "I listen patiently, quietly and reverently to the lessons, one by one, which Mother Nature has to teach, shedding light on that which before was a mystery."

No one can work with living matter, as Luther Burbank did, without gaining full reverence for the Spirit that animates every living thing, be it plant or animal or man.

"I am a sincere believer," says Luther Burbank, "in a higher power than that of man. All my investigations have led me away from the idea of a dead, material universe, tossed about by various forces, to that of a universe which is absolutely all force, life, soul, or thought, or whatever name we may choose to call it. . . . The universe is not half dead but all alive."

The new England transcendentalist philosopher, essayist, and poet, Ralph Waldo Emerson, had acquaintance with the great plant-grower's father, and also with his uncle, both of whom became, in a sense, his disciples. Certainly something of the spirit of Emerson appears in Burbank's work and in his writings. In twelve beautiful volumes entitled *Methods and Discoveries,* Burbank shows how much more he was than a mere grower of plants. He wrote with the spirit of a poet and a philosopher.

To read Burbank's text and to look at the numerous pictures made from color photographs with which he illustrated his books, is to walk with the master through his gardens, and to have him hold up, one by one, the marvelous things that he has grown. Perhaps no one in the entire country worked more patiently. In one test alone Burbank used 500,000 plum trees, an almost incredible number! In working with the white blackberry, in order to make a single selection, he examined 65,000 possibilities! In some cases, when he worked with small plants, he chose from millions! All that he did not find suited to his purposes, he destroyed. In numerous cases his patience extended over years.

As for working hours, Luther Burbank forgot all about such a thing as the "eight hour day." In fact, his interest was such that he made his day of labor more frequently one of eighteen hours than one of eight.

Luther Burbank's love for his chosen work was such that in labor he found the greatest pleasure. "No man," said he, ever did a great work for hire." In that, he sets forward one of the greatest prescriptions for happiness and contentment.

He was more than a worker: he was an altruist and an educator. He said: "The greatest happiness in the world is to make others happy; the next greatest is to make them think."

Visitors went to Burbank's experimental farm by the thousands, and letters poured in upon him at the rate of nearly 50,000 a year. Those fortunate people who visited his gardens found more than 3,000 experiments constantly under way, and more than 5,000 different botanical species under his daily painstaking observation.

In addition to his vigorous outdoor work he wrote frequently for magazines and newspaper syndicates. He served as special lecturer on evolution in Stanford University. He was a Fellow of the Royal Horticultural Society of London; Honorary Member of the Royal Botanical Society of Sweden; Member of the Italian Royal Agricultural Society; Life Fellow of the American Academy of Arts and Sciences, and member of numerous other learned and social bodies.

Of his work, the Dutch botanist Hugo De Vries said,

"The flowers and fruits of California are less wonderful than the flowers and fruits which Mr. Burbank has made."

Such a man sets an example of the joy and the success that one may gain when he has his heart in his work.

III

JOHN BURROUGHS

Naturalist and Essayist

John Burroughs' father had red hair and a freckled face. His mother's maiden name was Amy Kelly. Both parents came from pioneer American stock, his father's people having for generations cleared the land, tilled the soil, and made an obscure livelihood. His mother's father suffered at Valley Forge. Both parents might have traced their descent to adventurous Irish people who came to the New World to risk possible dangers from Indians and certain hardships in pioneer life. Both parents, without question, transmitted to John Burroughs, the much loved American naturalist and essayist, the Celtic spirit that made him so much a lover of nature.

The Burroughs family had no luxuries in their home. Instead, they found trouble enough in wresting a living from the earth. They did not even have the opportunity to go to near-by stores and buy whatever they needed, for they lived much closer to nature than that. They produced on their stony farm at Roxbury, New York, all the food that they ate, as well as the material from which they themselves made the clothing that they wore. In every sense of the word they lived hard-working, sturdy, independent, self-supporting lives.

John Burroughs had no opportunity to lead a lonely childhood, for he was the seventh child in a family of ten children, but on the other hand he had no opportunity to lead a childhood of pure play. Like all the members of his household, he had to do his full share of work, and he had to begin as soon as he was old enough to work at all.

The sort of life that Burroughs led in boyhood has disappeared in the eastern part of the United States. Today the tractor, the steam thrasher, the telephone, the radio, the automobile, good roads, ease of access to good stores, and railroad connections with great cities have entirely changed the lives of farmers. In John Burroughs' boyhood days the farmhouse was isolated from the rest of the world, every farm household being a community in and by itself, to a degree far more notable than is the case today. Perhaps, all this gave a greater opportunity for the development of individuality.

On the farm the father grew flax. That flax he turned into linen. The sheep that he sheared with clumsy shears, after he had washed their thick fleece under a great spout by the brook, gave the wool that the mother made into warm garments for the family. The mother made pillows and great beds soft with feathers that she herself picked from squawking live geese while she sat by the door of the house. The family had wheat to make into bread, because the father and his helpers thrashed the grain with primitive wooden flails, two wooden staves hinged together with leather. They had not bought those clumsy flails at a near-by store. They themselves had made them from wood that they had cut from their own forests and shaped in the workshop near the house.

The Burroughs family had sugar on the table, because, in the spring before the snow had gone, when the sap began to run, the men of the household had set out and tapped the maples, collected the sap, drawn it with the help of oxen to great open air vats, and there had boiled it over roaring fires in the maple grove, making it into syrup. That, in turn, the mother had made into maple sugar, brown, sweet, delicious, the greatest luxury in the house. People had zest in those days in using and in eating the things that came directly from the results of their own labor. They knew a poetry in life that people today, who buy almost all that they use, do not know.

On the Burroughs farm, which was small, even as farms went in that day, John Burroughs' father kept thirty cows, a number that called for a surprising amount of work in comparison with similar herds today. In the first place, the farmer had no milking machines, nor did he have any easy way to dispose of milk. After the milking, he set pans of milk on racks in a room cooled by running water, brought from a spring to which he himself had laid a line of bored logs as piping. When the cream was collected, he put it into a churn that the sturdy farm dog, or a stronger bullock, laboriously worked by means of a treadmill.

The mother spent weary hours making and packing butter. She pressed it down into tubs, fifty pounds to a tub, the very tubs themselves shaped and put together by the farmer or his neighbors.

Even then some one must work still more to gain money in exchange for the result of so much labor. John Burroughs often made the long journey of fifty miles or more from his farm home, to Catskill on the Hudson river, driving slow oxen over roads that people now would call impossible, and there putting the tubs of butter on board small boats that would convey them to New York. As the boy moved slowly along the uneven country roads he looked at the flowers and trees, watched chipmunks dart along the crooked lines of rail fences, noted the birds fly about in the air, and let his soul drink in the inspiration of the quiet scene.

At other times John Burroughs, as a boy, swung the scythe in the fields, cutting the tall grass. Occasionally, he would stop his work to rest, looking at the hills and mountains that rose on all sides, for the home at Roxbury lay in a region of rare beauty. With a naturally sensitive heart he felt a kinship with the nature that spread so much of her beauty before him. Like the American Indian he became an observer of the ways of nature; unlike the Indian he became an observer who understood and sympathized.

Through his farm life in boyhood John Burroughs prepared himself directly for his work as a man, for he began to notice nature then, and he continued with the broader, more penetrating, power of manhood. In all his later literary work he kept the simplicity, the enthusiasm, and the childlikeness, that he had had, when, as a boy, he whistled over his acres.

John Burroughs was born in Roxbury, New York, April 3, 1837, the son of a farmer. In spite of the fact that he spent many of his days in cities he remained a farmer all his life. So far as he knew, his people had tilled the soil for generations. They had learned the ways of nature in order to apply them to their own advantage, living close to the soil, observing carefully, and gaining a lively respect for the great life-forces that they saw around them. They did not become poets or essayists, but at least they led the way for their distinguished descendant.

Far back in the past, Great-Grandfather Burroughs, led by the pioneer spirit, had moved from the hill country near Danbury, Connecticut, where his own ancestors had established a home. His son, Grandfather Burroughs, following the spreading out of the settlements, moved to Roxbury, New York, the place where John Burroughs was born.

Did all these farmer generations before John Burroughs, speak through him? Had they looked at the squirrels, the birds, the wake-robins, the leaves and tendrils, and felt vague wonder, and wished for words with which to tell all that they saw and felt? Their descendant, at least, wrote essays on just those aspects of the outdoor world that they themselves had observed and loved.

The school that young Burroughs attended, a little country school, gave only the rudiments of education. The entire body of pupils consisted of less than three dozen children, and those of all ages, from the youngest toddler to hulking boys in their "teens." The training was without plan and often without results. The teachers, young people themselves who knew little more than their pupils, taught for a time and then withdrew, so that no one teacher remained long. There was little chance for the deep impression of personality, or for the development of a planned course of study. John Burroughs' early school is typified in Irving's

The Legend of Sleepy Hollow, and Edward Eggleston's *The Hoosier Schoolmaster.*

Oddly enough, in that little obscure school sat two country boys destined to make their names known, Jay Gould and John Burroughs. Jay Gould boasted that he was a year older than John Burroughs. He, too, had been born in Roxbury, and had the same surroundings and the same influences. Jay Gould lived to become a great financier and to accumulate over seventy million dollars; while at no time in his life did John Burroughs have more than enough money for necessities of work and simple travel. He had an immaterial fortune, however, that outweighed millions of dollars, and his words still enrich thousands of readers. Of the two, John Burroughs, the poor man, left the greater inheritance.

The fellowship of those two country boys, equally poor, equally gifted with opportunities for the future, who played and laughed and visited together, was commonplace enough, but the wide divergence in their lives presents one of the most remarkable contrasts in the stories of great Americans. Sharply indeed do their lives represent two contrasting ideals, the love of material power, and the love of that which is spiritual.

All his life John Burroughs desired to harm no man. He said that in his school days, even in the rough country school, he never struck a fellow student. He lived a happy-hearted and kindly life, always more inclined to withdraw into obscurity than to put himself forward. Even in the days of his fame, when all the world came to visit him, he continued to be shy and retiring.

When still little more than a boy, John Burroughs became a school teacher and for eight years had all the hard experiences of teachers of that day, never remaining long in a single school, going from locality to locality, constantly meeting new pupils and new conditions, gaining little money for his work, serving long hours, and "boarding out." In this uncertain life the future essayist drifted as far away from his native home as Illinois. Many a time in his wandering life he must have asked himself why he, the first of all his people to do so, had turned from the work of the farm.

How long John Burroughs might have remained a teacher if it had not been for the coming of the Civil War, is problematical. In spite of his Celtic blood he had too gentle a nature to enforce study and discipline. He could not play the tyrant, nor did he have any wish to develop himself into a Squeers, nor to turn his school into a Dotheboys Hall. As for himself, he delighted in study and in quiet pursuits, but if he wished to lead others at all, he did not wish to force them. In all his days, instead of becoming a fiery enthusiast, he remained a quiet philosopher. In spite of the fact that he taught for eight years, and in mature life, through his books, became one of the greatest teachers of mankind, he lacked many of the characteristics of a good teacher. After a struggle with a particularly obdurate boy he said he would no longer stay in work that he liked so little. And forthwith he left teaching.

Who was the "bad boy" who thus drove John Burroughs away from teaching, and turned him toward literature? Did the boy ever know what service he had performed for the world of letters? Did he know that he had aided in the development of genius?

Of a somewhat scientific turn of mind, the former teacher thought for a time of becoming a physician, and even made some preliminary studies. Certainly in medicine he would have succeeded. As it was, he had no opportunity to carry out his plans. When the Civil War made its ever increasing call for men, John Burroughs hurried to Washington with the full intention of becoming a soldier. At that time another lover of nature, Walt Whitman, then about forty-five years old, was serving as an army nurse. Henry D. Thoreau, two years older than Whitman, and also a lover of nature, remained quietly at home in New England. Fighting had no fascination whatever for either of those men. John Burroughs likewise must have thought of war as repugnant to all his instincts, but he intended to enter the conflict.

When the would-be volunteer found that he would have to spend many months in camp before going to the front, and when he saw the wretched conditions that the soldiers had to endure in their training grounds, he put his half-formed plans aside, and applied instead for a position in the Treasury Department, which was then calling for men.

For nine dreary years, from 1864 to 1873, John Burroughs, with the soul of a poet, worked as clerk in the Treasury of the United States at Washington, performing a humble task as vault-keeper. As one sees it now, this future American essayist had much in common with Charles Lamb, the "Gentle Elia," the humble clerk in the India House. There by the door of the vault, John Burroughs found himself far from the work of the farm, and set at monotonous, confining routine that by no means concerned nature or literature.

Instead of permitting his eight years of teaching and his nine years of serving in the United States Treasury to lead him from the outdoor influences that had exerted so strong an effect upon him in boyhood, he made those years emphasize similar influences. In the years when he taught, he used every opportunity to walk to beautiful places where he could observe and study plant and animal life. While he was teaching, he began also to make attempts to put into words what he noticed in the outdoor world. Even then he turned toward publication. When he was teaching in Newburgh, New York, he timidly sent his first essay to *The Atlantic Monthly,* and rejoiced in having it accepted.

While he served as clerk in Washington he lived in a house surrounded by a small amount of land. Both because he saved money by making a garden, and because he found garden work most congenial, he cultivated as much land as he could. He continued to take recreation in walks, and in loving observation of nature. Perhaps because of his long hours before the steel door of the vault, he found his excursions all the more delightful. In the evenings he continued to write, for he had something to say; and he wrote slowly and painstakingly because he wished to express himself well.

It was while he was still a clerk in the Treasury Department that he published his first book, *Notes on Walt Whitman as Poet and Person.* He was then, in 1867, thirty years old. Needless to say, he by no means expressed his full nature in that first book, nor did he meet success. Instead, he experienced such a sense of failure that he well might have become discouraged.

Because John Burroughs had something far more vital to say, he went on writing. Fortunately, in his second attempt, he expressed himself better. In 1871, when he was thirty-four, he published *Wake Robin,* a book whose cheery title tells its nature. In that book the Treasury clerk wrote of what he knew most intimately, of what he loved most deeply. In *Wake Robin* he gave the world a book that is still living, fresh, vigorous, interesting, and full of personality.

Now John Burroughs had found his real work in life. He had passed his period of preparation, development, training, wonderment, and drifting, and had found his place in the world.

From the earliest days the literature of the English race has expressed appreciation of nature; sometimes, as with Anglo-Saxon poets, turning to exaltation of the sea and the elements; sometimes, as with Chaucer, to admiration of a flower; sometimes, as with Shakespeare, to close and rapt descriptions; sometimes, with poets like Thompson, to pictures of scenes in various seasons; and sometimes, as with later writers, to lyric outbursts like those of Keats or Shelley or Byron; or to worshipful understanding of nature, as in the calmly deep lines of Wordsworth.

In this common love of nature, prose writers as well as poets have expressed themselves. Aside from men like Sidney, who wrote of unreal summer lands, there were others who wrote accurately of what they saw. In the seventeenth century, Izaak Walton, the patron of all anglers, wrote lovingly of fishing in the English streams. John Evelyn, a pioneer in the science of gardening and planting, called attention to the joys of observing nature. In the eighteenth century, Gilbert White, in his *Natural History of Selbourne,* told of observations of nature around his quiet English home, writing painstakingly and faithfully. Later, in the United States, men like Henry D. Thoreau wrote truthfully and well concerning the outdoor world.

Purely scientific observers, writers like John James Audubon, Louis Agassiz, Asa Gray and Hugh Miller, awoke new and lively interest in nature and its wonders. To that noble company of lovers of nature John Burroughs joined himself.

In 1872, the year after he had published *Wake Robin,* John Burroughs bought nine acres of land in the township of Esopus, New York, resolving, when the time came, to live close to the heart of nature, and to continue his work of writing about what gave him the greatest pleasure. Meanwhile he must earn a living. From 1873 to 1884 he served, with some distaste, we must imagine, as a National Bank examiner. Even then he spent a great deal of time on his little farm. There he worked in his vineyard and among his plants, and there he studied and wrote. The books that he published during that time suggested nothing whatever of ledgers and offices, but breathed the spirit of outdoors. He made even his titles suggestive of his happy heart: *Winter Sunshine,* 1875; *Birds and Poets,* 1877; *Locusts and Wild Honey,* 1879; *Pepacton,* 1881; *Fresh Fields,* 1884.

Who can think of John Burroughs as having anything whatever to do with accounts? Who can think of him as adding even a single column of figures in a dry-as-dust book of records?

It is easy indeed to picture him at work among his grapevines, pruning them as Virgil says the Romans pruned theirs centuries before, picking ripe clusters and laying them tenderly in cases for shipment. On his scant acres the naturelover grew grapes, apples and various other kinds of fruit. He found poetic delight in working far from the haunts of men but at the same time doing something useful for the world.

The Emperor Diocletian, says Gibbon in his *Decline and Fall of the Roman Empire,* having abdicated his throne, passed the last nine years of his life "in building, planting, and gardening." Solicited by Maximian to reassume the imperial purple, "he rejected the temptation with a smile of pity, calmly observing that, if he could show Maximian the cabbages which he had planted with his own hands at Salona, he should no longer be urged to relinquish the enjoyment of happiness for the pursuit of power." In such spirit John Burroughs worked, wrote and lived in the last twenty or more years of his life.

Nevertheless, he did not turn himself into a hermit. Often he went far afield from his orchards. In 1871, while he was still a Treasury clerk, he went to Europe for the United States Government, in company with three other employees of the Treasury Department, to convey $50,000,000 in bonds that were to be refunded. He must have thought that errand a curious one for a man of his nature, but perhaps he reflected that it was no more curious for him than it was for Chaucer, the "Father of English Poetry," to be Comptroller of Customs in London, or for Robert Burns, the delight of Scotland, to be an exciseman. Whatever he thought, he crossed the Atlantic and went as far as Paris.

Eleven years later John Burroughs again crossed the Atlantic, this time purely for pleasure, taking his family with him. In both journeys he broadened his view of men and events, increased his zest in reading, found material for comparison and contrast, and in no way changed his attitude toward the simple life.

Within the boundaries of North America the essayist made many trips. In 1899 he went, as a member of the Harriman Expedition, on a mildly adventurous trip to Alaska, learning much of science, and reaching such remote regions as the northeastern shores of Siberia. By accident, then, rather than from adventurous spirit, he played the part of explorer.

In 1903, in company with Theodore Roosevelt, a vigorous nature lover who had vast respect for the kindly essayist, he visited the most interesting parts of Yellowstone Park. He was then sixty-six years old, with much of his fame already won. Of that trip, and of somewhat similar experiences, he wrote in *Camping and Tramping with Roosevelt,* 1907.

Like Mark Twain, John Burroughs visited and enjoyed the semi-tropical comfort of Bermuda. He went still farther to the south, and rejoiced in the luxuriance of Jamaica.

Of camp life he was as fond as any Boy Scout. Every year, in company with some of his friends, among whom were Thomas A. Edison, the inventor, Henry Ford, the manufacturer, Harvey Firestone, the tiremaker, and other companionable people, he dropped back into primitive life in the woods. Beside the camp fire, before the group of his friends, he forgot the demands of the world, stretched at his ease, and told anecdotes from the years of his happy life. Sometimes he camped in the great forests of Maine, and on one or two occasions went into the Canadian wilderness.

When he was two years beyond three-score-and-ten, he journeyed to California, crossed the Pacific and visited Hawaii. In 1911 he again made the journey to California. It was in 1921, when he was returning from a similar trip that he died, far from his home among the trees. Certainly John Burroughs was no hermit. He had the instinct of the wanderer, the eager interests of the traveler, and the open mind of the scientist.

While John Burroughs was in no way inclined to put himself forward, he drew friends to him. He was only thirty-four when he talked with Thomas Carlyle in London, and with that very different person, the poet Dante Gabriel Rossetti. In addition to Carlyle, he met three other great essayists, Matthew Arnold, Ralph Waldo Emerson, and James Russell Lowell. He knew Walt Whitman well, and in 1867 wrote his first book about him, and in 1896 a later book, *Whitman, a Study*. In the United States he drew to himself a host of friends, active men of affairs, among whom were Theodore Roosevelt, Thomas A. Edison, and John Muir. The essayist's home became a place of pilgrimage, and he himself one of the notable national characters. His picture appeared in periodicals so frequently that he became one of the best known men in the land.

Perhaps he made and kept friends because he was an optimist. He had all the serenity of the proverbial philosopher, his attitude toward life being one of acceptance and not of battle. Believing that life is good, and that he himself had been especially fortunate, he expressed, in his writing and in his conversation, serene joy in existence. In one of his last books, *Accepting the Universe,* he set forward his belief in the oneness of man and nature, and his acceptance of all the conditions of life, whatever they may be.

His very appearance in his later days won friends. His white hair and beard gave him the look of a prophet; and his wish to live in a simple cottage whose door was of rough-cut slabs, and to lead a humble life, made him notable. In many ways, indeed, he allied himself in spirit with his first master, Walt Whitman.

Neither a poet nor a sentimental writer, John Burroughs was one of those men who write with charm about the world as it is, without need to exaggerate, or to ascribe to anything in nature characteristics that it does not have. Like Thomas Huxley he combined the powers of the scientist and the essayist. He had curiosity concerning all the facts of nature, and he endeavored to record his observations with minute fidelity to fact. Whenever he fell into mistakes, as he sometimes did, he did not do so because anything that he said was based on empty sentiment. His clearness of observation, a certain gentle childlikeness of thought, and his genuine interest in what he had to say, united to produce a charm that made his works popular. In his own lifetime his books became national classics, studied in schools throughout the country.

Probably he felt pleasure in knowing that he did his best work when he wrote about what he saw near his native Roxbury. When he went farther afield and wrote of scenes or conditions of which neither he nor his people had really intimate knowledge, or when he wrote of other subjects than those of the countryside, he wrote less well.

Photo from Kadel & Herbert, N. Y.

JOHN BURROUGHS

Thomas Carlyle said, "A blind man may travel from Dan
to Beersheba and find all barren." John Burroughs did not
concern himself with a wide territory. He had the power of
the seer, the man who sees and understands, and can show
to others what he sees, and interpret it for them. Naturally,
the essayist never gained distinction as a scientist, and he
made no pretense of having scientific ability. He knew that
he was merely an observer and an interpreter. Instead of
pointing out minute differences and variations, instead of
making classifications or setting forward theories that he
could support by an array of facts, he chose to awaken
people to the charm of the nature that lies around them.
Hence he gave some of his books such titles as *Signs and Seasons,* 1886; *The Ways of Nature,* 1905; *Leaf and Tendril,*
1908; and *Nature Near Home,* 1919.

In his later days John Burroughs gave to his writings a
deeper tone, becoming less the observer and more the philosopher. Then it was that he wrote *Time and Change,* 1912;
The Summit of the Years, 1913; *The Breath of Life,* 1915;
and *Accepting the Universe,* 1920.

In *My Boyhood,* 1922, the gray-haired naturalist wrote with
a reminiscent charm that made every reader feel a delightful companionship. Because he could convey so much of his
own pleasing personality, he deserved his popularity as one
of the most distinguished of American essayists. He made
himself a loving interpreter of nature, felt himself one with
nature and nature's forces, and led others to feel a similar
kinship.

John Burroughs died March 29, 1921. He was buried April
3, the day on which he had intended to celebrate his eighty-
fourth birthday. People noted that that date was the one
hundred and thirty-eighth anniversary of the birth of Washington Irving, another essayist who also had loved the beauties of the region along the valley of the Hudson River.

IV

ANDREW CARNEGIE

PHILANTHROPIST

WITH all his heart, young Andrew Carnegie longed to play
in Pittencrief Glen, where the Lyne Burn went roaring down
through the deep, crooked ravine and with its music tempted
him up the hill, where stood the ruins of old King Malcolm's
castle. The boy felt temptation as much as John Ridd had
felt it at the entrance of the Doone Valley. Every day he
saw the ravine, which cut right through Dunfermline and
constantly enticed him. However much he longed, he longed
in vain; for since his father was a poor weaver, neither he
nor the sons of the other weavers could go up Pittencrief Glen
to play on lands where kings once took their ease.

A few years passed; Andrew Carnegie went to Pittsburgh
in America, found Aladdin's lamp, rubbed it, came back to
Dunfermline, and, with one magnificent gesture, bought the
glen, the burn, the park, the castle, and all, and gave it forever to the common people of Dunfermline, to walk in and play
in all they pleased. He made it possible for every Dunfermline boy to fulfil the kind of desire that he himself had not
been able to realize.

Andrew Carnegie's father, the weaver, although poor,
owned a few books, and wished to own and read more, so he
made an agreement with four other weavers, each of whom
had a few volumes, and formed what was really a private cir-
culating library.

The boy Andrew, listening gravely to all that his elders
said, heard his father express the wish that he could find some

easy way to get enough books to read. Later, when young Andrew was a boy in Pittsburgh, he learned that a good-hearted man had established a library from which working boys could obtain books; and from his father's wish and that fact, he gained an idea that bore rich fruit for people in the future. When he had found a fortune, he gave Dunfermline a library that was free to any one, weaver or not; and what is more, he founded libraries all over the world, making it forever possible for any one who wished to do so to read to his heart's content. In building so many libraries, he made his father's wish come true.

As a boy, because a huge building of stone was such a very different residence from his simple cottage, Andrew Carnegie looked with awe upon even the ruins of a castle. As a man, he bought Skibo Castle, in Sutherlandshire, Scotland, and thus again fulfilled one of his boyhood desires. He appeared to be one of those happy mortals who know how to find the way to gain what they wish.

Instead of showing himself severely practical, as one might think the man would be who could accumulate many millions of dollars, Andrew Carnegie, in fulfilling his boyhood dreams, showed that he was an idealist, a visionary, a man who had set his heart on the "Never-Never Land."

Virtually all that the great millionaire and philanthropist ever did he based upon idealism. Perhaps more than any other man in our modern times he turned the world toward high ideals. Certainly, when he established the Peace Palace at the Hague, as well as the Hero Fund awards, now given in perpetuity in many lands, he attested his wish to make a world where every one should be kindly and noble.

The almost unbelievable romance of Andrew Carnegie, whose biography is one of the wonder stories of today, makes faint indeed the old tales of Aladdin and his lamp and Dick Whittington and his cat. It is the romance of one who made money without losing his dreams; of one who, in making a fortune for himself, made fortunes for others as well.

A hundred and seventeen years before Andrew Carnegie's birth, a certain James Blake had introduced into Dunfermline the art of weaving damask, a work that had developed until in Carnegie's time it had become the principal industry in the place.

In their cottages the Scotch weavers lived somewhat the same manner of life as did the English weaver, Silas Marner, in George Eliot's story, working long, hard hours, gaining little money, living the simplest lives, and remaining, like Silas Marner in his days of sanity, honest, honorable, and upright, "serving God and obeying the law."

When Andrew Carnegie first saw light in a little white one-story cottage in Dunfermline, November 25, 1835, conditions were beginning to be hard for the weavers. Steam and machinery, recently introduced, had led to putting away the old looms.

Among the many Scotch people who had already gone to America, where they had found greater opportunities, were two of Andrew Carnegie's aunts, sisters of his mother. The two good women had gone to Pittsburgh, Pennsylvania, where people made iron and glass, and where every one appeared to be prosperous. Their letters home led the entire family to determine to make their living in the new land.

It was in 1848, when Andrew Carnegie was thirteen years old, that the humble Scotch family made that momentous decision. They disposed of what they had and set out, only to find the sea voyage so long and so uncomfortable that they realized more than ever that they were going far from all that they knew. Nevertheless, not one of the family was despondent.

Those who saw the Carnegies land from the boat saw only a middle-aged man and woman, a boy of thirteen, and a younger boy who was only five, all roughly dressed in homespun, with little baggage, and with every evidence of poverty. Who could foresee what one, at least, of those uncouth immigrants would accomplish?

Instead of traveling across country as we do today, they took their places on a canal-boat, and for more than three weeks dragged along the quiet reaches of the Erie Canal to Buffalo, whence they went to Pittsburgh. Weary from weeks of travel, they had at once to go to work.

The father turned again to weaving, the one thing that he knew how to do well. Then, alas, he found that in America as well as in Scotland, steam was winning the day. With a sigh he surrendered and went to work in a factory, taking with him his son Andrew.

The Carnegies found their fortunes then at their lowest ebb. They had spent most of the money they had saved, and they had no definite plans for the future, and even no aims beyond supplying daily needs. Father and son, beginning work in the factory before daylight, continued all day long amid the roar of wheels, and did not end their toil until dark. When they went home in the evening and ate their simple supper they were tired enough to go to bed at once.

Andrew Carnegie, merely a boy, and finding such work especially hard, looked about and obtained a position more to his liking, one that any boy would have liked. He operated an engine for a man who made bobbins! Instead of the monotonous work of the cotton factory, he turned valves that set wheels in motion.

At no time in his life did Andrew Carnegie think of letting things stay as they were. When he went home from his work of operating the engine he saw other boys who earned money more easily than he did. Why should not he follow their example and turn from the hard work of the laborer? He again looked about him, and after a time became a messenger boy. He who some years later was to give away more than $300,000,000, at that time worked for $2.50 a week, and was exceedingly glad of the opportunity! In his work he found the chance to see many kinds of men and to gain a sort of education.

Like every messenger boy who listens to the click of telegraph instruments, young Carnegie had the opportunity to learn telegraphy. Instead of merely listening idly to the rattle of the instruments, as some might have done, he, with his mind always awake, learned the Morse code.

Very soon he entered the employ of the Pennsylvania Railroad as a telegraph operator. Once again he not only did all that his employers expected, but much more. In those days, when it was customary to receive telegraph messages by letting the instrument print dots and dashes on a strip of paper, Andrew Carnegie distinguished himself above other young operators by learning to read messages merely by sound. As a result of the energetic spirit that prompted him to do this, he advanced, by various promotions that he brought about by his own ability, faithfulness, and effort, to better and better positions.

In the meantime, long before this, he had taken advantage of the chance to read good books and to improve his mind. Throughout his life he felt a debt of gratitude to Colonel James Anderson, who had established the Library for Working Boys, from which, in those early days, he borrowed books. He allied himself with other young men who were intelligent enough to be serious minded, and, in what they called ''The Webster Literary Society,'' discussed with them various literary, historical, and social questions.

By nature, Andrew Carnegie had the spirit that led him to move ahead. He would not remain at the foot of the ladder. He believed in doing work well, for his own satisfaction—the true joy of the worker. By instinct, he sympathized with what Kipling had in mind when the poet wrote of those who should attain complete happiness:

''And no one shall work for money, and no one shall work for fame;
But each for the joy of the working. . . .''

An immediate result of working for work's sake is the attracting of special attention. The world has a habit of watching any worker, whether he be a man who molds a figure on the sand of the seashore, an artist who paints a picture in a public place, or a mechanic who works where people can see him. A man working at a lathe in a store window easily attracts a crowd. The true workman, by the fact that he does his work more lovingly, and therefore better, than most men, attracts more attention, and wins really influential friends.

Thomas A. Scott, superintendent of the Pittsburgh division of the Pennsylvania Railroad, noticed that one could rely upon young Andrew Carnegie and it was he who gave the young man the position of telegraph operator for the railroad, and thus set in motion one of the most remarkable careers of modern times. On February 1, 1853, when Andrew Carnegie was only a boy of eighteen, Scott made him his special clerk and operator at thirty-five dollars a month, a position far better than that of weaver's assistant in a cotton factory.

For a long time the immigrant Scotch boy worked in close contact with the railroad superintendent, and with such cheerfulness, such interest in what he had to do, and such skill that he made himself invaluable. If Superintendent Scott had gained a most energetic helper, Andrew Carnegie had gained a place where, unconsciously, he acquired training in being an executive, becoming superintendent himself, in time.

Then it came about that through Superintendent Scott, Andrew Carnegie entered the world of finance.

"Andrew," said Scott one day, "you are a thrifty lad. I know you are saving money. How would you like to do something with it?"

"What?" asked the canny Scot.

"I have a chance to buy ten shares of the stock of the Adams Express Company for six hundred dollars. Have you got five hundred? If you have, I'll lend you the other hundred."

When Scott explained the nature of the stock, told of its value, and advised the boy to invest, Andrew became enthusiastic. To be sure, he knew that the entire Carnegie family, at that time, did not have five hundred dollars that it could use for investment. Nevertheless, with his usual enthusiasm, he told his mother the opportunity that his friend had offered; and his mother, full of faith in her son and in her son's friend, promptly mortgaged her little home to raise the necessary money. When the time came for the purchase, and Andrew found that he needed still another hundred dollars, the good-natured railroad man advanced that money, in addition to the sum that he had originally promised. In this way Andrew Carnegie set in motion the wheels that made for him millions of dollars.

Some time after this, the young man accidentally met on a railroad train a man who gave him his first opportunity to carry on real work in organization. Young Carnegie, who was known to work in the office of the superintendent of the Pennsylvania Railroad, entered the car in which sat Thomas Woodruff, who had invented what today is so well known that it seems always to have been in use, the sleeping-car.

"Perhaps he can interest the superintendent," thought Woodruff.

The inventor went to the young man, entered into conversation with him, and showed him a small model of the sleeping-car. He aroused Carnegie's enthusiasm.

The result was the formation of the Woodruff Sleeping-car Company, that gave Andrew Carnegie the beginnings of his great fortune.

In order to join with Woodruff and Scott, Andrew Carnegie, who then had only a few hundred dollars, had to borrow more money. This time, without further possibility of raising money by mortgaging the family home, he mortgaged his reputation, or, rather, realized on the reputation that he had already made. Going to bankers who knew him, and therefore trusted him, he gave notes for the amounts he needed. Since the company prospered beyond measure, as he had led the bankers to expect, he soon repaid all that he had borrowed.

On the Pennsylvania streams, people had always noticed a scum that the Indians of early days had collected and sold for medicine. No one had thought it of much value. They did

not know it, but that scum was oil, the sign of vast stores of
wealth that lay underground. Little by little, people began
to find it useful.

The enterprising trio who had been so successful in the
sleeping-car venture found that they could buy the Storey
farm, one of the places where oil was most abundant. In
1860, when Andrew Carnegie was only twenty-five, he became
one of the owners of the richest oil land in Pennsylvania.
He, with Scott and Woodruff, paid forty thousand dollars for
the land that no one before had thought of much value.

If Andrew Carnegie and his associates had bought land
that contained the diamond minds of Golconda, they could
scarcely have done better than in buying the Storey farm.
With customary energy, the partners went to the expense and
took the risk of boring wells, believing that they could find a
market for the product. Later, in one year alone, the company took a million dollars from that rocky Pennsylvania
farm that no one before had noticed except to complain that
the streams were full of scum.

At the very time when fortune offered her gifts to Andrew
Carnegie, he put aside all his energetic money-making plans
in order to give patriotic service during the Civil War. His
associate, Thomas Scott, having been made assistant secretary
of war, Carnegie accompanied him to Washington and used
his ability as a telegraph operator, as well as an executive,
for the benefit of the national cause, becoming superintendent
of military railroads and government telegraph lines in the
East.

When the Civil War came to a close, Andrew Carnegie
went back to his enterprises in Pennsylvania. Now he turned
especially to the development of what he had long seen as the
great sources of prosperity in Pittsburgh, iron and steel.

At Pittsburgh, the far-seeing organizer established the
Keystone Bridge Works and the Union Iron Works. He had
real genius in seeing opportunities, in making plans by which
he could benefit many, always including the public, and in
organizing great enterprises. In other words, Andrew Car-

negie did not permit his horizon to be limited; he always looked beyond. It was a triumph of personality that early in life he could make himself the head of no less than seven great iron and steel works, all within such a limited circle that from his office he could see the smoke of every one.

From the time in 1861 when he associated himself with a certain Mr. Miller in a small, obscure iron works, to the time in 1866 when he organized the Pittsburgh Locomotive Works, he had constantly surprised every one; first, by his ability to see the work that needed to be done; and second, by his equal ability to plan how to do the work well and profitably.

Because of his forward look and his quick grasping of opportunity, he, of all the iron and steel makers in the United States, became the first to introduce into the country the Bessemer process of making steel. In one of his journeys to England he had seen the process, had at once realized its possibilities, and had resolved to carry it to the United States. Thus it came about that in 1868 he entirely revolutionized American methods of manufacturing steel.

Andrew Carnegie was always, at all times in his life, so much the dreamer, so much the idealist, that it is a pity to lay any stress whatever on his power to make money. At all times he found the real source of his power in his visions. In spite of the fact that he could foresee, plan, and organize in a way that made him superior to the most hard-headed, practical man of affairs, he remained from boyhood to old age essentially a supreme idealist.

One of the strongest possible proofs of his early idealism appears in a record written in his diary in 1868, a record written wholly for his own eye, with no thought that any one else would ever read what he wrote:

"By this time two years I can so arrange all my business as to secure at least $50,000 per annum. Beyond this never earn. Make no effort to increase fortune, but spend the surplus each year for benevolent purposes. Cast aside business forever except for others. . . . Man must have an idol. The amassing of wealth is one of the worst species of idolatry. No idol more debasing than worship of money."

That is a most remarkable resolution for a man thirty-three years old, with every prospect of rising to boundless wealth and power. That page from his own private diary shows how mistaken are those people who, not familiar with Andrew Carnegie's lifelong effort to help his fellow man, think of his charity as belonging purely to his old age.

Meanwhile, in spite of charities, the great iron-master's burning energy led to the accumulation of more money than he had ever dreamed of. He became principal owner of the huge Homestead and Edgar Thomson Steel Works and of a combination of other works. He presided as head of the firm of Carnegie, Phipps, and Company, and head of the firm of Carnegie Brothers and Company. In addition to all that, he associated with numerous men of high genius and ability, over whom he wielded influence as a king of the old days did over his great lords.

In 1889, when Mr. Carnegie led H. C. Frick to join forces with him, the Scotch genius became the virtual dictator over more than 40,000 acres of rich coal land in Pennsylvania, and the master of a pay roll that added its figures to $18,000,-000 a year. What a transformation from the immigrant boy, the weaver's assistant, the messenger boy, the telegraph operator, the boy whose father had worked from dawn until dark in dreary factory labor, the boy whose mother had bound shoes in the very city of Pittsburgh where the son became a multimillionaire and a manufacturing king!

In 1899, Andrew Carnegie consolidated all the vast properties in which he was interested, forming that powerful corporation known as the Carnegie Steel Company. Two years later, in 1901, when all these, in turn, became a part of the gigantic United States Steel Corporation, Andrew Carnegie, at that time sixty-six years old, withdrew forever from active business. Then for eighteen years, that is, until his death,

August 11, 1919, he amazed the world by his efforts to devote his wealth to the good of humanity.

In 1898, in an article in the *North American Review,* he had written that a man who accumulates great wealth is "the mere trustee and agent for his poorer brethren."

He made the startling statement that "It is a disgrace for a man to die rich," meaning, by that remark, that the person of great wealth should himself, in his own life-time, see that his fortune accomplishes public good.

In making every one of his gifts, Mr. Carnegie showed himself the idealist. He turned his fortune to the aiding of self-education, to the uplifting of working people, to the strengthening of educational work of all kinds, to the encouragement of self-sacrifice and the development of manhood, and to the establishment of peace and harmony among the nations of the world.

The amazing altruist, with more than the wealth of a Crœsus, or rather, with a purse like that of Fortunatus, gave away staggering sums. To the Carnegie Institute of Pittsburgh he gave $24,000,000; and to the Carnegie Institute of Washington, $22,000,000, hoping by these great gifts to make it possible for worthily ambitious young men to advance themselves in life. Remembering his father's unsatisfied desire for books, he established libraries throughout the United States and the British Empire, even in such remote places as the Fiji Islands. To the city of New York, for branch libraries, he gave $5,200,000; to the city of St. Louis, $1,000,000; and altogether, for municipal libraries for the good of the common people, the immense sum of $60,000,000.

To universities in the land of his birth, Scotland, where he might have remained a poor, obscure weaver, he gave $10,000,000; and to the Foundation for the Advancement of Teaching in the United States and in Canada and Newfoundland, he gave $16,250,000.

For the encouragement of knightly deeds he instituted in all the important lands of civilization the Carnegie Hero Fund awards. From the sums that he gave, he directed the commissions in charge in perpetuity to reward self-sacrifice, the saving of another's life at the risk of one's own. In his breadth of view, firmly believing in the unity of all mankind, he showed interest in common manhood, regardless of race or creed.

For the benefit of the employees of the Carnegie Steel Company he gave $5,000,000; to the Carnegie Dunfermline Trust he gave $3,500,000; to the United Engineering Society, $1,500,000. To the Carnegie Corporation of New York, of which he became a life member, he gave $125,000,000.

For the establishment of harmony among the nations of the world he gave $750,000 for a Pan-American Palace in Washington, D. C., to serve as the headquarters of the International Bureau of American Republics, and thus to help in bringing North and South America closer together in sympathy. To the Palace of Peace at the Hague, a place where the nations of the world might meet for a just settlement of all international difficulties, he gave $1,500,000. Besides these great gifts, he was always giving aid to all uplifting or educational causes, such as the work of Booker T. Washington for negro education at Tuskegee Institute.

In every one of his overwhelming gifts, Andrew Carnegie moved toward some lofty goal. He made the purpose of the Carnegie Corporation of New York "To promote the advancement and diffusion of knowledge and understanding among the people of the United States." To the Carnegie Corporation, when he died, he left nearly all of what remained of the fortune that he had piled up, so that today the Carnegie Foundation of New York has about $135,000,000 with which to carry on its work.

That Andrew Carnegie refused to cling to the old, merely because it is customary rather than because it is best, he showed by his gift of $280,000 to the Simplified Spelling Board, to aid in promoting not phonetic spelling, but simplified spelling, whereby, according to such a conservative educator as the late Superintendent William H. Maxwell, of New York City, school-children could save at least a full year of their school lives.

Never in the United States, nor anywhere else in the group of nations that we speak of as "civilized," had there appeared a more astonishing man. Andrew Carnegie became one of the best known men in the world. His short, sturdy figure, his genial smile, his happy, hearty look, became familiar to people on both sides of the Atlantic. Whether he went to visit his castle at Skibo in Scotland, or remained in his residence in East 91st Street, New York City, he moved like a king, but with the heart of a man of the common people.

Unparalleled honors showered upon him from all sides. Fifty-four cities in Great Britain and Ireland gave him their freedom. Great universities and colleges in the United States and in Scotland and England gave him degrees. France made him commander of the Legion of Honor, and other lands gave him similar distinguished tributes.

In 1883, when he was forty-eight, Andrew Carnegie had become an author, writing *An American Four-in-Hand in Britain*. Like most idealists, he had an itch for the pen, and from 1883 to his death he wrote many articles and books.

Andrew Carnegie had the pleasure of living in hearty health to the good age of eighty-four, and of knowing that every year that he lived he made himself more useful. Surely his was a triumphant career!

V

ALEXIS CARREL

Surgeon

At Compiègne in France, during the World War, a man worked miracles. He was a soldier, but he wore white. Instead of trying to kill he tried to save. From beyond where he had set his station he might have heard the roar of guns, had he not given all his attention to the men before him.

Grim, terrible figures came in endless procession, carried on stretchers, armless, legless, faceless, utter wrecks of suffering humanity. In any other period of history they would have died, and almost been glad to die rather than to live in torture. Over them bent the man in white, a young man, alert, keen-eyed, resourceful, able to fight Death, able even to make new men out of men who had been torn to pieces. He worked night and day, and he directed others. "Doctor Carrel," "Surgeon Alexis Carrel," they called him.

Great stories went from the place where he worked. Men who had been given up to die became well. Men who had expected to lose all use of their limbs found themselves strong. Men who had thought they never again wished any human being to look upon what had been their faces blessed the surgeon who had restored them to something like their former selves.

"He can do anything!" the soldiers said.

"Carrel is a miracle worker," wrote the war correspondents.

"He won the Noble Prize in 1912," said the people at home. "If any one can help the wounded, he can. He's as great a surgeon as we have."

In France, in the hard years of the War, Alexis Carrel, world famous surgeon, worked with all his skill. Long before that, however, he had made himself famous. In the World War he made himself loved.

Long before the World War, in 1912, three persons in the United States had won great honors in recognition of services done for mankind. Three Americans had won Nobel Prizes. One man came from native stock; the two others had chosen the United States as the land of their adoption. The first was Theodore Roosevelt, the statesman, who came from long-standing American ancestry of Dutch origin; the second was Albert Abraham Michelson, the physicist, who was born in Germany; the third was Dr. Alexis Carrel, the surgeon, who was born in France, the land where he was to serve so nobly.

Most people have respect for the work of physicians and surgeons because they see that the labor of such men represents the most kindly, the most altruistic motives that move mankind. They recognize that the object of the work is not personal aggrandizement, nor the gaining of power, nor even the winning of fame, but merely the helping of people who are afflicted. Instead of erecting statues in commemoration of conquerors, who, for the most part, are destroyers of life, people well might make statues in honor of physicians and surgeons, who save life.

From century to century, from earliest times, frightful plagues have swept over civilization, threatening it with extinction. Within the last century they have yielded almost entirely before the quiet, self-effacing work of physicians. Even the "black death," once the scourge of the world, has retreated to its African and Asiatic haunts. In former days surgery gave helpful service only in matters of minor moment, and even then often carried harm as well as healing. The work of a surgeon, however kindly his heart might be, was like the work of a torturer, for the methods of attempting major operations of any kind were too horrible to think of today with equanimity. All too frequently, major opera-

Photo from Brown Bros., N. Y.

ALEXIS CARREL

tions caused the unfortunate patient untold agony, continued pain, and ultimate death.

In spite of the stamping out of plagues by modern medicine, and the bringing of wonderful results through the miracles of surgery, people still speak more often of the soldier than of the doctor. They know the name of Julius Cæsar well, but how many know that of Lord Lister, the founder of antiseptic surgery, or that of Dr. William T. G. Morton, the discoverer of the uses of ether in anesthesia?

> "The evil that men do lives after them;
> The good is oft interred with their bones."

Probably most people, who could not name five of the world's leaders in the advance of surgery, could, with ease, name twenty of the world's great soldiers. Probably, therefore, many who read in 1912 that Dr. Alexis Carrel had won an award of the Nobel Prize in medicine, said: "Who is he?"

Of all the professions that men follow, medicine, most of all, forbids self-advertising. The practitioner must work with the utmost skill, but with great self-sacrifice, feeling satisfied to see the world look more to the result than to the man who brings it about; to think more of the patient and forget the man who restored him to life. Because the practice of medicine is so utterly unselfish in its aim and method, it is one of the most splendid of the professions.

Alfred Nobel, the Swedish chemist and philanthropist, who, in 1896, established the Nobel prizes, left directions that the trustees of the fund should make an award every year to the man who in that year made the greatest advance in the field of medicine. In 1912, Dr. Alexis Carrel, a surgeon of French birth, serving on the staff of the Rockefeller Institute for Medical Research, in New York City, won the distinguished award.

The advances made by Dr. Carrel in blood-vessel surgery represented discoveries of more significance than any that had been made in that field since 1616, when William Harvey had set forward the theory of the circulation of the blood. Dr. Carrel's investigations and experiments had the greatest effect upon that type of surgery, and made possible what surgeons had before thought impossible.

In comparatively recent times in the world's history, advances in surgery that former generations would have looked upon as miracles, have come to pass. Dr. William T. G. Morton, in 1846, announced the discovery of ether anesthesia, and thus making pain no longer necessary, set people free from the need of the grim stoicism or sheer terror with which they had met the surgeon. By his gift Dr. Morton made it possible to carry on the most serious surgical work without immediate pain to the patient. He ended forever the need of agony on the operating table. What gratitude he should have earned from the world, and yet how few know his name!

In 1860, Lord Lister, the father of antiseptic surgery, set forward the theory that absolute surgical cleanliness must prevail, and then showed how to maintain cleanliness and freedom from infection. He saved countless thousands from misery and early death. He brought it about that today surgical cleanliness is so fully recognized that it is difficult to believe there ever was a time when it was not insisted upon.

Once again, so far as ordinary people are concerned, how many who know of Napoleon or the Duke of Wellington, know the name of Lord Joseph Lister?

In 1895 Wilhelm Röntgen accomplished the unbelievable itself, making it possible to look, as it were, through the substantial flesh and see the exact condition of the bones beneath, by the amazing effect of X-rays. The German physicist enabled practitioners to make investigations that before they could not have made without recourse to the knife. Not long ago Dr. W. W. Kean showed that a skilled surgeon may cut into the brain itself without destroying life, may enter the temple of the mind and restore strength, health, and even sanity. In recent times many men, working in different fields of surgery, have learned to understand the body as if it were a machine, and to work upon it, take it apart, and restore it, as if they were highly skilled mechanics working with something far less delicate than flesh and blood, pulsing arteries and delicate nerves.

Dr. Alexis Carrel has done work as amazing as that of Dr. Morton or of Professor Röntgen, for he, like them, accomplished what people said man could not do. He has led in the surgery of blood-vessels, in the transplanting of limbs and organs, and in the preservation and growth of tissues outside of the body.

As is usually the case with people of substantial merit, Dr. Carrel is modest in the extreme, his heart so wholly in his work that he is thoughtless of himself. He had carried on his work so quietly that when he was awarded the Nobel Prize, many, even among leading surgeons, did not know the remarkable work he had done. Without in any way seeking publicity the surgeon had gone about his work for years, modestly and faithfully, with the spirit of the true investigator.

The winner of the Nobel Prize was born in Sainte Foy les Lyon, France, June 28, 1873. At seventeen he became a graduate of the University of Lyon and at eighteen gained the degree of bachelor of science. He at once interested himself in medical studies, and at the age of twenty-three became interne in the hospital at Lyon. There he studied and worked for four years, gaining the degree of Doctor of Medicine in 1900, at the age of twenty-seven.

Then, for two years longer, the young doctor continued in the University of Lyon, serving as prosector. While still a young man he drew attention to his work because of his unusual surgical skill, and his daring spirit of investigation. He had the ability to absorb all the old knowledge and the energy to look further for the new. He made himself an earnest, intelligent student, careful, painstaking, and brilliant. As house surgeon he showed not only the highest devotion to his work, but also a remarkable dexterity of manipulation. In all things, whether in study, in care of patients, or in investigation, he made the most conscientious, painstaking effort.

In 1905 the young surgeon left his native land and came to America, thus causing France to regret the loss of a brilliant surgeon. Even if Dr. Carrel had not come to the United States, and there found unparalleled opportunities, he still would have made himself one of the foremost surgeons of modern times. As it was, he gained a position that stimulated all his powers to the full. As one of the Staff of the Rockefeller Institute for Medical Research he had at command all the advantages that money could provide. Furthermore, instead of serving as an ordinary surgeon, he set to work as a scholar in surgical science, to study, to carry on experiments, and to devote his ability to the discovery of medical or surgical means of helping humankind.

The giving of such an opportunity is peculiarly characteristic of the people of the United States. Because the American people have been quick to recognize the worth of scholarly investigation, every American city of the first rank has provided for study along the principal lines of human interest. The givers of great gifts, the Carnegies, and especially the Rockefellers, have aimed to develop research, experiment, and the seeking of new ways. Under the direction of Simon Flexner, the Rockefeller Institute for Medical Research has for years carried on an active campaign for the development of new medical methods of benefiting humankind, and by its influence has stimulated medical study throughout the world. The work of the Institute in the investigation and the prevention of hookworm made a deep impression upon the public, while other work of almost equal value has been done but has gained less popular attention. Certainly the existence of the Institute has notably helped mankind. To Dr. Carrel it gave the means of accomplishing a great work.

It was Dr. Simon Flexner, the director of the laboratories of the Rockefeller Institute, who offered to Dr. Carrel the opportunity to work and study, surrounded by all the advantages that the Institute could give.

"America has every reason," said Warbuthnot Lane in an

article in the London *Lancet,* "to be proud of its capacity to present to the moving spirits of the world a soil in which they can grow with uninterrupted—nay, stimulated—vigor, and where merit and genius receive a recognition, unequaled, I believe, elsewhere. Carrel is a typical product of these conditions."

If the United States deserves such high praise from a citizen of another country, its own citizens may well believe that it is established upon a rock, its face set toward the development of all that is best in national life.

If it had not been for experiments of the type that Dr. Carrel and his associates carried on, the surgeons in the World War could not have performed their beneficent work in restoring parts of the face, or in giving back the use of limbs so severely injured that once amputations would have been necessary.

Before the surgeons of the World War could transfer living bone, Dr. Carrel and other men had had to learn, through experiment, how to perform such a miracle. In one experiment Dr. Carrel succeeded in removing the entire leg of a dog, and afterwards in replacing it, with every likelihood that the dog would regain full use of the leg, although while the operation itself was entirely successful, lack of proper care in bandaging led ultimately to the dog's death.

The same public that thinks nothing whatever of killing countless numbers of animals for the purpose of providing food for human beings, shudders at the thought of sacrificing an exceedingly small number of animal lives for the purpose of bringing about advances in medicine and surgery, advances that give blessings to the human race utterly incomparable with the blessings given by the deaths of an equal number of sheep or cattle killed for food. Dr. Carrel did not experiment in order to see what astonishing work he could perform, but to find how to aid human beings. He had a greater object than "acrobatic surgery."

In other experiments Dr. Carrel succeeded in transferring

various important organs from one animal to another of the same kind. Thus he removed a kidney from one cat and implanted it successfully in the body of another. To be sure, he had to work with a delicacy and skill far beyond the normal, but what one man can do is possible for another. His work pointed to the saving of human lives. Again, where surgeons had long thought they could not make sutures in arteries, Dr. Carrel showed how to take the cut ends of an artery, or of a vein, and bring them together by the process of anastomosis. By such demonstration he entirely changed the surgery of blood-vessels.

Then the skilful experimenter went still further and showed how to replace part of an artery by inserting part of a vein. In spite of the fact that surgeons had thought that the structure of a vein is such that it cannot withstand the arterial pressure, Dr. Carrel again did the impossible and brought about the anastomosis of veins with arteries.

In still other experiments Dr. Carrel astonished biologists and medical men by keeping alive parts, or even organs of the body, long after they had been severed from their original places. Thus he showed that life survives in the very cells that form the body. Taking part of an artery he preserved it for days, as a living thing, and even extended the period of days into a period of weeks! After he had long preserved, as living matter, such a part of a body, he transplanted it into an animal and saw it continue its existence! By such remarkable experiments he enabled surgeons to find a means of restoring, through the transplanting of new material, parts destroyed by the accidents of peace or of war.

Then Dr. Carrel showed that there is unity in living matter, and transplanted tissues from one type of creature to another, and made them live in their entirely new habitation. Thus he removed certain blood-vessels from a dog, preserved them for a time in the mysterious condition of life, and then transferred them into the body of a cat! At no time did he forget the serious object of his work, the giving of aid to suffering humanity.

For skill and ability in work of this sort he won the Nobel Prize in medicine. He had instituted new methods that surgeons could apply in the saving of human life. He departed far from all that physicians had believed before, and astonished even his close colleagues by a technical skill so delicate as to be almost miraculous. In his work he showed the brilliant powers of a man of genius, and the devoted enthusiasm of one who works for an unselfish and a noble cause.

When Dr. Carrel was at work in his laboratory at Lyon in France he had as one of his assistants a young woman, Anna de la Motte, who had unusual skill. She had been a laboratory student of the celebrated French surgeon Tuppier, but for a time had left laboratory work, only to return to it with new enthusiasm. The two found so much in common that romance developed, and they were married in 1913. In his wife, therefore, Dr. Carrel found a helper who not only gave him encouragement and inspiration for his work but had the highest technical skill. In that respect he had good fortune of the kind enjoyed by Professor Pierre Curie, whose work Madame Marie Curie so ably seconded, and so remarkably carried on after his death in 1906.

In winning the Nobel Prize in medicine Dr. Carrel first attracted public attention; in the World War he found a new opportunity for usefulness, and by his daring originality saved thousands of lives. In his work as a war surgeon, serving in France, he eclipsed the record he had made up to that time, brilliant as that was.

Being of French birth, Dr. Carrel could not remain quietly in his laboratory at a time when France had such great need. In 1914, in the very first year of the war, he went to France, prepared to give his services in any way in which they would be most useful. He became a major in the medical department of the French army, his work being to direct difficult surgical work, and to suggest new and improved methods of aiding wounded soldiers. Madame Carrel, herself a woman of France, likewise felt the call of the land of her birth. She also went to France in 1914, where she continued with her own great technical skill to aid her husband. From 1914 to 1919, the duration of the World War, the distinguished investigator and surgeon, together with his wife, gave all their attention to the needs of the soldiers.

In 1917 Dr. Carrel returned to the United States on a special furlough from his pressing work in France, temporarily leaving his war work, at the call of the Rockefeller Institute, to establish a hospital on the grounds of the Institute. When he had completed that work he again returned to Europe, where he continued war service until the end of hostilities.

In all wars, surgeons work under almost impossible conditions. They find the treatment of wounds a matter of the most serious moment. In a single day they receive more patients than they can possibly treat, and those patients with injuries of the most frightful description. They know that some of them have been without proper treatment for days, and that all have been quickly and rudely bandaged, and hurried back from the firing line by the roughest conveyances, under conditions that tend to increase rather than decrease their weakness.

In ancient times the wounded who could not help themselves lay in agony until death relieved them. In later times the best the unfortunate soldiers could hope for was the cauterizing of their wounds with boiling oil or with white-hot iron. In fact, because the advance of surgery was exceedingly slow, even as late as the period of the Civil War in the United States the wounded fared badly indeed as compared with the wounded of the World War.

In former times, as now, most war wounds were especially septic, that is, in popular language, poisoned. Such wounds, in periods when medical knowledge was not so great as at present, led to the most serious results. They brought rapid infection, made amputations necessary, and in all too many cases caused death. When the wounded lay some time before they received treatment they gave up all hope, but even when they were operated upon at once, they gained little except further agony. They suffered infection of their wounds, and then suppuration, and, if they lived to regain health, went through long and painful periods of anxiety. In former times the unfortunate wounded men confronted a thousand dangers. However careful surgeons might be, they could not, with the means once at hand, do much for the relief of the seriously wounded. When they operated on grave cases, they left the most troublesome scars and adhesions, that made the saving of life a blessing indeed, but one which did not restore full ability. When they amputated limbs they caused the ends of nerves gradually to lose function, with the result that muscles withered and became almost useless.

The celebrated French surgeon, Dr. Tuppier, found by investigation that only thirty per cent of wounds received in battle that called for operation were really serious enough in themselves to demand the knife. He found that seventy percent of the operations became necessary, not because of the nature of the wounds, but because of the infection of the wounds by the missiles that had made them, by clothing, by contact with the ground, or by other means all too common in warfare.

Dr. Carrel was one of many who changed all those conditions. He could not change the circumstances of warfare. As a matter of fact, he found the conditions that prevailed in the World War far more dangerous, from the point of view of the surgeon, than the conditions of the Civil War. What he could do was to change the treatment of wounds. He had left his laboratory in the Rockefeller Institute for Medical Research, but had found a greater laboratory on the battle field, a laboratory that stimulated him to the greatest possible exertions. At once he set about his work with the same spirit of daring originality that he had shown in times of peace, and with the same purpose of saving life and limb. The new method that Dr. Carrel found for healing desperate wounds was the simple one of saving the soldier from the very great danger of wound infection. That method became the means of saving not only the lives, but even the limbs of thousands of soldiers gravely wounded in the World War.

Dr. Carrel did not find his work in France in any respect easier than other war surgeons found theirs. He established a laboratory hospital at Compiègne and there gave himself heart and soul to his task. In 1918, the sweeping advance of the German forces drove him away from the place where he was working with such energy. Undaunted, like the good soldier that he was, he directed the establishment of a laboratory hospital in another place. Time and again he gave himself literally night and day to his work, and continued service until the signing of the Armistice.

Before his time, surgeons had endeavored to clean wounds, and then to keep them clean by excluding possibilities of infection. Dr. Carrel, of course, cleaned wounds, but he destroyed infection by using antiseptics in a new way. An English surgeon, Dr. H. D. Dakin, had found that a neutral solution of hypochlorite of lime is a strong antiseptic that does not in itself do harm to the patient. Dr. Carrel, learning the value of this antiseptic, devised a new method of applying it so that he kept the wound continually moistened with antiseptic.

The Carrel-Dakin method of treating wounds so that they are continually cleaned, continually free from all infection, and continually well drained, reduced the poisoning effects to the lowest degree. The method brought about results that would have vastly astonished the surgeons of the Napoleonic wars, those of the Civil War in the United States, or of the Franco-Prussian War in 1870. Destroying infection and putting aside all danger of new infection saved the lives of great numbers of soldiers who, under the methods of former times, most certainly would have died. The same method that saved life and limb also led to astonishingly rapid recovery. Chemotherapy, the method of healing by the use of chemicals rather than by making resort to the knife, made almost all wounds heal satisfactorily.

In Dr. Carrel's own book, *The Treatment of Infected Wounds,* all that the great surgeon learned in the World War appears in full. The Carrel-Dakin treatment of wounds is exceedingly simple, a treatment that can, of course, be applied to any of the wounds received in peace, but it has gained the honor of being called the greatest discovery in surgery since the time when Joseph Lister set forward his theory concerning antisepsis.

In six to eight days at the longest, Dr. Carrel made the most dreadful wounds sterile. Through an ingenious apparatus of tubes and drains, and the application of fresh antiseptic solution at frequent intervals, he destroyed bacteria and the possibility of infection. By this method he led to the immediate dissolution of tissues that had been torn apart or so severely injured that future value was out of the question, and likewise prevented the dissolution of injured tissues from becoming harmful. Thus he hurried the processes of healing.

Fortunately, while the Carrel-Dakin solution had such an effect on torn tissues, it had no harmful effect whatever on living tissues, but acted for them as a protector rather than as a destroyer. Likewise, it acted in all ways as a means of bringing about healing for the entire wound. The use of a neutral solution of hypochlorite of lime and the combination of tubes and drains increased the rate of the healing process to a degree that was astonishing.

To bring it about, even for a single soldier, that a wound of ugly nature that once would have called for eighty or ninety days of healing should heal in half that time, or at most in sixty days, was in itself a praiseworthy deed; but to provide the means of shortening the period of pain and anxiety, and of bringing restoration to many thousands of sufferers, was to confer incalculable benefits. Devoted surgeons, serving under the most difficult conditions during the World War, saved thousands of lives. They found their work aided immeasurably when they used the Carrel-Dakin treatment for wounds.

In thirty-three observational cases, in which severe lesions of the worst type were complicated by fractured bones, no deaths occurred; and what is still more remarkable, no amputations were necessary. In seventy-eight observational cases in which frightful wounds were not complicated by the breaking of bones, there were likewise neither deaths nor amputations.

What would the doctors of old times have said to the work of Dr. Carrel, who thus, as one writer put it, "healed wounded soldiers to order"?

Even in the worst cases that came under observation, cases in which bones were broken in confusing ways, in which arteries had been severed, or in which infection of a severe type had set in, the Carrel-Dakin treatment was most valuable, even if it could not always play the part of a miracle worker and restore function and life. Today there are living happily in their homes, veterans of the World War who owe their lives, as well as the fact that they can use muscles that might have been almost useless, to the work of army surgeons who learned from Dr. Alexis Carrel how to aid and heal.

When the war ended, the great surgeon and investigator returned once more to the quiet of his research in the laboratories of the Rockefeller Institute in New York. There he continued to serve as a soldier in the lasting war for the good of humanity. Some one said of him that his entire career is typical of the desire that people of modern times have to look to the future rather than to the past, and to find new ways of helping fellow men.

VI

SAMUEL LANGHORNE CLEMENS
(Mark Twain)

Humorist

Once a man who thought that he resembled Mark Twain, sent Mr. Clemens his photograph, and with it a letter commenting on what he considered a remarkable resemblance. At once the humorist sat down and wrote the following letter:

"My dear Sir—
Many thanks for your letter, with enclosed photograph. Your resemblance to me is remarkable. In fact, to be perfectly honest, you look more like me than I look like myself. I was so much impressed by the resemblance that I have had your picture framed, and am now using it regularly, in place of a mirror to shave by.
> Yours gratefully,
> S. L. Clemens."

A series of anecdotes of this sort endeared Mark Twain to the American people. His humor was spontaneous, unexpected, and always mirth-provoking. His casual remarks, quips from his frequent brief addresses, or quotations from his letters, were repeated from person to person, always preceded by the words, "Did you hear what Mark Twain said?" It was not alone the long series of books that Samuel Langhorne Clemens produced that gave him his popularity. It was the nature of the man himself, as well as the originality of his writing, that made him in many ways a most notable individual of his time.

Even in his own lifetime there grew about Mark Twain, the name by which Mr. Clemens became best known, a body of popular legend such as can come only about those who have won the public heart. The stories showed that he was looked upon as typically American in his freedom from restraint, in his boldness of expression, and in his originality, as well as in his lack of reverence for anything that involved sham or hypocrisy; also in his choice of subjects, his honesty, his keen sympathy, his democracy of spirit, and even in his appearance and manner of speech.

Especially in the last days of his life, Mr. Clemens looked the part that the popular mind had long ascribed to him. He appeared notable even when he stood among notable people. He had bushy, white hair, fine, strong features, and an easy and nonchalant bearing that made him stand out as the most distinguished person of any group. In 1907, when he was given the degree of doctor of literature at the University of Oxford, in England, he attracted all the attention, for the moment overshadowing such persons as Rudyard Kipling, General William Booth, and Sir Robert Ball, the distinguished astronomer, all of whom received degrees on the same occasion. Mark Twain was the central figure, for the moment the one great man at Oxford.

In 1902 the president of the University of Missouri, in conferring upon Mr. Clemens the degree of doctor of laws, called him "America's foremost author and best-loved citizen." Without question, Mark Twain, in his lifetime, became the best known of all American authors; he gained a fame that made it apparent that he will be remembered longer than any other writer of his period.

Most other really great American writers did not spring from American influences and American traditions in the sense that Mark Twain did. Washington Irving, the first American author to win recognition beyond his own country, modeled his work upon the writings of the English essayists and story-tellers. Like Mark Twain he had the gift of humor, but he had also the doubtful blessing of classical English reading and long residence abroad. Edgar Allan Poe, in his prose writings, followed the German models of Ludwig Tieck and Ernst Hoffman. The New England writers, even when highly gifted with humor, as were James Russell Lowell and Oliver Wendell Holmes, wrote under the influence of strong English and classical traditions. In great part, most American writers who were contemporary with Mark Twain read from so-called classical books, or gained education in classical colleges, and thus became more or less imitators of English or continental writers.

Mark Twain, to use the pseudonym, rather than the rightful ''Samuel Langhorne Clemens,'' was born in Florida, Missouri, November 30, 1835, far from the culture of New England. When he was three years old his people moved to Hannibal, Missouri, a place exactly like the town described in *Huckleberry Finn* and *Tom Sawyer*.

Hannibal, at that period, was little more than a collection of simple houses on the banks of the Mississippi River. It had no Harvard College and no literary traditions. In most respects the place was a frontier town, whose people were rough, even if they were kind-hearted; and uneducated, even if they had quick wit.

In his early days, instead of living in books, Mark Twain saw life, the moving drama that Carlyle said exists in the meanest hut. Instead of education based upon English traditions, and ultimately upon Latin and Greek, he had the brief training that he could gain in the poor common schools of Hannibal, and later the longer training that he obtained from adventures on the Mississippi river, picturesque experiences among the hills and mountains of the far west, and in the moving events of a wandering life. Instead of finding the nature of his early surroundings and the unusual conditions of his life a hindrance, he found them the means of giving to his writing, in later life, the spirit that people call so thoroughly American, so close to the lives and hearts of the common people. If he had had the opportunities to receive a classical education and to read much from British authors he might have lost his greatest advantage. He made his work racy, of the soil, because fortunately he fell only under American influences.

Mark Twain's descent was from Dutch and English stock. His people appear always to have been restless rovers, from the time when some of his ancestors had first crossed the sea to settle in a new land. The family lived in various parts of Virginia, until like Natty Bumppo in Cooper's *Leatherstocking Tales*, John Marshall Clemens, Mark Twain's father, found the Virginia hills too crowded, and moved to Kentucky. Carried by the pioneer spirit he moved on to Adair County, Tennessee, where he became owner of such a vast extent of land that Mark Twain afterwards spoke of it as "the landed possessions" of the family. At last the roving spirit took the man to Missouri, where in the little village of Florida, in a small, one story house, Mark Twain was born. Even after the boy's birth the father moved again, this time to Hannibal, Missouri, where Samuel Langhorne Clemens spent his boyhood.

Sam, the boy, led much the sort of life that Tom Sawyer and Huckleberry Finn did. He felt such an irresistible attraction for the Mississippi River that he fell into it and all but drowned no less than sixteen times before he was twelve years old. He talked with boatmen, went up and down the river, rambled about the country and did much as he pleased, keeping his parents and every one else wondering what he would do next. Instead of being the good boy of model stories, he delighted in mischief and in practical jokes.

As a small boy he saw his father, a local justice of the peace, hold frontier court, using a packing-box as a desk. He saw slaves, like "Nigger Jim," working for masters who could punish them or sell them whenever they pleased. He saw swindlers like the "king" and "the duke" of *Huckleberry Finn,* and the delightedly observed street fights of all degrees of violence. He went down the river a short distance, and explored the cave that every boy now knows so well as "Tom Sawyer's Cave." He lived in a two-story brick house before

Photo from Brown Bros., N. Y.

SAMUEL LANGHORNE CLEMENS—"MARK TWAIN"

which stood a great tree, a quiet, comfortable home that was the starting point for many an adventure.

When he was twelve years old he first met the serious side of life. His father died and he had to go to work to earn money. No longer could he spend his days in the vagabondage of childhood. Fortunately for the world he found a position as "printer's devil," and thus at the early age of twelve came into close and inky contact with publication. He had to do all the dirty or disagreeable work of the office, as well as to endure the gibes and practical jokes of the rough printers. On the score of mischief, however, he more than held his own, and frequently upset the office with his own practical jokes played in return. He swept the office, washed the rollers, built fires, picked up the scattered type, folded papers and did errands. When in school he had excelled in spelling and had learned to enjoy history. While in the printer's office, without his knowing it, he learned how to write, and increased his interest in the human drama.

From his father, Mark Twain had inherited the roving spirit. All his life he moved from place to place, never settling permanently in any one, however much he liked it. When he had worked for three years as "printer's devil" he started out to see the world. He was then fifteen years old. He could set type, manage a press, and carry on the work of a small printing office. Although it was a long way from Hannibal, Missouri, to New York, little by little the boy made his way across country, working now in one office and now in another, and at length arrived in New York with twelve dollars in his pocket. In the city where he was one day to be the most noted of persons, he looked about for work, wondering how long his twelve dollars would last. He fell in with a printer for whom he worked a dozen weeks, and then set off again, this time going to Philadelphia, where he spent some months in another printing office. Again he started off and went to Cincinnati, then to Louisville, and then to St. Louis, on the banks of his favorite river, the Mississippi.

Instead of thinking all this wandering sufficient for a boy

between fifteen and twenty, young Clemens longed for more. Some time later, learning that there were amazing lands far to the south, and that a vessel was about to set out for the reaches of the Amazon in South America, he at once wished to go beyond the equator, into the heart of unexplored regions. To fulfil that wish he spent two weeks in sailing down the Mississippi to New Orleans, from which place he hoped to sail for the tropics.

It is a pity that Mark Twain never put into the form of picaresque romance, in the style of *Huckleberry Finn,* the story of his early experiences as tramp printer. If he had told nothing except his own vagabond adventures, he would have made a book of most unusual interest.

Once in Philadelphia, he saw some rough men brutally treating a boy, and immediately sprang to the rescue. All that he gained by his chivalry was a thorough trouncing for himself. Throughout life, as then, he was always ready to defend the under dog.

When the would-be explorer of the Amazon arrived in New Orleans he found no chance to sail to the unknown, so he turned to an opportunity that really existed. He asked the pilot of the steamer on which he had come down the Mississippi to show him how to pilot a river boat. All the way to New Orleans he had felt the fascination of the pilot's work. He had watched with almost breathless interest the rounding of curves and points, the avoidance of mud bars and snags, the passing of other boats, and the approach to landings. "If I could be a river pilot I should be absolutely happy!" he thought.

"Yes, I'll teach you, if you pay me five hundred dollars," said the pilot.

Mark Twain, then about twenty-one years old, did not have five hundred dollars, but he did have high hopes.

"I'll pay you five hundred dollars when I get it," he answered.

"It's a bargain," said the pilot.

Sam Clemens had a happy day when he first stood at the

wheel of the clumsy old river boat and directed the course. He gained his wish, and became a full-fledged pilot. For about five years, from the time when he was twenty-one until he was twenty-six, he guided river steamers up and down the Mississippi. From those years, later in life, he drew the memories that went into the anecdotes of *Life on the Mississippi,* and the poetic descriptions of the Mississippi in *Huckleberry Finn.* As he earned at least $250 a month for his work, he became prosperous. For all that, as he stood at his wheel in his rough clothes, neither he nor any one else thought for a moment that he would ever find a welcome in the courts of kings and emperors. He had no thought that he would ever become a writer!

At the outbreak of the Civil War the pilot left his wheel, returned to his native Hannibal and enlisted in the Confederate army. For three months Mark Twain served as a soldier. When it happened that his brother, Orion Clemens, of whom he says much in his autobiography, gained an appointment as Territorial Secretary of Nevada, a place that then lay quite beyond the knowledge of most people, Mark Twain, as private secretary for Orion, went into the "wild west." The former Confederate soldier soon found that in the headquarters at Carson City he ran the risk of being recognized by Union soldiers. For that reason he left the more populous town and went to a small place called Aurora.

What adventures he had in Nevada! He loafed in country stores, played cards, smoked from morning to night, told stories without end, and listened to such yarns as *The Jumping Frog,* a frontier story that he afterwards told in most amusing way in print. At that time, in the rough surroundings of a frontier territory, he developed the humor that he had always had. In particular, he learned how to interest others.

Mark Twain enjoyed those months more than any others in all his life. He played practical jokes constantly, lived without responsibilities or worry, and simply enjoyed life. He did almost anything that came to hand. Sometimes, with pick and shovel on his shoulder, he set out as prospector, hoping to "strike it rich." For a short time, without his then knowing its value, he owned the famous Comstock Lode, that afterwards turned out millions of dollars. Sometimes he worked as day laborer in an ore crusher. He was "nobody," but he lived a life of supreme happiness.

Being a born story-teller, the young miner began sending humorous letters to Nevada papers. As might be expected, he wrote crudely, but he made his readers laugh. In 1862 he became local editor of the *Virginia City Enterprise*. It was then that he first used the pen name "Mark Twain," an expression that he drew from the report of soundings on the Mississippi river boats, "mark twain"—"up to the mark of two feet."

Too unsettled to remain long in any one place, or in any one occupation, the rising newspaper man left the mining camps of Nevada and went to San Francisco, then little better itself than a great mining camp. There he worked as city editor of the *Morning Call*, and later, in 1865, in connection with another adventurer, Bret Harte, as editor of the *Californian*.

What a rare partnership that was: Mark Twain and Bret Harte, both of them born story-tellers, both of them lovers of romance and adventure, trying to make a living from the practical work of the newspaper! Finally the two "great writers-to-be" trudged off into the hills, hunting for gold. In each case they were to find gold by developing ability to write, but at that time each was looking for nothing less than the pot of gold at the end of the rainbow.

Mark Twain, the born adventurer, could not remain long in San Francisco. He heard that over the ocean lay the Sandwich Islands, then less visited than the South Sea Islands are today. Off he sailed, in 1866, for the land of palm trees and dusky natives, prepared to pay his way by writing letters to the *Sacramento Union*. He was then thirty-one years old.

When the traveler came back to San Francisco, after interesting adventures that he had reported most entertainingly, he had spent his money and again had to set to work in the newspaper field. Now he added something new; he began to give public lectures, and to play the part of professional humorist.

He wrote a lecture on coarse brown wrapping paper, pasted the sheets together, and let a prodigious strip unroll when he stood before an audience in any of the small towns of California or Nevada; then he went on, with his slow drawl, to give a humorous talk that set the house into roars of laughter. He had learned the art of public entertainment in the days when he had loafed in the country stores of crude mining towns.

But why stay long in California and Nevada? The restless seeker for something new turned his thoughts to the East, and promptly secured passage on a vessel sailing for the Isthmus of Panama. Since in those days there was no Panama Canal, nor any security against yellow fever, he went on a real adventure. He made his way across the Isthmus in safety, took another vessel, and landed in New York. From there he proceeded to Washington, where for a time he earned a living by writing Washington Letters for the San Francisco *Alta,* and by giving humorous lectures.

Hearing that a steamer called *The Quaker City* was to sail for Europe and Palestine, the wanderer was on fire to go as a passenger. On the promise of writing humorous accounts of the trip he secured $1200 from the *Alta,* and joined what was really a selected company of people of scholarship and refinement. Among them the man who had spent so many days "roughing it," to use the title of one of his books, in which he afterwards told of some of his early experiences, must have felt somewhat out of place. However he felt, he wrote articles, afterwards printed as *Innocents Abroad,* that set the world laughing. He now came into his own as a humorous writer of national interest.

Strange as it seems today, Mark Twain did not find it easy to secure a publisher for his articles in book form. He offered the manuscript to publishers in New York, in Boston and in Philadelphia, but they all declined to print what became one of the best selling books ever published in the United States. Finally the humorist met Albert D. Richardson who had relations with the American Publishing Company of Hartford, Connecticut. He arranged through Mr. Richardson that the Hartford company would print the book. In that way Mark Twain became connected with Hartford, a city that he was to make famous.

To the chagrin of the publishers who had refused the manuscript, and to the delight of the author, *Innocents Abroad* had an unparalleled sale, selling at once over 200,000 copies, and bringing profits of many thousands of dollars. From that time to the present the book has continued to produce royalties.

Meanwhile Mark Twain had sailed again, had made the long journey to San Francisco, and then had turned and come back to New York. He had a romantic reason for wishing to remain in the East. On *The Quaker City* he had seen the picture of a young woman, Olivia Langdon, of Elmira, New York, and had fallen in love with the picture. He was so successful a wooer that he married the woman of his choice, the daughter of a prosperous judge.

After his marriage Mark Twain expected to live in a simple boarding-house in Buffalo, New York, where he had a position on the *Buffalo Express.* When he and his bride arrived in Buffalo he was surprised to be met by a carriage drawn by beautiful horses, and to be taken to an imposing house. Amazed, he asked what it all meant. Then he learned that his father-in-law had played a practical joke upon him, in fact had given him horses, carriage, house and all!

On his visit to Hartford at the time of the publication of *Innocents Abroad,* the author gained an impression that stayed with him. He thought it good to live in the city that had first welcomed his book. About 1870, therefore, he moved to Hartford, and there erected a beautiful, castle-like, brick and stone house. Since money had poured upon him he was able to furnish his new house with every luxury.

The erection of the Hartford residence by Mark Twain and the princely way in which he entertained guests there, remind one of the erection of Abbotsford by Sir Walter Scott, and the lavish hospitality of "the wizard of the North."

There are, in fact, many parallels between the lives of Mark Twain and Sir Walter Scott. Both men wrote under pseudonyms, one calling himself "Mark Twain"; the other styling himself merely "The Author of 'Waverley.'" Both men rapidly won public favor and accumulated large sums of money. Both built great houses in which they entertained freely. Both met great financial disasters through the failures of publishing houses. Both men, without being legally bound to do so, gave themselves heart and soul to the payments of huge debts. Both achieved their purposes, and both won lasting fame, alike as writers and as men.

In the summers Mark Twain, with his family, went to the "Quarry Farm" at Elmira, near his wife's former home. There he enjoyed days of triumph. He saw himself the head of a growing family; he found his fame increasing daily; and from his books he gained a great income, from his first books alone receiving as much as $30,000 a year.

Indeed, at most times in his life the great humorist found it far easier to make money than to keep it. Like Sir Walter Scott he enjoyed the success of a magician who had only to wave his magic wand to discover gold. From the dramatization of *The Gilded Age*, a book that he wrote in connection with Charles Dudley Warner and published in 1873, he received in one year alone as much as $70,000!

People do not generally realize that Mark Twain was not only a writer but also a successful inventor. He was forever devising some useful or oddly ingenious contrivance. Among such devices he made the celebrated *Mark Twain's Scrap Book*, a simple means of filing clippings on already gummed strips and pages. From that invention alone he gained more than $100,000! In his entire lifetime he earned perhaps $2,000,000.

In spite of his ability to earn, and in spite of the long

hours of work that he gave to his writing, people still think of the author of *Huckleberry Finn* as a man slow in speech and in action, a lover of ease, and even of indolence.

In 1872 Mark Twain went to England, where he lectured, and made arrangements for the foreign publication of his writings. In 1873 he came back for a time to the United States. Then in 1878 he and his whole family were off for a sixteen months stay in France, Switzerland and Germany. He simply could not remain quietly in one place.

In 1876, stirred by memories of his boyhood days in Hannibal, he wrote the immortal *Tom Sawyer*. Nine years later, in 1885, he published the sequel, *Huckleberry Finn,* perhaps the most vital of all American books of fiction.

Mark Twain alone knew to what an extent he drew the material of those two books from real life. He himself, in spite of the fact that others have been pointed out, was both Tom Sawyer and Huckleberry Finn. He described the cave because he had played in it as a boy. He wrote about Injun Jo and other persons in the stories because he had seen them in real life. He made his books so real that he gave them lasting life. He wrote about boys that are genuine boys, combining good and evil, mischief, chivalry, trickery, fun, and heroism. In those two stories he reached his highest achievements in writing.

In 1884 Mark Twain, like Sir Walter Scott, entered into partnership in a publishing house, becoming one of the founders of the printing firm of C. L. Webster and Company. At first he delighted to see the great successes the new firm made, but in the end he became involved in a failure that made him, as he believed, morally responsible for a debt of more than $200,000.

Under circumstances that some others would have evaded without much pricking of conscience, Mark Twain showed himself a man of the highest honor. He gave up his beautiful house and its furniture; sacrificed all that he had, and went to work manfully to repay every cent of the debt. That was something that even he could not do quickly, but he continued writing and lecturing, until he paid the entire amount, great as it was.

In those years of struggle he traveled much, visiting Europe, and residing there, and even making a lecture tour of the world under the management of J. B. Pond. At that time he wandered farther than he had ever done before, going to New Zealand, Australia, Ceylon, India, South Africa, and England. From that long trip he drew *Following the Equator,* which he published in 1898.

Like all humorists Mark Twain had a deep vein of melancholy, and at many times in his life became deeply depressed. In more than one of his books he shows the serious side of his nature. In 1896, when he published his *Joan of Arc,* he issued it anonymously, fearing that the public would refuse, as it often did, to take a humorist seriously. Once, at a girls' college, Mark Twain attempted to read a really serious poem that he had written. Thinking the audience an appropriate one to which to read the poem, he said, "I have written a poem." He awoke shrieks of laughter.

"I have written a serious poem! I mean it!" he said earnestly. He drew forth still more laughter.

"Here it is!" he said, as he showed the manuscript. He made the house laugh and applaud more than before.

"I shall not read it," he announced in despair, putting the manuscript away amid the laughter and applause of a highly amused audience. It is small wonder that he chose to print *Joan of Arc* anonymously.

In mature life Mark Twain had great reason for depression. He felt keenly the sting of the failure of his publishing house, and staggered under the burden of repaying such great sums as he believed himself accountable for. He sorrowed for many years to see his wife an invalid, and he grieved over the deaths of favorite children. At an age when he expected to enjoy life the most, he felt himself obliged to work the hardest. Nevertheless, he kept his wit and humor alive.

When his fortunes were at the lowest ebb, and a report went through the United States saying that Mark Twain was dead, he received a dispatch from a newspaper asking for details. The humorist immediately sent a message that made all the world laugh: "The report of my death is greatly exaggerated."

In 1893, when under the darkest clouds, he had the good fortune to make the acquaintance of the Standard Oil magnate, Henry H. Rogers. Too proud and independent to take any financial help from a man who was eager to give it, he did accept a friendship that ripened, with the years, into closest intimacy. When, three years later, in 1896, Mark Twain's daughter Susie, a young woman of twenty-four, died, he had every reason to feel the value of friendship.

In the latter years of his life, except for frequent visits to Bermuda and other places, Mark Twain lived in New York City. There he wrote industriously, spending much time on his *Autobiography*, a work that he intended should be the most truthful, most nearly complete, and most self-revealing autobiography ever written. In order to avoid giving immediate offense he directed that the book should not be published until long after his death.

Having a rare gift as an after-dinner speaker, Mark Twain spoke often on public occasions. He told anecdotes inimitably, and could set a house into roars of laughter, while at the same time giving shrewd comment on current affairs. Speaking in a comically lazy, slow drawl, with a fund of wisdom such as appears in the original epigrams that he placed at the headings of chapters of *Pudd'nhead Wilson*, he could sway an audience at will.

In his later days Mark Twain won great public honors. He received honorary degrees from Yale and Oxford. He became a member of the American Academy of Arts and Letters. Everywhere he met people who welcomed him with enthusiasm. In fact, he became the most noted public person in the United States, one whom every one knew.

Nevertheless, in his last years, the humorist was a sad and lonely man. He grieved for his wife, who had been the greatest help to him in all his work and in all his troubles, and who had died while they were living in Europe. He sorrowed likewise for his daughter Susie, who died at twenty-four, and for his daughter Jean, for whom he had had an especial love, who died at twenty-nine, when he himself was in his seventy-fourth year. He missed another daughter who had left home to marry Ossip Gabrilowitsch, the distinguished Russian pianist. Old, lonely, and sad, Mark Twain lived on. He who had given so much of laughter to the world found for himself much of sadness. Propped on pillows, white-haired and venerable, looking like a seer or a great poet of dim old times, he dictated his autobiography. Finally, in 1910, at the age of seventy-five, he died.

Always a wanderer, always restless, he had won success. A visionary and a dreamer, he had maintained absolute honesty in the face of utmost difficulties. Thoroughly honest himself, he hated all hypocrisy and all sham and pretense. He was a maker of laughter but also a man of the deepest sympathies and the most tender heart. A true American, he liked all types of people. In many respects he is the most notable author in the history of American literature.

VII

THOMAS ALVA EDISON

Inventor

To sit in one's old age and see the world made happy by the inventions one has made must be delightful. Few are they who achieve this high success, and fewer still are they who live to enjoy to the full the results of it.

Thomas A. Edison saw the entire world literally brought from darkness to light through his perfection of the electric light and of electric lighting systems. He saw the world turned from coarser enjoyments to the educating influence of moving pictures through his development of the kinetoscope. He saw music, song, jest and laughter brought to all the lonely places in the world through his invention of the phonograph. He saw the world benefited in business and in pleasure, through more than a thousand other inventions that he had made. He heard himself called "wizard" because he had accomplished marvels beyond the dreams of all magicians. He knew that he had lifted himself, without the benefits of ordinary school and college training, into a position of genuine greatness. He knew that he had the gratitude of all people. Such an old age must be truly delightful.

One naturally asks, "How did it happen that one could do so much? The answer is, "Through the hardest kind of work."

In old times, a wizard, so people said, had a familiar spirit as the source of his wonder-working power. This modern wizard, at all times in his life, from boyhood to extreme old age, had as his familiar the spirit of work. He made his

tireless energy his most notable characteristic. Putting aside
sleep, rest, and amusements of the idler sort, for years he
worked fifteen to twenty hours a day. Any man who so
sets for himself the ideal of hard work is certain to go far
on the road to success. When he can unite such energy with
real genius, as did Mr. Edison, he can go still further.

When Thomas A. Edison was only a small boy eleven
years old, he went into partnership with another boy, cultivated a piece of land, seeded it and planted it, weeded it,
raised vegetables, found purchasers, delivered his product,
and made about $600 in one year! Find any boy of that
age who is able and willing to do so much work and you
will find one who gives real promise for the future. "Genius," says the epigram, "is one-tenth inspiration and nine-
tenths perspiration." Through his energy as a newsboy
Thomas A. Edison earned from eight to ten dollars a day.
At the same time he never failed to give to his mother, every
day, at least a dollar of his earnings. He showed even then
that he was not wholly self-centered.

Natural brilliance, ability to work, and substantial character
are three great reasons for Mr. Edison's great success.

Thomas A. Edison's parents were not poor, as one might
think from the fact that Mr. Edison, in his early days, was
a newsboy and a telegraph operator. His people belonged
to the middle class, neither enjoying great fortune nor suffering from want. His father dealt in grain and various farm
products, sold lumber, acted as an intermediary in the sale of
farms, and raised plants and trees as a kind of nurseryman.
By such business he did not bring great fortune, but he did
much more than keep the wolf from the door.

Apparently the Edisons, for many generations, had been
hardworking, prosperous people. The family had originated
in a land of work and of thrift, Holland. There, like so many
in that land of windmills, they had been millers. The Edisons, like many other people from Holland, emigrated to
what is now New York, land that the Dutch had discovered and settled. Nearly fifty years before the American

Revolution one of the Edisons sailed from the land of dikes and established himself in the new world. He had strength that came from generations of good living and of hard work in the open air, and a physique that made him capable of much labor. Edison's great-grandfather lived until he was one hundred and two; his grandfather lived until he was one hundred and three. Edison himself drew from countless Dutch millers and farmers a strength that enabled him to work until he changed the ways of the world.

If his father and his father's ancestry gave Edison vitality, his mother gave him inspiration. She, the daughter of a clergyman, was the descendant of people who lived in America long before the Revolution. Her family, like so many families that aided in making the United States, was of Scotch origin. How frequently forgotten are the mothers of great men, and yet how often they not only guide infant steps but shape destinies! Nancy Elliot had gained an unusually good education for a woman of her day, and was distinctly an intellectual woman. Brought up in Canada, whither her people had moved, she had become a school teacher who had real enthusiasm for her work.

Thomas A. Edison, it is true, attended school for only a few weeks, but he gained at home more education from his mother, an experienced teacher, than ordinary boys of his acquaintance obtained from much unwilling attendance at school.

Day after day, patiently and conscientiously, Nancy Elliot Edison taught her chubby little son. How could she know that she was guiding the mind of a genius? How could she know that those hours of teaching in the plain little home were of significance to the entire world? In her teaching she stimulated the boy to investigate for himself, to test and to prove everything, and to add more, when it was possible, to what he had learned from books. For that work she should be named among the great teachers, even though she taught but a single pupil.

Thomas Alva Edison was born in Milan, Ohio, February

11, 1847. When he was about seven years old his parents moved to Port Huron, Michigan. The boy, a healthy, hearty, rosy-cheeked youngster, was an out-of-doors boy who played vigorously with other boys. Instead of going to school, he studied with his mother.

By the time the youngster was twelve years old he wished to do something to make himself more or less independent. He had enjoyed gardening but he wished to do something even better. After some urging for permission from his parents, he became a train newsboy on the Grand Trunk Railroad. Now he turned his work as train-boy into a means of gaining an education, making his railroad train both a library and a laboratory. From the boy's earliest days he had found encouragement to read, his father, who appreciated books, sometimes paying him a stipulated sum of money for every book read. Thus, early in life the inventor had respect for books and a belief that reading is worth while. On the train young Edison took advantage of the opportunity to read the papers and other publications that he sold. He learned what was happening in the world, and thus lifted himself from the limited surroundings. Once he set out bravely with the determination to read every book in the Detroit Free Library.

"How much have you read?" a man asked him.

"Fifteen feet!" he answered. And as a matter of fact he had begun at one end of a shelf and had read book after book religiously!

His questioner told him that that sort of reading would give mental indigestion, and lead to nothing. He taught the boy how to select his reading wisely. The result was that in all his later life Mr. Edison found great pleasure in omnivorous but well-directed reading. He made himself a broadly educated man.

As a newsboy Edison was most energetic. When he was fifteen years old he read one day in his paper that fifty thousand soldiers had been killed or wounded in the battle of Pittsburgh Landing. He knew that people would want to read the story of the battle. Therefore he sent telegraph messages along the line of the railroad, asking operators to post in the railroad stations bulletins about the battle. The far-seeing newsboy felt sure that such bulletins would increase the demand for papers when he arrived on the train. Although he could not pay for as many papers as he thought he could sell, he persuaded the newspaper managers to let him take 1500 papers on his promise to pay later. In the end he sold all his papers and might have sold more.

Young Edison's interest in newspapers led him to print a newspaper of his own, photographic facsimiles of which are still extant. It was printed from some old type that he procured, on a crude press and was twelve by sixteen inches in size. He was reporter, editor, typesetter, and pressman, all in one. As for his printing room, he established that in the baggage car.

Ever since he had been a small child Edison had liked to experiment, that is, to find out things for himself, an instinct that his mother had greatly cultivated. When he was only a child of six years, hearing that geese are hatched from eggs, he at once took a number of eggs and tried to hatch them by putting them in his bed and keeping them close to himself while he slept. In that experiment, unfortunately, he failed.

On the train he kept his newspapers, and the other things he had for sale, in the baggage car. There also he began to experiment in chemistry, trying to apply principles that he had studied about in books. This was not at all a new thing for him. When he was only ten years old he had set up a sort of laboratory in the cellar of his home, where he had carried on experiments that had kept his mother continually anxious. All went well with the boy scientist's experiments in the railroad car until one day when some phosphorus with which the youngster had been working occasioned a fire. The conductor of the train became so indignant that he did what many another conductor would have done under similar circumstances; he put the boy off the train, chemicals, apparatus and all. Unfortunately, the conductor went much

THOMAS ALVA EDISON

further and boxed the boy's ears severely in righteous indignation at having the train set on fire. If the conductor lived to learn the importance of the experiments that he had interrupted, and the greatness of the injury that his anger had inflicted, he must have had more than one qualm of conscience, for by that blow he made Edison partially deaf for the rest of his life.

In 1862, when the enterprising lad was fifteen years old, he risked his life to save a small child from being run over, a heroic deed done on the spur of the moment, but one that was a turning point in the life of the inventor. When the grateful father asked what he could do in return to help Edison, the boy answered: "I'd like to learn how to telegraph," for the child's father was a telegraph operator. From that man the fifteen-year-old Edison learned telegraphy. From that slight beginning in electricity he went forward toward his first inventions in connection with the telegraph, and toward the great work of his career. In risking his life to save another he had determined his own future.

Even before that time, however, he had studied electricity to some extent, and had set up a crude telegraph line made from stovepipe wire. Now he made a better line, setting it so that he connected the railroad station with the town. Over his little telegraph system he now sent messages of real importance. In that way the wizard of electricity earned the first money that he ever gained from the employment of electricity.

For the next ten years and more Thomas A. Edison was a telegraph operator, but he had one characteristic that distinguished him from other telegraph operators; he was forever experimenting, seeing what new device he could contrive, or how he could accomplish work in easier, quicker or more satisfactory ways. Where others were contented to do what they had been told to do, merely to earn their pay, and to find real enjoyment outside of their work, Edison fussed with wires, batteries and instruments, not in the hope of gaining money, but out of sheer interest in seeing what he could do. At the same time, in an effort to find guidance, he continued to study books about electricity.

The officials of the Grand Trunk Railroad paid the telegrapher $25 a month for his services as night operator. They thought they had hired an operator; really they had engaged a student who turned every place into a laboratory or a shop. Generally speaking, Edison's employers did not approve of his experiments. Like the conductor of the train, they looked upon such "fooling" as a wilful waste of time and material, as well as a source of trouble. Some of them reprimanded Edison; others discharged him.

Meanwhile, young Edison worked faithfully, increasing his ability as an operator and enlarging his knowledge of electricity. At second-hand bookstores he bought books about electricity and devoted himself to them, no college student ever giving himself more thoroughly to study than did this strange young telegrapher. One day he found a book by the great Michael Faraday. That night, entranced, he sat up all night and read its pages, finding it far more interesting than most people find fiction.

"Oh, he was a genius!" people say in explanation of Edison's greatness; they might better say: "He was a worker! He was a student!"

As telegraph operator, for a dozen years or so, Edison worked in many places in the United States and in Canada. He was forever moving from one place to another, partly because people did not like his constant experimenting; partly because, being mischievous, he played practical jokes; partly because, being quick, he won promotion. He worked in Adrian, Michigan; in Fort Wayne and Indianapolis, in Indiana; in Cincinnati, Ohio; in Memphis, Tennessee; in Louisville, Kentucky; in Boston; in New York, and in a number of other places. Beginning at $25 a month, he went on to $60, and $125, and finally to much more. Before Edison had ended his work with the telegraph, he had invented the automatic repeater, the quadruplex telegraph, and the printing telegraph, besides other inventions that aided in perfect-

ing the art of telegraphy. Although only a young man he
made himself known as one of the men who best understood
telegraphy and electricity. He made himself recognized as
a great inventor, whose work was worth observation, and
whose experiments were worth paying for.

In 1873, when he was twenty-six, he found the Western
Union Telegraph Company eager to contract with him to pay
him for experimenting, if he would give that company the
benefit of his experiments. He must have felt a sense of
triumph over those who had discharged him for the very
thing that he now found the world most eager to have him
do.

Nevertheless, he must have annoyed people by his experiments. In one position that he held, he had to send the
letters "S-I-X" every half hour to indicate that he was present
and at work. He amused himself by making a series of cogged
wheels, connecting the series with a clock, and letting the
clock do the sending even more accurately as to time and
telegraphy than he himself could have done it. Unfortunately
he found that his employers did not approve of his clock
device.

Whatever instruments Edison worked with he changed in
some way to suit his convenience. Beginning at first in a
simple way, he gained the ability to work with more complex apparatus. Instead of theorizing, he tried to bring
about practical results that would help people to work more
easily and more quickly.

Instead of finding his employers eager to have him try to
make ingenious devices to save labor, he found them slow
to recognize that that was the very thing in which they
should be most interested. Once when he found it most
difficult to receive rapidly sent messages he devised an apparatus that would automatically record the messages at a fast
rate, and a second bit of apparatus that would permit him
to transcribe them at his own rate. Thus he devised something of utmost practical utility, but because he had spent
time in making it and had used instruments not officially

sanctioned for the purpose, he lost his position. Later he had the pleasure of seeing the Edison automatic repeater looked upon as one of the great inventions of telegraphy.

The inventor was twenty-seven when he perfected another notable improvement. He wished to enable people to send more than one message on a single wire, but he found many difficulties to overcome before he could lead the way to multiple telegraphy. When Edison was first beginning his work in telegraphy, he had invented a device for the employment of two circuits on a submarine cable. From year to year he had continued to experiment. In 1874, he brought about, not a perfection of duplex telegraphy, but a perfection of quadruplex telegraphy! By that invention he made possible a saving of nearly three-quarters of a million dollars a year for the Western Union Telegraph Company. This showed the company that it was worth while to interest itself in experiments that a mere telegraph operator chose to perform, and to pay him to do nothing else except to experiment.

Edison had gone to New York, a telegraph operator with little money, and practically unknown. He had been able in a short space of time, through his genius and his ability to work, to command a salary of $3600 a year, in those days a large salary. He had made ingenious stock-tickers that printed market quotations so rapidly and legibly that they came into general use. He had sold these for about $40,000, and had set up a laboratory of his own for further experiment.

So when he was only twenty-six, he was no longer an unknown telegraph operator, but the head of a great experimental laboratory where he directed some three hundred men along lines of scientific inquiry. This laboratory he established in Newark, New Jersey. From that day to this he made New Jersey the scene of his researches, experiments, and triumphs. There, as it were, he drew his magic circle and called forth the spirits of earth, air, fire and water to do his bidding for the good and the pleasure of mankind.

In 1876 he moved to Menlo Park, New Jersey, and in 1887 to West Orange, but he remained in the State where he had first given himself, on a large scale, to investigation. In the first period of Mr. Edison's work he devoted himself to telegraphy, then a comparatively new invention, for it was in 1837, only ten years before his birth, that S. F. B. Morse had invented it. To that he gave all his time and energy, and from that work he developed all that he did in the years that followed. To the telegraph Edison gave the automatic repeater, quadruplex and sextuplex telegraphy, the printing telegraph, and many other remarkable inventions, among which we may name further developments of telegraphy, such as the telescribe, the electric valve that is the basis of all wireless telegraphy, and wireless telegraphy to and from moving trains. Surely it was a happy day for the world when a railroad newsboy determined to rise in life.

As is shown by the later inventions connected with telegraphy, especially with wireless telegraphy, Mr. Edison never lost his interest in the subject. He continued to think of the work of communicating human thought as a life task. From telegraphy, that is, communication by electrically sent dots and dashes, he broadened his work to telephony, in which electricity conveys actual speech; and to wireless telegraphy and telephony. As a matter of fact, when he invented the phonograph, the megaphone, and the motion pictures, he was still employing himself in the art of conveying messages of some kind or other through the agency of electricity. Where some men invent devices for the manufacture of goods, Edison invented devices for the transmission of thought. Every invention for that purpose grew out of his boyhood interest in telegraphy.

For more than a year, 1876 to 1878, Edison combined his work with the telegraph with work on the telephone. It was he who made the carbon transmitter, one of the greatest improvements ever made in the telephone. Even before Alexander Graham Bell had completed his invention of the telephone, Edison had worked along the same lines, and had achieved notable results. As it was, he very narrowly missed being the actual inventor of the telephone.

Mr. Edison's invention of the phonograph came about through an accident. He pricked his finger. Where most people would have thought the accident a mere annoyance, Mr. Edison was curious to learn why he had pricked his finger. On investigation he found that when he talked into the telephone he was working on, he set in motion the tiny steel point that had pricked him. From that he at once gained the idea of making a record of the voice by pin-pricks, and reproducing the sound by reversing the process. While the idea was simple enough, he found the practical working out of the thought was not so simple. For a long time Mr. Edison experimented with all his ingenuity, but he could not bring about the reproduction of the voice.

After some time he made an instrument that would repeat at least part of what he said. With certain sounds, especially the "S" and "Z" sounds, he had great difficulty. For weary hours, day after day, he experimented, repeating again and again into the machine words that contained the troublesome sounds. Thus he repeated the word "S-P-E-Z-I-A" thousands of times, and at last, through sheer tireless effort, overcame all difficulties.

When the inventor had made a machine that would actually "talk" like a human being, he was as pleased as a child might be with a new toy. Calling together some of his assistants, he proudly exhibited the marvelous instrument.

Perhaps none of all Mr. Edison's thousand inventions amazed people more than the phonograph and the moving pictures. In both cases he seemed to perform the miraculous, and thoroughly to deserve the title of wizard. Even today a savage, hearing a phonograph or seeing moving pictures for the first time, is far more awe-struck than when he sees a telegraph, a telephone, or an electric light.

Edison introduced the phonograph to the outside world in an amusing manner. One day he conveyed a bundle to the office of *The Scientific American*. Placing the bulky package on the desk of an editor whom he knew, Mr. Converse Beach, he unwrapped it, but said nothing. With a smile he watched the editor look curiously at the unknown apparatus.   Still Mr. Edison said nothing.

Mr. Beach saw a crank handle, evidently to be turned.   He gave it a turn or two, not knowing what would happen, and from the machine, as if a magician had enchanted it, came the words: "Good morning!   What do you think of the phonograph?"

From 1878 to 1887 Mr. Edison concerned himself with experiments relating to light and power.   In that time he made, perhaps, the most beneficial of all his inventions.   In his task of perfecting the electric light the inventor found much difficulty and many annoyances.   Of all his inventions, he says, the electric light called for the greatest care and the greatest persistence.   When he had perfected the apparatus he found that others, who had experimented along somewhat similar lines, contested his claims, and so he became involved in a series of law suits, from all of which he emerged triumphant.

In this day when the entire world is lighted by electricity, people are still living who went to see a single electric light exhibited as a curiosity.   Those who first saw the invention, which Mr. Edison openly demonstrated in 1880, at once recognized its usefulness.   From the days of camp-fires, crude oil lamps, candles, and illuminating gas, people had struggled to make the night as light as day.   They had found no good means to accomplish their purpose until Mr. Edison showed the way.

The ingenious inventor found the principal difficulty not in making an electric light but in making an electric light that would not burn out.   He found it easy enough to send a current of electricity through a conductor that would then glow, but difficult to keep the glowing conductor from burning into nothingness.   Through his agents, the persistent experimenter hunted in all parts of the world for a conductor that he could use as a filament.   At last he made the first durable carbon filament, enclosed in a vacuum.   Since that time other inventors have made great improvements, especially in making filaments that glow with any desired brilliance, but the man who first bridged the gap and led the way was Thomas A. Edison.

From the electric light, more than from anything else, the "wizard of electricity" gained great sums of money, for almost every one wishes to use the convenient and powerful means of illumination. As a reward for his work, he saw money pour in in a golden flood. In this he rejoiced, for it gave him the means of carrying on other experiments.

In 1887 the wonder-worker brought forward the kinetoscope, the ancestor of our modern moving picture machines. He thought such an invention would at once spring into popularity, as had the electric light, but such was not the case. Although he exhibited the kinetoscope in many places, he found difficulty in arousing people to enthusiasm. Edison's original moving picture machine was a sort of peepshow that could amuse only one person at a time. Nevertheless, it did present pictures that moved. The idea, however, was appealing enough to interest a French inventor, Antoine Lumière, who carried it to perfection. Again Mr. Edison found himself involved in a long series of distressing and time-consuming lawsuits, but again he emerged triumphant. He had been the first to find the way and he deserved the honors and the rewards.

It is impossible even to mention the numerous inventions that Thomas A. Edison gave to the world. In one way or another every one of them is marvelous. For example there is the microtasimeter, an instrument that can detect even the most minute change in temperature, noting the heat of the body even when at a distance of eight feet. There is the microphone, that magnifies the slightest sound and makes it audible, magnifying the step of a fly and making it sound like the tramp of an elephant. There is the megaphone, that magnifies sound electrically and carries the voice to a great distance. There is the mimeograph, that enables a person to make a thousand copies of a single letter, making every copy clear and perfect. In addition to all these things there are numerous other inventions that come less before the public attention but that are valuable. Among such are devices for the making of Portland cement, machines for the milling of ore, an alkaline storage battery, and other useful inventions without end.

During the World War, when the United States Government naturally called upon Mr. Edison to use his inventive and scientific skill for war purposes, he gave help of the utmost value, much of which has not been revealed. He designed, constructed and carried on factories for the manufacture of benzol, and factories for the making of carbolic acid, aniline salt and other chemical products.

Altogether, through life, Thomas A. Edison fulfilled the promise that his energetic boyhood had made. He continued to inquire into things, and to find new ways of carrying on useful work. At no time did he learn how to live idly. In spite of wealth and fame, his life continued to be simple and without ostentation. As might be expected, Mr. Edison never became conventional, never learned how to follow in a rut. He developed idiosyncracies without number, as befits a genius, but all centered around his interest in work and his wish to do something useful.

A man of his type must look upon so-called honors bestowed by societies or governments as meaningless. Of awards, of tributes, of medals, of degrees, Mr. Edison has had plenty, but a man whose name is to be found wherever the electric light glows, wherever the phonograph speaks, and wherever moving pictures give delight, needs no formal honors. In his home at Llewellyn Park, Orange, New Jersey, his once dark hair now white, his eyes gray and keen, his figure strong and sturdy, his manner open and pleasing, his talk quick and intelligent whatever the subject, the many-sided magician who refuses ever to lay aside his magic wand works on into extreme old age, finding now, as he found in youth, that in hard work he wins greatest pleasure.

VIII

GEORGE WASHINGTON GOETHALS

Engineer

Once a United States official, worried by the failure of the French to succeed in the attempt to make a canal across the isthmus of Panama, and staggered by the vastness of the undertaking, said to Colonel Goethals, the engineer in charge:

"Colonel, this is a big job. Some people think we won't have any better luck than the French did. What would you say if foreign ministers, representatives of the great nations, told you we are making a mistake even in trying to make a canal in Panama?"

"I wouldn't say anything," Colonel Goethals answered quietly. "Just make the canal, that's all."

That was the man's way; he was a doer, not a talker. He did make the canal, and by so doing gave the best answer to all who had criticized the United States for entering into what they called a rash undertaking, the digging of a great ship canal through mountains and across the jungles of a fever-haunted tropical land.

The day came when the first boat was to pass through the Canal, a day of triumph and rejoicing. On the shore, watching the working of the locks, stood a tall man, middle-aged, gray-haired, dressed in ordinary civilian clothes. He acted as if he were especially interested in seeing how the locks worked. He was an onlooker, that was all, and yet it was he who had made the canal; for the plain man in civilian clothes was Colonel George W. Goethals, the chief engineer. He was not a man who cared to make a display; he was too interested in his work.

Furthermore, he had made others interested in it, too. By force of will, by determination, by power to lead others, he had done what the French, by sacrificing $300,000,000, had not been able to do.

"To accomplish any task successfully it is necessary not only that you should give it the best that is in you, but that you should obtain for it the best that there is in those who are under your guidance." That was what Colonel Goethals said.

In every way he fulfilled the requirements of his own saying. In his work in constructing what people called "The Big Ditch" he gave himself utterly to his task. He worked as long, as hard, and as faithfully as any one of the many thousands who aided in cutting the waterway across the isthmus. In spite of the fact that he drove men as no other man had ever driven them, he was a leader, too, who had at heart the interests of those whom he led. As a result, Colonel Goethals created in the force in the Canal Zone a spirit that made them able to do what people at other times had found impossible.

All great leaders of men have ability in special fields, determination, and a love of fair play. Through such characteristics Lord Nelson made himself and his fleet invincible, and led even the humblest powder-boy to love him, because, as every one knew, the great admiral thought both of his duty and of the needs of every person on every ship. Then, too, every powder-boy trusted Nelson because he believed the commander capable beyond all others, a man who aimed at nothing less than victory. That, too, was the way the canal laborers looked upon Colonel Goethals.

Fear drove laborers to construct such stupendous works as the Pyramids and the Great Wall of China. Supreme authority gave the command, and then brute force drove the thousands of workers, regardless of the cost in energy or in lives.

Such conditions could not hold in the making of the Panama Canal. A higher recognition of the rights of man called for a leadership which ancient times never knew.

The modern leader had to have greater knowledge than any of the ancient engineers ever possessed; he had to have far greater determination; and instead of thinking nothing whatever of the interests of his workmen, he had to think everything of them. He had to recognize that as civilization advances, the character of real leadership advances with it.

Compared with the Panama Canal the seven wonders of the ancient world appear less great. The construction of the walls and hanging gardens of Babylon, the pyramids of Egypt, the mausoleum at Halicarnassus, and the temple of Artemis at Ephesus, called for far less technical skill and far less patience; the making of the pharos of Alexandria, the colossus of Rhodes, or the statue of Zeus at Olympia called for far less effort and determination.

The megalithic works of man, such as the Druid arches at Stonehenge, the rock-cuttings of the Incas in Peru, and the stupendous temples in Egypt, certainly awaken respect. So, too, does the Great Wall of China, which stretches over mountains and plains for fifteen hundred miles. Nevertheless, none of these approach in wonder the Panama Canal, one of the greatest accomplishments in human engineering.

Although the people of the classical world, as well as the good Caliph Haroun al Raschid in the eighth century, had the daring conception of cutting what is now the Suez Canal, no one made the attempt successful before Ferdinand de Lesseps in 1869. That great engineer made a canal about one hundred miles long, cutting it through a level region, and linking bodies of water that have similar levels.

In 1893 the Greeks did what Cæsar had thought of doing, and dug a canal about four miles long through the Isthmus of Corinth, conquering the difficulty of a hill 170 feet high. When one speaks of canals he must think also of the great Caledonian Canal, for which James Watt made the surveys, sixty miles long; of the Kiel Canal that connects the Baltic and the North Seas; of the Manchester Ship Canal; and the canal from Bruges to Zeebrugge. And then, although it is not a ship canal, as are the others just named, the Grand Canal of China, reaching from Hangchow to Tientsin, is no less than 650 miles long.

No doubt the tragedy of the various attempts to dig a canal at the Isthmus of Panama had much to do with making the American achievement under the direction of Colonel Goethals appear the more remarkable.

Because of the disagreeable necessity of making a long voyage around Cape Horn, very early in American history people began to wish for some means of making a waterway across the narrow isthmus. Even the Spaniards, in the days of the conquistadores, thought of making a canal. In 1849, on the discovery of gold in California, men took the first steps toward a canal by constructing a railway from Colon to Panama.

In 1879 Count Ferdinand de Lesseps, the promoter of the Suez Canal, having formed a French company, purchased the Panama railroad, and began work in 1881. He led the French to work pertinaciously, but he met defeat because of disease, dishonesty, and the difficulty of the task. Today the rusting wrecks of the French machinery and a short length of canal are all that is left for the $300,000,000 that De Lesseps spent. Mountains, swamps, malaria and yellow fever played havoc with human lives, and drove De Lesseps from his work. Theft and fraud, and lack of sufficiently great leadership, made further procedure with the work out of the question.

In 1902 the United States Congress authorized the purchase of the French canal and of the railroad at Panama. In 1913 President Wilson, sitting at his desk in Washington, touched an electric button and thereby brought about an explosion of dynamite that tore to pieces the last obstruction between the waters of the Pacific and of the Atlantic. In the following year the Panama Canal, one of the great waterways of the world, came to completion.

For more than fifty miles, in a tropical land, it makes its

way over level regions, across swamps and lakes, and through mountains, maintaining a depth of over forty feet, and a width that at its narrowest is 300 feet. The Panama Canal cost over $368,000,000. At the Culebra Cut it pierces hills for nine continuous miles, cutting through a depth of 375 feet. Two hundred and thirty million cubic yards of rock and earth were removed. In the face of countless slides that threatened to destroy men and canal alike, the workers persisted and won the victory. They did a task worthy of Titans, a colossal accomplishment that staggers the imagination. No one can pass through the Panama Canal without using the word "giant."

Since the tides of the Atlantic rise and fall only one foot, while the tides of the Pacific rise and fall over twelve feet, and sometimes over twenty-one feet; and since the Pacific, at that place, is eight inches higher than the Atlantic, gigantic locks must control the waters and make it possible for vessels to proceed in either direction. The gates of some of these locks are eighty-two feet high, sixty-five feet long, and seven feet thick, and weigh seven hundred and thirty tons. What other works of man can compare, in immensity, with those gates, so colossal that no teller of wildest romance would ever have dared to mention them?

Such facts give one respect for the character of the man who successfully directed thousands upon thousands of workers, ranging from men with the highest technical skill to those who could do no more than wield picks or drive mules. They make one wonder at the ability of a man who carried in his mind all the details of an undertaking so highly complex, involving both destruction and creation. They make one honor the powers of leadership of one who so commanded the respect of all that he filled every man with enthusiasm like his own, and for years maintained an *esprit de corps* that made it seem as if one single giant with a giant's power, were digging the canal.

"Tell the Colonel!" they said on the Isthmus. No matter what question arose, they looked to one man to make a right decision, and that man was Colonel Goethals, the engineer in charge.

Like so many really great men, this master of men, this conqueror of nature, was extremely modest and unassuming. In all the time that he worked on the Isthmus, in charge of so many individuals, and master of such great forces, he never wore a uniform. Instead, he went about always dressed simply, in civilian clothing, a worker and not at all a man on parade.

A Secretary of War, the head of that department of State under which Colonel Goethals worked, visited the Canal during its construction. Looking sternly at Colonel Goethals, who was an officer of the United States Army, he said: "Sir, I expected to find you in uniform."

"I never wear a uniform," answered the Colonel.

"Perhaps I shall order you to wear one."

"I couldn't. I don't have a uniform here!"

On the day when the Canal opened, when of all times it might have been expected that Colonel Goethals, after years of unremitting labor and responsibility, would wish to be the first man to pass through, he went to one of the locks, and carefully watched its operation. At the very last, he was more interested in making a satisfactory canal than in making a name for himself.

As the men on the Canal said of him during the time when they were working, "The Colonel took the Canal to bed with him every night." He was a man with a duty to perform, and he intended to perform that duty to the best of his ability. For that reason he was a leader who won respect.

"He was on the job every minute," as one of his subordinates said. He cared nothing for rest, recreation, pomp or ceremony. Apparently, too, he did not think of his work as anything else than the carrying out of a duty that had been assigned to him. When he had completed the work on the Canal, in spite of the fact that it was entirely natural that the people of the United States should wish to honor the man who had represented them so well, Colonel Goethals did his best to forestall public testimonials. He thought it improper that Congress should honor him for having carried out orders. When called upon, in New York, in Washington, or elsewhere, to stand forward as one who had accomplished something beyond the ordinary, he became as embarrassed as any one could well be. He had been willing to work months and years in the broiling heat of the tropical sun, but he was not willing to stand before an audience and hear himself praised.

In that modesty, Colonel Goethals showed genuine character, for the boaster, the man of over-weening conceit who enjoys hearing himself praised usually thinks far more of himself than he does of his work.

"If Colonel Goethals has a weakness," said one who knew him, "it is that when he makes up his mind that a certain way is right, you cannot change him: you might as well talk to a stone."

President Roosevelt, who always admired real manhood, called upon Colonel Goethals to take charge of the work of carrying the Panama Canal to completion, because he believed Colonel Goethals had both the ability and the character to do the thing to be done. President Roosevelt always considered his own work in urging the construction of the Canal and in leading to the negotiations with the new Republic of Panama that made the Canal possible the greatest thing that he did while President. He might well have thought of his selection of Colonel Goethals as leader of the work of construction as at least second in importance.

It is an interesting fact that the chief engineer of the Panama Canal was named after the first President of the United States; he was George Washington Goethals. That was because his parents had believed in the sort of things for which George Washington had stood, and they wished their son to uphold such principles.

It is even more interesting to learn the origin of the name Goethals. Back in the year 806 A.D., a certain ancestor of the Canal builder, a rough and hardy Roman soldier called

Photo from Brown Bros., N. Y.

GEORGE WASHINGTON GOETHALS

"Honorius," believed in fighting but not in yielding. In one of his many battles, when an arrow hit him on the neck, he remained unharmed because the armor that he wore turned the weapon aside. He appeared to have escaped because his neck had been too hard for the arrow. At once he earned from his follow soldiers the nickname "Boni Coli" or "Stiff Neck." Later, as a reward for many valorous services, "Boni Coli" was given lands in the Low Countries. There, after a time, he or his people changed the Latin name, which had stuck, into the low country name, "Goet Hals"—"Stiff Neck."

Colonel Goethals' own record shows how well he upheld the family name.

The centuries passed, and at last one of the Goethals, with his wife, both of them Dutch, emigrated from Holland to the United States. They were the father and mother of the maker of the Canal.

Throwing themselves at once into the spirit of American life, these Dutch immigrants, the Goethals, named their son, who was born June 29, 1858, George Washington Goethals. Like most of the Dutch people, the parents of the Canal maker were hard-working, prosperous people. They made their home in Brooklyn, New York, and there they proposed to do what they could to make their son more truly American than they themselves might ever hope to be. They sent him to school, and then to the College of the City of New York, which he entered at the age of fifteen.

George Goethals remained in college for three years, at the end of which time he received an appointment to the United States Military Academy at West Point. There he upheld his family name of "Stiff Neck" by sticking to his studies so well that when he was graduated in 1880 he stood second in his class. From such a person, with such antecedents, one might expect something.

The young student, at not quite twenty-two years of age, became second lieutenant of engineers, and two years later first lieutenant. Since promotions in the army in time of peace are slow, he patiently served nine years before he became captain. At the time of that promotion he was thirty-three years old.

As a student at West Point, Cadet Goethals had devoted himself to study, not in any perfunctory way, but through real interest. Having acquired studious habits before graduation, he continued to study afterwards. Perhaps he realized that any good school or college is not merely a place where one may acquire sufficient learning, but also a place where one may learn how to gain a real education by reading and study throughout life. George W. Goethals remained an intense student. If later he understood engineering, and was able to comprehend all the varied work that went into the making of the Panama Canal, he had the knowledge and the ability, not through lucky accident nor natural brilliance, but through hard study.

Some time after his graduation, he attended the Engineering School at Willett's Point, where he continued the studies that he had begun at the Military Academy, work that involved difficult problems in engineering. Naturally he perfected himself in higher mathematics. Later, in 1905, after further studies, he was graduated from the Army War College.

Being a lover of learning, Colonel Goethals inspired others and thus won marked success as an educator. For a time he taught astronomy at West Point. For four years he taught civil and military engineering in this institution, at the same time studying by himself, thus making his work both accurate and progressive. From the time when he first entered school, until 1888, when he was thirty years of age, Colonel Goethals lived in the classroom. He felt interest in higher mathematics and in engineering, rather than in what the world commonly regards as the work of a soldier. He never cared for military display. Instead of destructive, he had constructive interests.

Early habits, early training, early interests, do much to

form mature life. To say that Colonel Goethals, an officer of the United States Army, directed the work of making the Panama Canal, by no means explains the man's ability. His devotion to study, his mastery of engineering, his experience in teaching, did far more to aid him than did any specific military training.

While some civilians have become far more military than Colonel Goethals, he remained, perhaps, the least military, in spirit, of all great soldiers who have won world fame. Nevertheless, as a United States Army officer, Colonel Goethals saw active service in warfare. During the short war with Spain he went to Porto Rico as Lieutenant Colonel and Chief of Engineers in the volunteer service. There he did excellent work in difficult engineering, building docks under almost impossible conditions and supervising work of various kinds in the interests of the United States forces.

Once, in the campaign, he received orders to make a landing place where the surf dashed wildly upon the shore. Under any circumstances he would have found the task difficult. As it was, he had too little material. Near by he saw some barges that the naval forces had captured.

"Get those barges; fill them with sand; sink them here," he ordered, knowing that they alone would enable him to carry out instructions. His men had scarcely begun work when an orderly came from one of the naval officers, who, of course, had no authority over Colonel Goethals, ordering him to stop work at once, since the barges were prizes of war.

"Tell him I have been ordered to make a wharf," said Colonel Goethals, "and say that I shall make it in any way I can."

Back came the orderly with the words, "Stop work at once, or I shall fire!"

"Tell him to fire away," said Colonel Goethals.

That was all. He made his wharf, and the ship did not fire upon him.

"When he has his mind set you cannot change him," men who worked with Colonel Goethals said.

Before the great engineer took charge of the work of making the Panama Canal, he had already directed several important engineering enterprises in the United States. He served as Chief Engineer of the work the Government carried on in the District of Columbia; for a year or more he worked on dikes and dams along the Ohio River, in an effort to control its characteristic devastating floods. Then, too, he had charge of engineering work in Tennessee.

When President Roosevelt wished to find a man great enough in ability and in personal power to take charge of the unparalleled work of making the Panama Canal, he turned at once to Colonel Goethals. In him, no doubt, he saw a reflection of himself. Both men were doers rather than observers; both were forceful, energetic, and utterly tireless; both were fighters for what they believed right; both were natural leaders; and both had high ability.

The orders to construct the Panama Canal were certainly overwhelming. In effect they were as follows:

"Go to the most unhealthful place in the world, where men die by the thousands; make a canal fifty miles long right across the backbone of the Americas; dig it forty feet deep and three hundred feet wide. You'll come to a mountain nine miles across; dig a cañon right through the mountain. Control the rivers that are always having floods; control the tides in the two oceans; make about fifty steel gates, every one as big as a six-story building; make canal locks on such a scale that they can lift the largest battleship; organize and control thousands of all kinds of unruly men; direct experts; keep every one happy; see that no one cheats the Government; hurry up."

Colonel Goethals went to Panama, and there from 1907 to 1914, obeyed orders and carried out all instructions, accomplishing one of the greatest feats of modern times.

In one of his orders especially he showed his individuality:

"Culebra, Canal Zone,
August 14, 1911.

Circular No. 400

The use of profane or abusive language by foremen or others in authority, when addressing subordinates, will not be tolerated.

Geo. W. Goethals,
Chairman and Chief Engineer."

That order appeared to upset the old saying, "Swear like a trooper." What was its object? Not at all the stopping of profanity, but the stopping of abuse of inferiors. That meant good spirit, genuine team work, in which every man was to have his part, and to play it.

In that order General Goethals himself explains why he had the power to lead. Without posing as a military autocrat he insisted that men should work without shirking, without rascality, and without fear of contemptuous slave-driving.

When contractors sent tainted meat Colonel Goethals sent it back by the first boat. When still other contractors delivered screening for the protection of the men that did not come up to the very letter of specifications, he condemned the screening by thousands of yards. When some of his subordinates protested at orders for supplies on a scale beyond all previous experience, he merely remarked, "I take the responsibility."

In his civilian clothes he went everywhere up and down the Canal, observing every detail. When men at work saw Colonel Goethals go by in his car they said, "There goes the brain-wagon!"

He had given orders that train engineers should obey all signals, however unwise they might seem. When an engineer disobeyed a signal and, as a result, killed a man, Colonel Goethals sentenced the disobedient worker to a year's imprisonment. The transportation men held a meeting and sent word to Colonel Goethals that if he did not free the engineer by seven o'clock that day they would quit in a body. They received no answer. At ten minutes past seven that evening the leader of the strikers called up Colonel Goethals on the telephone.

"What is your answer?" he asked.

"It is ten minutes past seven," said Colonel Goethals. "Call up the jail. You'll find the engineer still there."

"What are you going to do?"

"Every man not at work promptly on time tomorrow morning will be transported to the United States on the first steamer."

The engineer was not released; there was no strike; the men all went to work bright and early next morning and obeyed all further orders.

As part of his work at Panama, Colonel Goethals practically played the king. He went to a tropical jungle, where he organized a government that included all that goes with good government in any civilized part of the world. Instead of having under him people of one language and one race, as almost every king does, he had people of all languages, races, and degrees of intelligence, and not only men, but also women and children. He had to think of the needs of every individual; establish courts of justice; organize a police force; plan a system of taxation for common benefit; organize a school system; install a postal system; and aid in the building of churches. In fact, he had to act much like the most autocratic of kings in order to establish a self-respecting republic. In doing all that successfully he showed the highest powers of leadership.

One incident shows what slight respect Colonel Goethals had for politicians. Congress was forever sending to Panama committees of investigation, the members of which knew little if anything about the needs of the canal work. One Congressman, more active than the others, insisted upon looking into everything. Finally he climbed eighty-two feet up an iron ladder, from which a swinging derrick all but knocked him to the ground. The Congressman came down jubilant,

and said to Colonel Goethals: "What do you think of that?
What degree should I get for that?"

"The degree of 'D. F.,' " said Colonel Goethals.

Quietly, efficiently, tactfully, the engineer worked on the
construction of the Canal from 1907 to 1914. He gave spirit
to the work, united the men, and through powers of organization, engineering skill and sheer leadership, at last brought
the work to a triumphant close.

For that work, "For Distinguished Service in the Construction of the Panama Canal," the United States gave him
"The Thanks of Congress;" the United States Army promoted him from the rank of colonel to that of major general;
and the University of Pennsylvania and Princeton University
conferred upon him honorary degrees.

Upon the completion of the canal construction, Colonel,
now General, Goethals became first civil governor of the
Panama Canal Zone, a strip of land about ten miles wide,
following the Canal in its entire extent, and including a
number of islands in the Gulf of Panama. He held this
position for two years, from 1914 to 1916, his promotion from
chief engineer to governor oddly enough giving him a smaller
salary.

As governor, General Goethals served in the same efficient
manner as before, looking after the interests of all types of
people on the Canal. In reality, he merely continued the
great administrative work he had previously inaugurated.

On final retirement from public service to civil life General
Goethals found that people still wished his help. In 1916,
officials asked him to serve as chairman of a board to investigate and report on the Adamson Eight Hour Law, his known
ability and high sense of fair play making him most ac-
ceptable to all concerned. In 1917, the State of New Jersey
made him state engineer. In addition to such official work,
General Goethals entered actively into various plans for the
public good and showed himself always ready to play a full
part as useful citizen.

During the World War, when it became necessary for

every country involved in the struggle to call to its aid all men of great ability, General Goethals found himself again at the head of great undertakings in the interests of the United States. For a time he worked as general manager of the Emergency Fleet Corporation. When he resigned from that position, he became Acting Quartermaster-General of the United States Army. In 1918 the energetic executive became chief of the Division of Purchase, Storage and Traffic of the General Staff. He accomplished the great task of entirely reorganizing the Quartermaster's Department and placing it on a war basis.

The authorities again awarded him the Distinguished Service Medal, this time "For Especially Meritorious and Conspicuous Service in Re-Organizing the Quartermaster's Department." At that time General Goethals was sixty years of age! Through many years of active and exhausting work the great leader had maintained his energy, his health, and his power to accomplish great tasks.

In March, 1919, at his own request, at the age of sixty-one, General Goethals retired once more from active service. In the same year, the Republic of France conferred on him the honor of making him commander of the Legion of Honor. In private life this most useful of Americans continued his interest in engineering, devoted much time to study and to writing, and remained, in a quiet way, a forceful figure.

Throughout a long life General Goethals represented American ability and activity at their very best. In making the Panama Canal he did work that will rank, for centuries to come, among the greatest of human achievements.

IX

WILLIAM CRAWFORD GORGAS

CONQUEROR OF YELLOW FEVER

ON the walls of a church on one of the islands of the Caribbean Sea is a marble tablet that bears a pathetic inscription to a young soldier who, "Escaping the dangers especially incident to his profession, particularly those of the Siege of New Orleans and the ever-memorable Battle of Waterloo, was cut off, when on the eve of promotion, by the yellow fever, after only five days illness, whilst stationed with his regiment on this island." In the same church are many other memorials to those who died of yellow fever, one inscription saying that the persons named "Fell victims of this fatal climate."

Today that island of the "fatal climate" is one of the most healthful places in the world. Other islands and other lands that travelers of former days hesitated to visit because of constantly recurring plagues of yellow fever, are now vacation resorts.

Years ago along all the coasts of the Caribbean Sea and the Gulf of Mexico; along most of the coasts of South America; in New Orleans, Memphis, and Philadelphia; and along the coasts of Spain, people literally by thousands fell victims to yellow fever, a disease that today scarcely exists anywhere in the world.

Inscriptions in the cemeteries of New Orleans, giving names, dates, and ages, and adding the words, "Died of Yellow Fever," make somewhat personal the great fatality of the disease; for in that city, in 1853, 7970 people died in an epidemic of yellow fever; in 1867, 3093; in 1878, 4056.

Yellow fever was one of the things that drove Count Ferdinand de Lesseps and the French from their work of making a canal at Panama. Yellow fever, doing more damage than war, swept away 69 per cent of a regiment stationed in British Guiana. Every year it spread by leaps and bounds, threatening to do ever increasing damage. The more energetically physicians endeavored to find some way to check its ravages, often to fall victims to it themselves, the more scornfully the spirit of yellow fever laughed at their every effort.

According to the Anglo-Saxon epic, *Beowulf,* a terrible monster named Grendel lurked in hiding places by the sea, came forth at night, and destroyed human life, making all people despair. Then, from a distance, came the hero, Beowulf, who followed the monster to its lair, attacked it, and after a terrible struggle, overcame it and freed the land from danger.

Although no poet has told in epic form of the work of William Crawford Gorgas, Surgeon-General of the United States Army, in overcoming yellow fever, that man fought monsters more terrible than Grendel, or Grendel's Mother, and he won a victory that meant far more to civilization than did any of Beowulf's exploits. General Gorgas, having found the means of combating yellow fever, made the disease practically nonexistent.

In thirteen years in Rio de Janeiro, 28,078 people died of yellow fever; in recent years, in that once plague-infested spot, not one has died of the disease.

General Gorgas carried on a fight with yellow fever that one might tell as a romance as astonishing as any of the hero tales of old. Since yellow fever had something to do with every period of his career, he lived under circumstances that made it appear that destiny had appointed him to overcome the disease. Unintentionally, without knowing the path he followed, the great physician moved steadily to his work, accomplished it, and where others had failed, won victory.

General Gorgas' father, when a lieutenant in the Mexican War, had a light attack of yellow fever. His mother, in another place, had to flee from her home to escape the disease.

When General Gorgas himself was only a medical student he volunteered to go to Memphis, Tennessee, to aid in caring for yellow fever sufferers in a great epidemic. Although he did not succeed in having his services accepted he made an effort to begin his lifelong battle. As a young surgeon in the United States Army he took care of yellow fever patients, contracted the disease, and all but died. In the hospital where he lay he became acquainted with another patient, the young woman who became his wife. In the Spanish War he took charge of a yellow fever camp. Then he became chief sanitary officer of Havana, and began organized efforts to conquer the dreadful disease. He brought about such wonderful results that he became, a little later, chief sanitary officer of the Panama Canal Zone. In the Canal Zone, by his wonderful work, he made the construction and later the maintenance of the Panama Canal possible. Before he died, in 1920, at the age of sixty-six, he had seen his work carried to every part of the world where yellow fever had ever existed. Without at all intending it, he had made his entire life a unified struggle with yellow fever. To all intents and purposes he killed the disease.

Curiously enough, in his youth, William Gorgas believed that all his plans for life had been blasted. He had wished to go to West Point and become a soldier, but had not been able to obtain admission, not because of any inability to pass examinations, but because he could not gain the political appointment. In after years he looked upon his early "misfortune" as the stepping stone to all his great work.

General Gorgas' father was a soldier, a graduate of West Point, of the class of 1841. He had stood high in his class, and had made himself an expert in ordnance. He served in the Mexican War, and later in the Civil War, giving himself heart and soul to the cause of the South, and becoming chief ordnance officer of the Confederate Army. He had been a hard-riding, adventurous man, a dashing soldier and a commander of men.

It is small wonder that the son of such a man should wish to go to West Point, to follow in his father's steps and become a soldier. Young Gorgas felt the disappointment keenly. He did not know that he was to become one of the world's greatest soldiers in a warfare far nobler than that of the sword. All his life the boy had lived in a military atmosphere. He had seen his father in the uniform of active service. He had seen some of the stirring events of the Civil War. He believed that he must become a soldier in spite of all and therefore he determined to enter the army through the medical service.

If William Gorgas had gone to West Point, as he desired, he might have remained unknown. As it was, he went to Bellevue Medical College, and ultimately became Surgeon-General of the United States Army, making a record far more brilliant and far more useful than that of his father.

The name Gorgas apparently indicates a Spanish origin for the family, a peculiarly interesting origin in view of the fact that the people of the Caribbean regions and of South America, for whom General Gorgas did so much, likewise drew their origin from Spain. So far as General Gorgas knew, his people were Dutch in origin. They had settled originally in the North, in Pennsylvania. Long before the Civil War, General Gorgas' father was stationed in Alabama, and there married Amelia Gayle, daughter of a governor of Alabama.

William Crawford Gorgas, a true son of the South, was born in Mobile, Alabama, October 3, 1854. He spent the first seven years of his life in a typical southern mansion, a place of serene quiet and comfort, around which stood great oak trees that spoke of age and solidity. When, as a child, he went up the long approach to the house, he passed along a road bordered with great cedars. In that place, where he romped and played, he gained dream-like memories that he carried to old age. The boy was only seven years old when he saw his paradise desolated by the Civil War. In company with his mother he fled from his beautiful home; remained in Richmond in its days of terror; saw that city in flames; and then made his way to Baltimore, hungry, poorly-clothed, barefoot, and wishing with every inch of him that he were old enough to fight.

General Gorgas was not a man of peace; even in his boyhood he was a born fighter, always able and ready to use his fists at a moment's notice. He had great pride and a temper that took fire at the least touch of insult, perhaps because his father had been a soldier, and his mother a woman accustomed to ride spirited horses; perhaps because in the background lurked the influence of Spanish ancestors. Later, General Gorgas used all his hot fighting spirit in his determined conflict with yellow fever.

After the Civil War General Gorgas' father found his occupation gone. For a time the man who had been a soldier, an officer and a gentleman managed a blast furnace in Alabama, willing to turn his hand to anything. Four years after the close of the Civil War he became president of the University of the South at Sewanee, Tennessee, where he gave his high ability to the cause of education.

William Gorgas, in his home surroundings, had especial advantages. In the first place, he had family traditions that he wished to uphold; in the second, he lived surrounded by people of culture and of refinement, in an atmosphere of books. Like any high-spirited boy, "Will" Gorgas entered vigorously into all athletic games and sports. Although distinctly an out-door boy he maintained excellence in all his studies. Naturally he became a student in the institution of which his father was the head, and from that place, the University of the South, he was graduated in 1875, at the age of twenty-one, with the degree of B. A.

For a year, despairing of gaining the political appointment to West Point, he studied law in New Orleans; but study as he might, he felt the insistent call of military life. With little money with which to pay his expenses, he went to New York, where he entered Bellevue Hospital Medical College, a branch of New York University. Here for the first time in his life he found himself in surroundings other than those of the South. Now, more than ever, he turned to books, finding in them what he had before found in human companionship. Since the distance between New York City and his southern home was too great to permit him to afford either the time or the money for vacation trips, he lived somewhat like an exile. To be sure he had companions, but for the most part he relied upon his books and became a tireless student. In this way he laid a solid foundation for his work in mature life.

The two years between 1878 and 1880, the young man spent as interne in Bellevue Hospital, gaining practical experience in hospital work. At the end of that time, in June, 1880, being then twenty-six years old, he gained his long-coveted appointment as surgeon in the United States Army. In a way he had now fulfilled his ambition. Naturally he wished for promotions as the years should go on, but he had no further definite ambition. He had become a soldier! He had done his best to follow in his father's footsteps; and surely that was enough. As for planning to attack and conquer yellow fever, of that the young army surgeon did not even dream.

Nevertheless, as it appears now, his destiny had been leading him on, forcing him into medical study, giving him just the right preparation, and training him for his work. Now fate gave him his first opportunity to meet his lifelong enemy.

The new army surgeon received orders to proceed at once to an army post in the West. For some years he served in various forts, carrying on useful work in Texas, in North Dakota, and in Florida. When an epidemic of yellow fever occurred at Fort Brown, Texas, and over two thousand soldiers became sick with the disease, Surgeon Gorgas was sent, not to care for yellow fever patients, but to set other surgeons free for that duty.

All his life, even in childhood, he had known that obedience to orders is the first and most necessary requirement of military life. What unexplained impulse, what influence of fate, what divine command, led the soldier and the son of a soldier, deliberately to disobey orders, and dissect the body of a patient who had died of yellow fever? He was detected, arrested, and placed at once in the yellow fever wards. In that moment he began the great work of his life. He took care of yellow fever patients, contracted the disease, and all but died, making it appear now as if the spirit of yellow fever had recognized its enemy and inflicted upon him one of the most severe cases in the hospital. Somehow the young army surgeon lived through it.

Because of that illness Surgeon Gorgas gained an armor against the enemy, for one who has once had yellow fever, even in its mildest form, will not have it again. The doctor was now free to be with yellow fever patients as much as he chose. Because of his immunity to yellow fever he accomplished his notable work in overcoming it. At whatever army posts there were cases of yellow fever, there Surgeon Gorgas went, under orders from his superiors. He worked hard and faithfully, and won promotion to a commission of captain assistant surgeon, and continued to study and to investigate along every line that might make him more useful.

When the war with Spain led to the invasion of Cuba and Porto Rico, and to the United States' control of those islands, the military authorities sent Surgeon Gorgas to Havana, a place that, for years, had been one of the disease centers of the Caribbean, and especially a center from which yellow fever spread to other places. Surgeon Gorgas, by this time promoted to the rank of major surgeon, became chief sanitary officer of a foreign and tropical city, with orders to free it from disease. That work he began in 1898 and continued until 1902.

With American love of cleanliness, Surgeon Gorgas looked with disgust upon the festering filth of tropical Havana. The streets of the city, according to photographs taken in 1898, apparently had never been cleaned, for heaps of rubbish and garbage lay everywhere, as did also stagnant pools in which disease bred. Some of the streets, filled with mud and filth, had not shown their pavements in the memory of man. The house interiors, according to other photographs, were unsanitary beyond belief.

Havana was a great city with innumerable crooked, narrow streets, the principal business street, the *Calle Obispo,* being then only eighteen feet wide. The oldest European city in the western hemisphere, well over a hundrd years old when the "Mayflower" came to Plymouth, Havana had never known a house cleaning!

Such was the city that Surgeon Gorgas was to free from disease!

One of the twelve labors of Hercules was to cleanse the Augean Stables, an easy task compared with the cleansing of Havana. The inhabitants of the Cuban city, people of all races, most of them ignorant, and through every habit of life accustomed to filth, cared nothing whatever about making the city clean. They laughed at the suggestion, thinking the task impossible.

What a house cleaning Havana received! The Americans dug down through the dirt and found the pavements; they carted away the rubbish; they went into houses and into stables, and cleaned and inspected everything. They did an overwhelming work, but they did it thoroughly, and made Havana look like any other self-respecting American city.

"Now," thought General Gorgas, "we shall have no more yellow fever."

The event that occurred was most astonishing. Yellow fever increased! The cleaner the city, the more people died. Yellow fever existed on every street in the place. Most surprising of all, in the crooked, narrow streets where ignorant people crowded together like animals and did the least to observe sanitary laws, yellow fever appeared less than elsewhere. The disease attacked soldiers, officers, people of high worth; those who lived in clean houses! Here was a puzzle.

Photo from Kadel & Herbert, N. Y.

WILLIAM CRAWFORD GORGAS

Although yellow fever had always existed, no one knew what caused it. In 1495 Columbus had found the disease at San Domingo. Some thought it came through the peculiar air of the tropics; others related it to dirt; some referred it to decaying coffee. In the meantime, the real bearer of the disease, a certain kind of mosquito, flew about merrily; for the most part leading an unsuspected life of crime. Here and there people were beginning to wonder just what carried yellow fever. Dr. Mott, in Mobile, in 1848, thought that some kind of insect might carry the disease. Dr. Beauperthuis, in Guadeloupe, in 1853, thought that insects might carry both malaria and yellow fever, the two great scourges of his island.

For twenty years, in Havana, Dr. Carlos J. Finlay had insisted that a very particular kind of mosquito, and no other, carried yellow fever. Dr. Finlay would talk of nothing else, but he could make no one believe him. He talked to citizens, he talked to physicians, he read papers before medical conventions, but all in vain. In his house he kept a jar in which he confined the kind of mosquito that he accused, the *stegomyia*.

"Show us," said every one.

Dr. Finlay let his mosquitoes bite yellow fever patients, and then bite people who were not immune to the disease, but nothing happened! He was unable to prove his case. Nevertheless, he was right. Almost through inspiration the wise doctor had found the cause, but unfortunately he could not demonstrate it.

Various men had attacked the character of mosquitoes in general, and the insects had very little reputation left. In 1880, Sir Patrick Manson discovered that one kind of mosquito carries filariasis; in 1897 Ronald Ross discovered that the *anopheles* mosquito carries malaria. In 1881, at a medical congress in Washington, Dr. Finlay accused the *stegomyia* of carrying yellow fever. There are some eight hundred different kinds of mosquitoes, all of them most industrious, but not all of them equally guilty of inflict-

ing harm.   The *stegomyia* had been accused; he must be
tried.

At the order of the Surgeon-General of the United States
Army, there went to Cuba a commission, the names of whose
members should be written in letters of gold: Walter Reed,
James Carroll, Jesse Lazear, and Aristides Agramonte.   They
and their assistants did heroic work of a type that can never
be forgotten.   They experimented on themselves!   Dr.
Lazear, bitten by a mosquito, died of yellow fever; Dr. Carroll, likewise bitten, all but died.

The commission built two little houses, fourteen by twenty
feet in size, both of them thoroughly screened.   One of them
they made clean and well ventilated, but in it they put fifteen
mosquitoes known to have bitten yellow fever patients; the
other they made dark and badly ventilated, and in it they
put the bedding and the clothing worn by patients who had
died of yellow fever.

In the clean, well-ventilated house that contained infected
mosquitoes, the volunteer soldiers contracted yellow fever.
Fortunately all recovered.   In the second house, in spite of
the closest possible contact with the bedding and clothing of
yellow fever patients, and in spite of the lack of cleanliness,
sunshine, and good air, three heroic men, a medical officer and
two privates of the medical corps, slept for twenty days without contracting the disease.   Here was a clear demonstration.

The American commission now made a careful study of the
stegomyia fasciata, the convicted mosquito.   They found it a
beautiful black insect, with long delicate wings, and white
silver marks.   They observed that the *stegomyia*, like most
mosquitoes, comes from stagnant water, but unlike other
mosquitoes it never flies to any distance, nor does it live away
from houses.   They learned further that once in a room the
stegomyia stays there and continues to be a source of infection, once infected being able to carry yellow fever for fifty-
seven days!

Thus, of forty-six people who entered a single house, forty-
five contracted yellow fever, because infected mosquitoes re-

mained in the building. Of two hundred and forty-nine who went on a single boat, two hundred and forty-two took the disease for a similar reason. And the seven who did not take it were immune.

The American commission had proved by experiments that there is no danger from contact with patients, with their clothing, or from breathing the air of places where yellow fever rages, but that the danger from the *stegomyia*, the one source of all danger, is very great.

Even the *stegomyia*, the commission discovered to their astonishment, is not dangerous at all times. The male mosquito never carries the disease, and even the female is not dangerous unless it has bitten a person suffering from yellow fever, and that within the first three days of the attack, when, it appears, a peculiar virus exists in the patient's blood. Even then, for twelve to fourteen days more the mosquito is harmless. After that lapse of time it spreads the disease, to whatever susceptible person it bites, for fifty-seven days. The *stegomyia*, so the investigators learned, has many curious habits. In the short time just before the mosquito lays its eggs, it bites both day and night. After that time it bites at night only, thereby making it much more likely that a person will contract yellow fever after dark than in the daytime.

The entire investigation, on which Dr. Gorgas based his later work, was one of the most remarkable scientific investigations of modern times. It was self-sacrificing, patient, heroic work of the noblest kind, carried to absolute completion and finality.

At once, on learning the conclusions of the commission, Dr. Gorgas set to work to destroy every *stegomyia* in and near Havana. He might have planned to destroy human armies and have awakened respect, but when he planned to destroy insect hosts that bred by thousands in all manner of unreachable places, in and near a tropical city whose people laughed at the surprising thought of a great government making a serious attack upon mosquitoes, he awoke ridicule.

Dr. Gorgas knew that the *stegomyia* does not fly about

from place to place, and is not blown about by the wind. He knew that if he could kill it within the houses and in its breeding places he would win the victory. To that end, as Chief Sanitary Officer of Havana, he divided the city into districts, and then, through his agents, invaded every street, every house, and every stable, and looked into every possible container. From his searching eyes he brought it about that there was no privacy. He made the amazed people exhibit, and even list, all their containers, big or little. Over every bit of water where mosquitoes might breed he spread a film of kerosene that killed the larvæ. Wherever there were cases of yellow fever he screened the houses thoroughly, so that no mosquitoes could possibly reach the patients. He maintained a constant inspection of drainage, houses, and puddles. He made all Havana laugh or grumble but he also made every one obey orders. The determined sanitary officer, with the hot fighting spirit, gave Havana such a disciplining as it had never had before in all its existence.

For nearly one hundred and fifty years, according to the records, Havana had had yellow fever every day in the year. After Dr. Gorgas had completed his work, Havana had no more yellow fever except the chance cases brought to it on vessels, and those imported cases, under the new methods, brought no danger for any one. The whole world was amazed at the result, for Dr. Gorgas had laid low an enemy of humankind that ever before had admitted no master, as easily as David had overcome Goliath.

The researches of the American commission, and the vigorous, unrelenting, fighting quality of the work of Dr. Gorgas, gave new life to Havana, and new hope to mankind. Since that time, physicians in every part of the world where yellow fever existed have employed the methods used in Havana, with the result that the disease is no longer a menace to human existence.

In 1903 a special act of Congress promoted Dr. Gorgas to the rank of colonel assistant surgeon for his accomplishments in overcoming yellow fever in Havana.

When the United States took measures to construct the Panama Canal, people remembered how yellow fever had driven the French from the work. The authorities therefore sent Dr. Gorgas to do in a tropical jungle what he had done in a tropical city, but how different was the situation! At Panama they expected him to kill all the mosquitoes in a strip of land ten miles wide and fifty miles long, a region of swamps, jungle, and tropical vegetation, whose inhabitants were utterly indifferent.

Many people of intelligence, even in the United States, believed that the expensive war on the mosquito was a mistake. Admiral Walker, who had charge of work on the Panama Canal before Colonel Goethals, thought it most ridiculous. Politicians, who had other uses for the public money, made vigorous protests against what they regarded as a nonsensical attack on an insect that was a mere annoyance and nothing more. General Davis, the first governor of the Canal Zone, had no patience with the cost of destroying mosquitoes. Even Colonel Goethals, great man as he was, did not sympathize with Dr. Gorgas and his work. Most surprising of all, such a broad-minded man as Theodore Roosevelt was not at first fully appreciative.

In spite of everything, the doctor who had been so ready to use his fists when a boy, redoubled his courage and went ahead with his work. He made the people along the Panama Canal keep every can, pot, pan and barrel free from breeding mosquitoes. Then he sent his men into the jungles. Like a crusader, he attacked the Panama region, that had reeked with yellow fever, and made it what it is today, a health resort! He made the construction of the Panama Canal possible without the expenditure of thousands of lives, and he made its maintenance forever secure.

In his work in Havana and in the Canal Zone, Dr. Gorgas himself was more active than any of his men. He went everywhere, did everything, cared for no rest, and without doubt by such labors shortened his life. In 1914, in recognition of all that he had done, the authorities promoted Dr.

Gorgas to the rank of brigadier general, and at the same time made him Surgeon-General of the United States Army. In the following year, 1915, they again promoted him, this time to the rank of major general.

Colleges and universities conferred high degrees upon General Gorgas; medical societies in Great Britain, in France. in Italy, and in the United States gave him the highest honors. Every one hailed him as a man who had done for all lands an utterly priceless service. Probably the great physician felt that the consciousness of the value of his work, of the hundreds of thousands of lives that he had saved, of the fact that he had changed tropical regions from places to be avoided into places suitable for full development, was his highest reward.

In 1916 General Gorgas made a long trip to South American countries, places that he had benefited so greatly. He visited Ecuador, Peru, Colombia, Venezuela, and Brazil, places where yellow fever had prevailed for generations. Then he visited Mexico and Central America. On that trip he proposed plans to eliminate yellow fever from the entire world, and with such good effect that today one may travel anywhere in the once afflicted lands and fear no danger from the once ever-threatening disease.

Dr. Gorgas also made a trip to South Africa, this time not in connection with yellow fever, but to find means to aid in overcoming pneumonia, so prevalent among African laborers.

In 1918, at the age of sixty-four, General Gorgas retired from active service, but could not permit himself to retire from the service of humanity. He became director of yellow fever research under the Rockefeller Foundation, and everywhere gave his influence and his active help toward combating disease.

Beginning with humble work in obscure army posts in the West, he had made the whole world the scene of his medical labors. He had carried hope to all lands as few have ever done. To the very last he remained a hard-working, hard-fighting, determined man. General Gorgas had more than fulfilled the ambitions of his boyhood: he had become a soldier, an officer, and even a major general, but in an army far nobler, far more worthy of praise than any army equipped with swords and cannon, the army of those who work to save life, not to destroy. In his last days, in London, England, Dr. Gorgas received the Harbin Gold Medal for "Services to Mankind." How much those words must have meant to him! How deeply he must have realized that satisfaction in life comes from being of use, and that supreme satisfaction comes from being of use on a great scale. The great physician died in London in 1920, at the age of sixty-six. His funeral was held in St. Paul's Cathedral, a place sacred to the great dead of the British service. The people of England, like the people of many other lands, thought of Dr. Gorgas as one who had risen beyond all bounds of nationalities and made himself a citizen of the world.

His body is buried in the national cemetery at Arlington, Virginia.

X

ALBERT ABRAHAM MICHELSON

PHYSICIST

ON a clear winter night look high above the horizon. There, brightest of all the constellations, you see the great rectangle of Orion, the Hunter. In the center of the rectangle you see three bright stars, "Orion's Belt." How beautiful that great constellation is! How wonderful! How bright it is, brighter far than any other group of stars in the entire sky! You stand awe-struck. You look upon the eternal, the unapproachable, the infinitely remote and the infinitely beautiful.

If you remember your Homer at all, you may remember that the ancient Greek writer, perhaps a thousand years before Christ, looked in the same way upon Orion, and wondered; for he mentioned the constellation twice in the *Iliad,* and once in the *Odyssey.* You may think of Amos, the "herdsman of Tekoa," who lived perhaps eight hundred years before Christ; and of the writer of *Job,* who lived perhaps five hundred years before Christ, both of whom spoke of the beauty of these great stars.

There the stars are, immensely brilliant. One in the great rectangle, brighter than the others, is Betelgeuse, or *Alpha Orionis,* a yellowish-red star that strongly attracts attention. Bright as it is, it is infinitely remote, for it is much farther away than the nearest of our star neighbors, *Alpha Centauri,* which is 25,000,000,000,000 miles distant! Who, then, would dream of measuring the size of what is so far away that even the telescope cannot magnify it beyond a point of light?

136

In 1920, Albert Abraham Michelson, a physicist, by means of an ingenious apparatus called the interferometer, measured the size of Betelgeuse, finding the star an unthinkably vast mass 260,000,000 miles in diameter. Professor Michelson was the first man to measure the size of a fixed star.

Thirteen years before he announced the measurement of Betelgeuse, he had become the first person in the United States to win a Nobel Prize, receiving that great award in 1907 for his remarkable work in the study of light, a work that called for much ingenuity, and great patience, combined with power to work accurately under almost impossible conditions.

Like so many who have brought honor to the United States, Professor Michelson was born in a foreign land; his birthplace being Strelno, in Germany, where he was born December 19, 1852.

While the first American winner of the Nobel Prize was born in a foreign land, he is not to be thought of as a foreigner. Professor Michelson brought from his German birthplace, strength, energy, and good inheritance, to which he added a thoroughly American education. In 1873 he was graduated from the United States Naval Academy at Annapolis, with every prospect of becoming an officer in the United States Navy. With such thoroughly American training as that, he became an American of the Americans.

Devoting himself at first, after his graduation, to teaching in the United States Naval Academy, he steadily developed unusual powers of research, and ultimately became head of the department of physics in the University of Chicago, a position that he has held since 1892.

In addition to the Nobel Prize, which brought with it, as well as the usual money award of $40,000, world-wide distinction, Professor Michelson has won so many other prizes notable in the world of learning, that it is more than evident that he is one of the greatest investigators and scholars of modern times.

Thus in 1889 he won the Rumford Medal; in 1900 the

Grand Prix at the Paris Exposition: in 1904 the Matteucci Medal of the Italian Society at Rome; in 1907 the Copley Medal of the Royal Society of London; in 1912 the Elliott Cresson Medal; and in 1916 the Draper Medal, all for studies in physics in connection with light. In 1921 he won the Gold Medal of the Society of Arts, of London, for the Michelson-Morley experiments on the interference of light as it bears on the Einstein Theory.

In addition to all these great honors, educational institutions have conferred upon him high degrees, Western Reserve University, Stevens Institute of Technology, Yale University, the University of Pennsylvania, the great German universities at Leipzig and at Göttingen, and the historic Cambridge University in England, alike honoring him. Learned societies in the United States and in Europe have welcomed him to membership, among them being the famous Royal Society of London, the Royal Astronomical Society, the British Association for the Advancement of Science, the Royal Academy of Sweden, the Academy of Sciences of the Institute of France, and even the French Academy, of which he is a Foreign Associate. In the United States, Professor Michelson is Fellow of the American Academy of Arts and Sciences and member of many other distinguished bodies. He is one of the greatest leaders in the advancement of learning.

Some time ago, while Professor Michelson was in Germany, one of his former classmates at the Naval Academy at Annapolis, a man who had continued in the naval service, and had been so fortunate as to rise to the rank of admiral in the United States Navy, met the learned scientist at a public reception. Realizing how far Professor Michelson had risen beyond all distinctions of military and naval rank, and how much greater is the accomplishment of sheer intellect than the exercise of power, the admiral said in self-satirizing jest: "You made a great mistake, Mike; you might have been an admiral by now!"

Instead of concerning himself with the waves of the ocean,

Professor Michelson had made himself familiar with the waves of light; instead of measuring the velocity of cannon balls he had measured the velocity of light, which moves most rapidly of all things in the universe; instead of taking latitude and longitude, he had measured stars that are only pin points of light; instead of sailing on oceans of the earth to familiar ports, Professor Michelson had chosen to sail, by thought, across the vast, uncharted seas of stellar space, and there to discover new knowledge.

Without question Professor Michelson owes much of his brilliant power to a strong inheritance. In the first place he was as naturally gifted in intellectual power as was Raphael in painting, or Mozart in music, or Tennyson in poetry. He was born with potential capacities that he developed into scholarly ability of the highest rank.

Another person, given precisely the same opportunities, and the same education, might have become an entirely different sort of individual; for the qualities of inheritance, that every one recognizes as important in the race horse, are important in human beings. Whatever training it receives, the drayhorse will not develop into a racer, nor will its descendants make new records on the track. A natural aristocracy of blood both in animals and in men makes itself felt. Professor Michelson's sister became a writer of popular novels, and his brother became a leading editor.

As a boy Albert Michelson was a careful student. At the United States Naval Academy he made a notable record, showing himself especially strong in mathematics, in physics and in chemistry. For that reason, two years after his graduation in 1873, he was asked to become instructor in physics and chemistry. In that position he served at the Naval Academy for four years, teaching classes, and making further and advanced studies because of his natural delight in study, as well as performing the first of his really important experiments. He was not satisfied merely to accept what other men had discovered. He had taken to heart the first lesson of all science: "Seek further knowledge." To that end, having mastered what others had learned, he set out to find new truths.

Science is not so much a mastery of truth as it is a search for new truth. The scientist will forever have the joy of sailing into the unknown, because the universe is so complex that much will always remain to be discovered.

After four years of teaching at the United States Naval Academy, Professor Michelson took a position in the office of the *Nautical Almanac*. He was then twenty-eight. In the work of the office, which naturally has much to do with astronomy, he increased his interest in the measurement of light. Although the ardent student continued to study and to experiment, he felt the need of association with the greatest scientists, and wished to sit as a humble disciple at the feet of great masters. To that end he went abroad, and studied in the University of Berlin, and in the old University at Heidelberg. A little later he went to France, where he studied with French scientists at the Collège de France, and the École Polytechnique. As a result, by the time he was thirty, he had gained a firm basis on which he could rear his own studies and investigations.

From the very first, even as a young student, Professor Michelson had marked love of accuracy. At all times he was willing to go to any amount of pains, and to devote any amount of time, in order to gain this quality most necessary for the scientist. When Albert Michelson was only a young man, at an age when most young men are students who accept blindly instead of investigating for themselves, he resolved to advance the work of measuring the velocity of light. To that end he made long and careful preparation, and considered every element that might enter into the problem. Then he carried out his work with such utterly painstaking care that he achieved complete success. He worked with such accuracy that even at the present time no one has surpassed what he did as a young man. Out of his conscientiousness as a young student developed his greatness as a mature scientist.

On his return from his foreign studies, Professor Michelson became professor of physics in the Case School of Applied Science in Cleveland, Ohio. In that school he taught, studied and experimented for six years. Then for three years he taught in Clark University. In 1892, at the age of forty, he became professor of physics and head of the department of physics in the University of Chicago.

In 1752 Benjamin Franklin, by his famous kite experiment, showed that a flash of lightning is really merely an electrical discharge. Thereby he led people in America to interest themselves more in careful study of the laws of nature. Benjamin Franklin, whose methods were the fundamental ones of investigation and experiment, became the first American physicist.

Professor Michelson made investigations of light as dramatic as Franklin's investigations of electricity, and with as far-reaching results. Where Franklin changed the conception of a common phenomenon of nature, Professor Michelson changed the conception of the universe itself. By his measurements of the size of some of the stars, the great modern investigator of light showed that our world and our sun are more utterly insignificant, as compared with the immensity of certain stars, than even imaginative astronomers had dared think them to be. By careful measurements Professor Michelson found the diameter of the star Betelgeuse, or *Alpha Orionis*, to be 260,000,000 miles, no less than three hundred times the diameter of our sun, a body that itself has the great diameter of 864,000 miles! When one remembers that the sun has a diameter about one hundred and ten times that of the approximate 8000 mile diameter of the earth, a size so great that it could permit the earth and all its inhabitants to fall into its immense body with no more comparative disturbance than when a small pebble drops into a pail of water; and that at the same time, Betelgeuse is so great that it could receive the sun itself, with all its attendant planets, as if it were no more than a wind-blown seed, he realizes in a faint degree something of what Professor Michelson revealed concerning the staggering size of the vast bodies that float forever through space.

Up to the time of Professor Michelson, astronomers had thought it impossible to measure the diameters of stars. Using the most powerful telescopes ever made, they still saw the stars only as tiny points of light. While with great telescopes they brought into view many more stars than people with unaided vision can see, they resolved the image of no star into a disk like that of the moon or of any one of the planets.

Professor Michelson had for his problem the measuring of the width of something that he could not possibly see in completeness or touch, or apparently reach sufficiently, either through any of the senses, or with any of the instruments in use up to his time.

What good is it to measure the stars? Who cares whether they are large or small, far or near, moving or standing still, increasing or decreasing in brilliance, attended, like our sun, by planets, or moving in loneliness through space? Much of astronomical research contributes little if anything to the ordinary ways of life. The true scientist, however, never concerns himself much with practical utility. He keeps for his one object the finding of truth. He wishes to add to the fund of human knowledge, to discover all that he can concerning the world in which we live, and the worlds that exist around us. The true scientist leaves it to others who follow after him to use the knowledge that he reveals. He holds to his work of patiently discovering, one by one, the secrets of nature, the mysteries of the universe. Nevertheless, he leaves behind him a rich legacy of practical advantage.

Out of such scientific studies, pursued solely in the interests of learning new truth, came much of the art of navigation. Because of the work of astronomers who, for mere love of knowledge, found the relation of the earth to the heavenly bodies, the sea captain on his bridge can find with his sextant the altitude of the sun, and with his chronometer his distance from a known meridian, and thus learn the exact position of his vessel, although he may not have seen land for many days. In some future time, it may be, from the work of such men as Professor Michelson in measuring the stars and in studying light, will come great practical benefits.

What is that mysterious thing that we call "light"? It appears to be a kind of wave-motion of the ether, with waves that move back and forth across the direction in which the light is going. It travels at the inconceivable velocity of over 186,000 miles per second, the greatest velocity, according to Professor Einstein, that can possibly exist. When two waves of light in the same phase arrive at the same place the light appears to increase. When two waves in opposite phase arrive at the same place the light appears to decrease.

On this basis Professor Michelson made his interferometer, an instrument for detecting the interference of waves of light. The ingenious experimenter, splitting a narrow beam of light into two identical parts, made the parts travel over separate paths and then arrive at the same place. When he observed the result of bringing together the two separate parts of the beam, he saw a series of interferences, that showed as a regular series of light and dark bands. Then he found that when such interference is caused by rays of light that come from each of the opposite edges of a luminous object of sufficient size, he could, by observation of the interference bands, determine the diameter of the source of light. He had discovered something new and startling. By that most wonderful of modern inventions, the interferometer, he could, as it were, lay a foot-rule across the very faces of the stars.

In 1890, when he was thirty-eight years old, Professor Michelson wrote an article for the *London Philosophical Magazine* on "The Application of Interference Methods to Astronomical Measurements." As a physicist, he suggested to his brother scientists, the astronomers, the utilization of his investigations of the results of the interference of light waves. He wrote:

"If among the nearer fixed stars there is any as large as our sun, it would subtend an angle of about one-hundredth of a second of arc."

That very minute angle, he thought, could be observed by the use of the interference method. This was seventeen years before the Swedish Academy of Sciences awarded him the Nobel Prize for his work in the study of light.

At a meeting of the American Physical Society in Chicago, Professor Michelson announced that he had found the way to measure the fixed stars, an announcement that meant that further study would reveal new truths about the heavenly bodies. His suggestion proved of the utmost importance. Today every astronomer in the world looks upon the work of Professor Michelson as the beginning of a new day in astronomy.

Curiously enough Professor Michelson was not, and is not, an astronomer. He is a physicist, and in particular a student of light. At the time when he first thought of using the interferometer for the measure of the fixed stars he was professor of physics in Clark University. In his investigations of the action of light he happened to find the possibility of making practical application of principles that he had discovered.

At the great observatory at Mount Wilson, California, Professor Michelson and others, by the use of the interference method, measured the diameters of the planets and thus established the worth of the method, as well as a closer acquaintance with the members of our solar family.

Professor Michelson now turned his interferometer upon those mysterious bodies, the double stars, stars that appear to the ordinary eye as single but that are really two stars moving together in harmony. By his wonderful instrument he measured their distances apart. The brilliant investigator used the great mirror telescope at Mount Wilson, the largest telescope in the world, as well as if he were an astronomer,

ALBERT ABRAHAM MICHELSON

and although only a student of light he changed the work of astronomers for all time to come.

In noting the results of Professor Michelson's work in measuring the stars, people are too likely to forget his long hours of patient effort, his all-absorbing care in making delicate adjustments, and his repeated attempts to succeed in spite of repeated failures.

In much of his work the scientist had to devise and to make the instruments with which he worked. In order to make diffraction gratings sufficiently good to enable him to make satisfactory studies of spectra, he spent several years in work. He made his ability to be painstaking in the extreme, the means of gaining success.

In all probability Professor Michelson made the most accurate measurements ever made by any human being up to his time. In his apparatus for the measurement of the lengths of light waves he secured an accuracy that left a possible error of only one part in ten million, an accuracy little short of miraculous, so close does it approach absolute perfection.

Professor Michelson's experiments in connection with Edward W. Morley, to determine if the earth moves through imponderable ether, were so important that they led the way to the theory of relativity propounded by Professor Albert Einstein, a theory that gave entirely new conceptions of the nature of the universe, and upset, in a most relentless way, much that scholars had always accepted as ordinary matter of fact. In that work Professor Michelson and Edward W. Morley again made use of the wonderful interferometer. The two scientists found results that raised most serious questions, whose answers could not be given until 1905 when Professor Einstein proposed his remarkable hypothesis.

In many other ways, and with equal ingenuity, Professor Michelson applied his interferometer to other problems of science, finding results that awakened new lines of interest.

Every one is familiar with the great movement of the sea

that we call the tide. Few know that the land itself, that appears to be so solid and substantial, so unmoving, set fast "like the everlasting hills," likewise moves, although, of course, in a degree not noticeable to the unaided senses. By making use of the interferometer Professor Michelson detected the extremely minute angular shift of a long level space several hundred feet in length, thus proving that the bosom of the earth moves, as if Mother Nature actually lived, and breathed with great regular breaths.

Thus, with the marvelous apparatus that he had devised, on the one hand he reached out into the depths of space and applied measuring devices to the invisible surfaces of distant stars; on the other he so magnified human perceptions that he detected the "breathing" of the earth. In such work, delicate, exacting, demanding most minute and painstaking care, he accomplished results little short of the miraculous.

Through the interferometer Professor Michelson found new information, not only concerning the size but also concerning the distance of the stars. Thus when he examined Betelgeuse he found that immense star not so near as astronomers had supposed it to be, but at an immensely greater distance from the earth.

By the interferometer this annihilator of old conceptions determined new facts concerning the movements of the stars, which for many years people had spoken of as "fixed," assuming that they had no movement. By the use of his magic instrument Professor Michelson showed that some of the stars are moving toward the earth; that some are moving away from it; and that all the stars are in motion, reminding one of Shakespeare's lines:

"There's not the smallest orb, which thou behold'st,
　　But in his motion like an angel sings,
　　Still quiring to the young-eyed cherubins:
　　Such harmony is in immortal souls;
　　But, whilst this muddy vesture of decay
　　Doth grossly close it in, we cannot hear it."

Professor Michelson and other scientists are doing much to enable us know something of the harmony of the stars, of which Shakespeare spoke, but they are showing us a grander harmony than any that poet ever imagined. Through the interferometer they are making revelations of sizes, distances and movements on a scale so unthinkably great that it staggers thought, and lifts even the grossest materialist to a lively sense of awe.

What is the use of knowing the size, the distance, or the movements of the stars? What is the use, one might ask, of revealing anything of beauty or of sublimity, that lifts the soul in admiration or in awe? Professor Michelson, in his work with light, shows the kinship of the scientist with the poet, the artist, the musician, and even the preacher of a noble faith, and how much he adds to life. Many people, indeed, in such scientific revelation, find very real spiritual revelation.

As one of his admirable characteristics Professor Michelson has marked adaptability. When it became necessary for him to make his delicate diffraction gratings he adapted himself at once to the work, and spent years in making it perfect. In fact, he made a new and better device for the construction of diffraction gratings for spectroscopic work, and he improved the spectroscope itself.

When his fame went abroad he was asked to speak before various scientific bodies, among these being scientific societies in South America, whither he was asked to proceed to explain the diffraction gratings by means of which he had been able to make important discoveries. At that time Professor Michelson did not know Spanish. He accepted the invitation, brought together material, and set out on the voyage to South America. On the vessel he devoted himself to the study of Spanish, with such power of work and such concentration, even in the indolent atmosphere of a passenger steamship, that he learned Spanish on the trip sufficiently well to enable him to cast his lecture into Spanish, and to give it in Spanish before a congress of scientists in South

America. In 1899 Professor Michelson gave the Lowell Lectures in Boston, an honor given only to leaders in thought. On that occasion he took for his subject, *Light Waves and Their Uses.*

In a certain way Professor Michelson has served as foreign representative of the United States, for he and men like him have done much to awaken the respect of the scholars of Europe for the intellectual life of the United States. In such work he is perhaps a more successful representative than are many politically appointed ambassadors. For example, it was at the invitation of the International Bureau of Weights and Measures, at Paris, that he found the length of the standard meter, expressing it in terms of the wave length of cadmium light.

When one reads that Professor Michelson is a member of the Societé Hollandaise Vetenskapsakademien des Sciences, of the Societé Française de Physique, of the Cambridge Philosophical Society, the Royal Institute, and the Bureau International des Poids et Mesures, as well as other foreign societies, he sees in what a broad way the scientist serves as a kind of national representative.

In 1911 Professor Michelson became exchange professor at the University of Göttingen in Germany, and there, in one of the strongholds of science, in the land of his birth, represented the scientific work of the United States. An ambassador of learning has great opportunities to bring about friendly relations between great peoples.

In his books, likewise, Professor Michelson has appealed to every scientist throughout the world. In 1902 he published a work on *The Velocity of Light,* and in 1903 his Lowell Lectures, *Light Waves and Their Uses.* In both books he spoke to the scientists of all lands and directed their attention to new developments. In various magazine articles, in scientific publications, especially the *American Journal of Science,* he has spoken from time to time to great bodies of people, and almost always on his favorite subject, light.

The great scientist is still leading an intensely busy but

intensely happy life; still making an eager and unselfish search for knowledge; still finding constant joy in its achievements; and still, through his revelations, lifting the imagination to new heights.

XI

ROBERT ANDREWS MILLIKAN

PHYSICIST

"WITHIN the past seventy-five years, the merest drop in the bucket of time, the conditions of human life on this earth have been completely revolutionized, and that solely because, for the first time in history, man has become interested in considerable numbers, rather than, as heretofore in isolated instances, in patiently and persistently seeking merely to uncover nature's 'useless' secrets, and then, when the inner workings have been laid bare, has in many cases seen a way to put his brain inside the machine and drive it where he would. Every increase thus in man's knowledge of the way in which nature works must in the long run increase by just so much man's ability to control nature and turn her hidden forces to his own account."

So said Robert Andrews Millikan, winner of the Nobel Prize in physics in 1923. The words show that the man is not only a physicist but that he is also a philosopher.

Up to the period of what we call modern times, most people were content to accept the conditions of life without inquiring into them. So great a ruler as Queen Elizabeth had almost nothing of what we regard as essential for the carrying on of daily life. She could not travel in train or in automobile; she could not send Sir Francis Drake and his men on swift steamships to move against the enemy; she could not communicate by telegraph or telephone; she could not illuminate her castle with electric light; she could not even maintain proper conditions of health for herself and those around her; she could not protect herself and her court from infectious diseases; she could not enjoy the comfort that springs from modern methods of heating houses, and from a thousand and one useful devices that we enjoy. She lacked the advantages that we have gained through the work of scientists who tried, first of all, to discover the secrets of nature.

Scientist, a word derived from the Latin *scire,* to know, in its root significance, at least, means "one who seeks to know," and not "one who seeks to use."

In former ages only here and there, in the person of some Archimedes, some Roger Bacon, or some Isaac Newton was there an eager search for knowledge of the facts of nature. In the past, such men, like lighthouses, indicated something of the way that men should go. Those early investigators, men of the highest genius, had too few followers. Too often, as in the case of Roger Bacon and of Galileo, they drew upon themselves suspicion or suffering because of their eager search for knowledge. The alchemists and the astrologers learned facts of great importance to mankind, but because of the trend of opinion in the ages in which they lived, they posed more as magicians than as seekers for truth.

Somehow, in spite of their own pretense at having mysterious powers, and in spite of the threat of prison and execution, or the charge of being in league with demons, such men continued their work, and led the way, however slowly, to the science of the nineteenth and of the twentieth centuries.

In modern times, freedom from many bonds that shackled people in the past, together with the wide development of general education, make it possible for ingenious people to find how to make use of the secrets that the scientists reveal. Because people have thus taken advantage of the discoveries of science, the queen of today may live in what Elizabeth would have regarded as a magic castle.

Robert Andrews Millikan is among the scientists who delve most deeply into that which is hidden. Where another

American winner of the Nobel Prize in physics, Albert A. Michelson, with his interferometer, reached across the unbelievable distances of space and measured the stupendous size of the stars, bodies utterly gigantic as compared with our earth or our sister planets, or even with the mighty sun itself, Professor Millikan reached into the very heart, and almost into the very soul, of matter, and measured the infinitely small. He won the Nobel Prize in physics, in 1923, for his astonishing work in isolating and in measuring the ultimate unit, the electron. Professor Millikan's work lies as far beyond ordinary comprehension and ordinary imagination as does the work of Professor Michelson, for the work of one man concerns the infinitely small, and the work of the other the infinitely great.

While Professor Michelson found a universe of immense bodies, all in motion, following laws that belittle all with which we are familiar, Professor Millikan, going into regions that lie beyond the most powerful microscope that has ever been made or that, in all probability, ever will be made, found conditions that suggest a parallel, bodies, if we may call them such, or electrons, that move in appointed orbits, with inconceivable velocity, in accordance with laws as definite as the laws that govern the stars. He found the means to determine the charge on a single electron, leaving it to other investigators, such as Niels Bohr, and Sir Ernest Rutherford, to investigate further.

Whereas to the ancient world matter was merely "matter," solid, substantial, and unmoving, to the scientists of today it is vibrant with energy and motion. The atom is no longer thought of as the ultimate, but as something itself composed of parts, in fact, as a system not unlike our solar system; in which around a central "sun," speed bodies in unimaginable, but measurable, motion. An atom of hydrogen has but one revolving body; an atom of helium, two; of carbon, six; of nitrogen, seven; of oxygen, eight; of sodium, eleven; and so on, different conditions existing in different elements. Professor Millikan found the way to isolate one of

ROBERT ANDREWS MILLIKAN

those mysterious electrons that revolve within the atom, to attach it to a drop of oil, and to measure both it and its speed. He uncovered what today may be a useless secret of nature, but tomorrow may be a source of limitless power.

All that is is in motion. The earth on which we walk, the implements that we use, our very selves, are alike composed of atoms, and they, in turn, of ions and electrons in motion swifter than thought. No longer is "matter" a base and substantial thing, but it is vibrant, filled with power, elemental in beauty, and suggesting an order poetic beyond anything ever before conceived.

Professor Millikan is especially fortunate in his use of clear, plain English in explanation of scientific facts. When some people spoke of what they called "revolutionary conceptions of science," he answered:

"Nine-tenths of them are just as revolutionary as was the discovery of the seven year old boy who came home from school one day altogether disgusted, saying that for a week his teacher had been teaching him that three and four made seven, and he had just got it well learned when she told him that five and two make seven. So it is with our discoveries in science."

Nature remains the same, whether we look upon her with the childlike eyes of primitive man, or with the clear vision of the scientist.

Although Professor Millikan has made himself one of the greatest of scholars, a man who will be remembered for centuries, who led in bringing about new conceptions of matter, he has retained an intensely human, companionable quality that makes him a delightful exponent of scientific truth. Never content to make his work dry, technical, and abstruse, he draws constantly, in his exposition, upon a fund of familiar illustrations; nor is he afraid to mingle shrewd humor with scientific fact.

Both in his lectures and his books he refers constantly to

such common, matter-of-fact things as "a man on a bridge," "a football," "a bullet," and "snails." In speaking of the moving components of matter, he says they "dart hither and thither like gnats in a swarm." He refuses to bury himself in the abstract, and thus gives to his words a human quality that shows how thoroughly he enjoys life and the ordinary ways of humanity.

Like every good scientist he makes accuracy the keynote of his work. In one of his lectures he said, "There is no science without exact measurement." Only because of his intense belief in that thesis, could he carry on his difficult work of measuring the electron, work that called for such extreme accuracy that it demanded almost superhuman power.

How did Professor Millikan gain the training that enabled him to carry on such difficult work and win recognition as one of the most accurate of scientists? In the first place, from his father, Rev. Silas Franklin Millikan, an educated man who had a good library, the boy very early learned to derive pleasure from books. Under the direction of that wise father, he read and studied and grew up in an atmosphere of learning. In those early days, when he first learned how to study, he unconsciously turned his steps towards a scholarly career.

Robert Andrews Millikan was born in Morrison, Illinois, March 22, 1868. If it were not for the fact that he has become, as does almost every great scientist, a citizen of the world rather than of any definite section of the world, one would say that he is thoroughly a son of the Middle West, where he was born, where he gained his early training, and where he went to college.

In the early days of the United States, the leaders in all fields of thought came from somewhere near the seacoast, from Massachusetts, New York, Pennsylvania, Virginia, and the Carolinas. In the days when the population became such that men moved on to open new lands to the west, many of the strongest, the most vigorous, the most active, as well as the most daring and the most original, went to find fortune in new lands. From the descendants of such forward-looking people the leaders in the Middle West have sprung. Having a good inheritance, they have shown "the mettle of their pasture."

After his training in the home and in the small preparatory schools of the day, the young student, who had already become interested in the elements of science, went to Oberlin College in Ohio. There, more than ever before, he followed his inclinations and gave much time and effort to the study of physics and of chemistry under the direction of skilled, well-informed teachers. He was graduated from Oberlin in 1893, with a degree of B. A.

Fortunately for him, he gained inspiration to carry his studies still further. Having succeeded, and having developed strong interests, he wished to continue in the work that he had begun. Therefore he went to New York City where he continued to study physics. There he did conscientious, careful work, and in 1895 received from Columbia University the degree of doctor of philosophy.

The enthusiastic worker had now shown himself remarkably able to grasp details and to carry on difficult undertakings. When circumstances made it possible for him to go to Europe, and there study under the most expert teachers of science, he went to Germany, where he studied in the University of Berlin, and the University of Göttingen, ultimately obtaining a German degree. In those days of student life in Germany he came into intimate contact with leaders of the highest rank, from whom he received new inspiration.

In the meanwhile the young scientist had already begun to teach. In his first college days in Oberlin he had shown himself so capable a student that he was given the opportunity to tutor in physics at the same time that he carried on his own studies, and thus, during three of his college years, taught others. Naturally, in so doing, he strengthened his own work as a student. The authorities at Oberlin noticed that the young tutor showed especial promise. Therefore, when he had completed his studies in the German universities, they invited him to return to his own college as assistant professor of physics. That was in 1896, when he was twenty-eight years old.

For a young man of his age, Robert A. Millikan had made a most creditable record. He had won his bachelor's degree with great credit, had won his doctor's degree, had studied abroad under distinguished masters, had won a foreign degree, and now had gained an honorable position in an institution of recognized high rank.

If Professor Millikan had been content to assume that he had now reached success, he might have continued quietly in his work as teacher of physics, very largely abandoning intensive study and research, and have taken pride chiefly in transmitting to others what he himself had learned. He would have had every reason to think of his life as a success, and he would have had the consciousness of doing a useful and necessary work.

Most men, whether in business or in professional life, "arrive" comparatively early. They become mature, "settled," and cease, in any great way, to grow. The true scientist can never possibly "arrive." One great scientist spoke of the gaining of knowledge as merely the picking up, here and there, of a few poor pebbles on the beach of the great ocean of the unknown. By that, he meant that the lover of knowledge will always find more to learn. Although he might live to more than the allotted three score years and ten, and in all his years of mature life give himself to intense study and devoted research, he would always wish for more time in which to work, and would always try to learn something new. To the search for knowledge he would find no end.

Because the young professor at Oberlin was at heart a true scientist he did not fall into the easy rut of college life and become merely a routine teacher. He did his work well and thoroughly, and a year after he had accepted his appointment won promotion to the position of associate professor. In his laboratory he studied and experimented more than his

pupils did, and made himself more truly a student than most
of those whom he taught.

When he was thirty-one years old he found the opportunity
to go to the University of Chicago, and there to take part
in the work of a larger institution. Like Gareth who, though
he aspired to be one of Arthur's knights, was willing to serve
in a menial position, Millikan was content to go to the bottom
of the ladder, and begin work as instructor. Where Gareth
developed into a hero who did knightly deeds, the young instructor developed into a scientist who won the Nobel Prize
in physics.

In 1901, two years after he had gone to the University of
Chicago, the man who had his heart in his work became
assistant professor of physics; six years later, associate professor; and after three more years, full professor in the
University of Chicago. He was then forty-two years old.
For the next eleven years Professor Millikan carried on
scholarly work in instruction, guiding younger instructors,
directing research, and more eagerly than ever continuing
his own studies and experiments.

In his work as college instructor Professor Millikan did
not believe in dead, formal methods of lecture instruction,
although much of his work called for lecture methods. He
believed in stimulating students to individual experimental
work and to gaining knowledge for themselves. He could not
think of students as so many containers into which he could
pour information. He thought them as active and as eager
in the search for knowledge as he himself. "In all branches
of instruction," he said, "the formal lecture is a most in-
efficient means either of imparting knowledge or of training the powers of the student."

Scholarly as he was, he wished his students, instead of sitting receptive at his feet and learning from him what he
had learned, to go with him into his laboratory and there
to study and experiment as companion seekers for knowledge. Of his teaching he said, "I would not infuse the ele-

ment of amusement, but rather the element of intelligibility, the element of interest.'' In that position he took a stand quite the opposite of one common in education in recent years in the United States.

A century and more ago, when schools were few and teachers far from well trained, only a small number of people made any serious effort to gain learning. Because they had to depend so much upon their own efforts, they looked upon education as a citadel that they must take by long and patient siege. Such people, whose interests lay deeply in study, and who, by every necessity, had to work long and hard, became genuine scholars, taking pride in their attainments.

Then the people of the United States made an attempt, never before made in the history of the world, to give education to all, even to force education upon them. They filled thousands of schools with students who had no deep desire for learning. In an effort to create that desire, teachers endeavored to turn study into play. Sometimes, even in the laboratory, they gave demonstrations to give amusement rather than to create interest in making original investigations. Against such teaching, which can result in no substantial education, Professor Millikan set his face. He wished his pupils to have the characteristic that he himself had, that of intense interest in learning new truth through original work. In that respect he made himself one of the leaders in the modern method of teaching science.

In lectures that he gave before groups of teachers of science, in articles that he wrote for scientific publications, and in text books that he prepared for class use, Professor Millikan expressed his beliefs in the weakness of the lecture method of instruction, and in the necessity of leading students to rely upon themselves in seeking truth, not from books and instructors, but from observation and experiment.

In speaking, whether in the class room or on the lecture platform, he is most engaging in delivery, carrying his hearers along with him, and making them think as he thinks. In his laboratory he is unconventional, quick to fall into some unexpected pose, or to twist upon a chair, his whole thought in his work.

In 1898, when he first entered upon his duties in the University of Chicago, this professor who believed in work published a book called *A Course of College Experiments in Physics*. In that book he endeavored to lead students to discover for themselves the important principles of the laws of matter. Some years later he published a text book called *A Laboratory Course in Physics for Secondary Schools*. In that book he gave to young students, just beginning to study, an opportunity to cultivate original power, and through their own effort to gain some mastery of principles, an opportunity that once only advanced college students had had.

He believed that out of early work, begun in the secondary schools, students should gain training that would enable them to go on to more difficult problems in college study. He wished young students to think of the study of physics as something that they might follow to new heights. Because of that belief Professor Millikan, at the same time scientist and educator, wrote his treatise on *The Correlation of High School and College Physics*. Thus, instead of remaining a scholar among scholars, he made himself a powerful force in the world of education.

In spite of his demanding labors in the laboratory, he found time in which to prepare talks on methods of teaching physics, in which to write text books, and to make valuable reports concerning his own work. In 1900 he translated from the German a valuable book on *The Theory of Optics*. For classroom study he wrote *A First Course in Physics; Mechanics, Molecular Physics and Heat; Electricity, Sound and Light;* and *Practical Lessons in Electricity*. For more general reading he wrote *The Electron, etc.*, and *Science and Life*. Himself a student, he helped others to study.

Out of his own researches he prepared a number of illuminating papers that inspired scholars and turned attention to new theories. Among these he wrote:

The Electron, Its Isolation and Measurement.

*The Isolation of an Ion, a Precision Measure of Its Charge.
New Instruments of Precision.*

*New Modifications on the Cloud Method of Determining the
Elementary Electrical Charge, and the Most Probable Value
of That Charge.*

*New Proof of the Kinetic Theory of Matter and the Atomic
Theory of Electricity.*

The Significance of Radium.

The paper on *The Significance of Radium* Professor Millikan gave under most interesting circumstances. Professor
Pierre Curie and his scholarly wife, Madame Marie Curie, in
their laboratory in Paris, had made the initial investigations
of radium.   Beginning with the accidental discovery of
strange properties in pitchblende, they had gone on tirelessly
in their work, and had made fundamental discoveries.   In
1906 when Professor Curie died, his wife continued the work
and made herself the leading investigator in the subject.

On her visit to the United States in 1921, in appreciation of
the remarkable work that she had carried on, scholars wished
to present to her some token of recognition.   They decided,
most appropriately, upon a gram of radium, the product of
many tons of pitchblende and the result of an enormous
amount of labor, a gift having a cash value of about $35,000.
For the presentation of this remarkable gift they called upon
Professor Millikan, because of his researches into the nature
of the atom.   At the National Museum in Washington, D. C.,
May 25, 1921, the American scholar presented the gift to the
great French investigator, and spoke on the importance of
radium.

Professor Millikan himself, at various times, received public honors.   In 1913 he won the Comstock Prize, awarded by
the National Academy of Science for researches in electricity;
in 1922, the Edison Medal, awarded by the American Institute of Electrical Engineers; in 1923, the Hughes Medal,
awarded by the Royal Society of Great Britain; and in the
same year, the Nobel Prize in physics, awarded by the Swedish Academy of Science.

From Oberlin College, Northwestern University, the University of Pennsylvania, Columbia University, Amherst College, and the University of Dublin he received honorary degrees. He became a member of the American Academy of Arts and Science; of the National Academy of Sciences; of the Royal Institute of Great Britain; of the Academy of Science of Leyden, in Holland; and president of the American Philosophical Society.

At no time a recluse in his laboratory, the scholar has given much public service. In 1917 he became a trustee of Oberlin; and in 1921 chairman of the administrative council of the California Institute of Technology. During the World War he employed his technical and scientific skill in the service of the United States, holding the rank of commanding lieutenant colonel in the Signal Corps, U.S.R., in 1918, and Chief of the Science and Research Division of the Signal Corps.

In 1922 Professor Millikan became the first Exchange Professor to Belgium, where he ably represented the scientific ability of the United States.

Professor Millikan has shown that the old conception that the great scholar lives apart from active affairs is now without foundation. He sets forward the new conception that the scholar, while forever seeking knowledge, still lives a practical and useful life.

XII

ROBERT EDWIN PEARY

Arctic Explorer

Who can look upon a range of hills or mountains without
wondering what lies beyond?

> "One day I know, shall my free soul roam
> Over the lofty mountains."

So wrote Björnstjerne Björnsen in one of Norway's favorite poems, expressing man's common desire to go beyond
familiar limits, to explore new regions, and to learn new conditions. Every mountain peak is a challenge to climb; every
land that men do not ordinarily visit is an invitation; every
star dares one to inquire into its nature, its distance, and its
motion; while the infinitesimal world that lies within reach
of the microscope, or even beyond such reach, calls to the
seeker after knowledge.

In answer to such challenging calls, men and women venture into the Sahara, cross the jungles of Africa, work their
way through the sodden depths of the regions of the Amazon, or explore the frozen lands of the Arctic or the Antarctic.
Eric the Red, Christopher Columbus, Ferdinand Magellan,
Henry Hudson and Sir Francis Drake belong to the company of those who answered the call of the unknown. Sir
Martin Frobisher, William Baffin, and Vitus Bering belong
to another company of adventurers. They ventured into the
cold and desolation of the north, content to risk everything in
order to learn what lies in the forbidden regions.

The question whose answer they sought still presents itself. A great frozen sea and possible expanses of ice-covered land await full investigation. On all sides men are making the effort to learn more about the regions around the poles of the earth. Ships go into the ice, and remain frozen in for dark, weary months, while brave souls that sail on them do their best to learn what the north has to reveal. One man, Salomon Andrée, dies in an attempt to fly across in an old-fashioned balloon; others, Roald Amundsen and Richard E. Byrd, imperil their lives in modern aircraft. One man of self-sacrificing courage, Captain Robert Scott, staggers and dies in the frightful cold and winds near the south pole, but in his last words he writes:

"I do not regret this journey, which has shown that Englishmen can endure hardship, help one another, and meet death with as great fortitude as ever in the past. . . . We have been willing to give our lives for this enterprise, which is for the honor of our country."

What good is all this effort, all this sacrifice of money and lives? Men have given various reasons for entering the uninhabited, frozen expanses. Some said they looked for a northwest passage; some, for new lands to bring under the dominion of their countries; some, to learn facts concerning the shape of the earth, the movements of the tides, the nature of strange electrical phenomena visible in northern regions, or to learn more about mineral or animal wealth concealed in the north. In most cases the real reason is man's deep desire to learn about the unknown.

To discover the facts about the polar regions may bring few practical results, but it will at least bring infinite satisfaction in having met and conquered the challenge of nature.

Of the daring of Americans in entering the polar regions, Edmund Burke said: "Whilst we follow them among the tumbling mountains of ice, and behold them penetrating into the deepest frozen recesses of Hudson's Bay and Davis's Straits, whilst we are looking for them beneath the Arctic circle, we hear that they have pierced into the opposite region of polar cold, that they are at the Antipodes, and engaged under the frozen serpent of the south.''

Of all the long list of men whom America has sent into the far north, one man alone will always hold the place of distinction as having first reached the goal. That man is Robert Edwin Peary, rear admiral in the United States Navy, the discoverer of the North Pole.

Beside the place where Admiral Peary is buried in the National Cemetery at Arlington, just beyond the Capitol of the United States, stands his monument, an immense globe of granite, representing the earth. That globe bears a sculptured map that shows the frozen places into which Admiral Peary ventured from the time when he was a young man of thirty until, at the age of fifty-three, in 1909, he succeeded in reaching the North Pole.

For all the greater part of his mature life Robert Edwin Peary lived with practically one object, to reach the North Pole. He met difficulties that at first appeared insurmountable; he endured hardships of the most extreme kind; he found himself beyond the age of fifty with his ambition still unsatisfied; then, in one last great effort, in a marvelous dash that he had planned as skilfully as a general plans a campaign, he succeeded. Without question, Admiral Peary shortened his life by his years of struggle with the north. He knew the sacrifices that would be necessary, and he was prepared to make them. He gained the supreme satisfaction of his life in placing the United States flag on the North Pole. The fact that he also placed there the flag of his college fraternity is a personal touch that shows that the great explorer never ceased to have the interested spirit of a boy.

In the nature of Robert E. Peary, in the spirit that moved him, in his dogged determination, in his patience and his skill, there was everything that is admirable. About him, too, was something so intensely human, so within reach of the understanding, that he made himself one of the most loved of explorers. Throughout life he made and kept many friends. He met strangers with a kindly look and a warm clasp of the hand. He so kept the devotion of his wife that she went with him more than once into the desolate regions. Instead of being forbidding and austere, he was kindly and well-disposed to all. He made himself a hero of modern times, a romantic hero, as notable as any whose praises have been sung by poets.

"The true explorer," said Peary himself, "does his work not for any hopes of reward or honor, but because the thing he has set himself to do is a part of his being, and must be accomplished for the sake of the accomplishment."

These are brave words and worthy of being remembered.

Curiously enough, originally Robert E. Peary was not a seafaring man. He began the work of life as civil engineer. The conqueror of the polar regions gained his interest in polar exploration through the chance reading of a book on the subject. He was then only a young man but he formed the wish to go himself, and to do what others had not been able to do.

Robert Edwin Peary was born in Cresson, Pennsylvania, May 6, 1856. After his boyhood days he went to Bowdoin College in Brunswick, Maine, the college in which Nathaniel Hawthorne and President Franklin Pierce had been companions, and from which Longfellow had been graduated. Although there were fifty-one students in his class, his was the distinction of winning next to the highest honors. When he was graduated in 1877 it was with the degree of C.E.

Misfortune had carried him to Maine. His father had died when Robert was a child only three years old. His mother had taken him to the state in which his ancestors had lived. Those ancestors of the future explorer had been hard-working woodsmen in the Maine forests, every one accustomed to hardships. No doubt they bequeathed to the explorer much of his power of physical endurance.

In Maine, then, near Portland, Robert Peary grew up. Like all people who live on the coast of Maine, he became familiar with the sea, of which Longfellow, who lived in Portland, at one time, wrote:

> "Only those who brave its dangers
> Comprehend its mystery."

As a boy Robert Peary led a distinctly vigorous outdoor life. He went in boats on the sea, and very early learned how to trap and hunt on the land. Although a hard-working muscular boy, he showed scientific spirit early. Instead of being satisfied merely with hunting, he prepared and mounted the specimens that he shot and made a collection that was a noteworthy piece of work for a boy. Probably some of his Maine ancestors had been hardy Frenchmen who had come to northern New England early in the history of the Colonies, for the name of Peary suggests the French "Pierre." If that is so, then with that strong French stock, whose virtues Francis Parkman made so emphatic in his story of the struggle of France and England for America, there was mixed a strong English strain. The inheritance was good; the surroundings were healthful, both physically and morally, and the boy grew into a sturdy youth.

Robert Peary had the good fortune of having a mother who was an inspiration to him. Mary Wiley Peary, left a widow, devoted herself to her son, and guided his education. When he went to Bowdoin she moved to Brunswick, where she followed his work with interest.

Young Peary was a thoroughgoing, "all-around" college student, good in studies and good in athletics. In mathematics and engineering he showed natural ability, while at the same time he was interested in writing and won prizes for essays. He took a prominent part in the work of the track team, and became one of the college runners and jumpers.

He had always enjoyed taking long walks into the country, and that exercise, together with his attention to athletics, had developed an especially strong, lithe physique. Without knowing for what important work he was training, he made his college study and his college athletics prepare him for his life task. He became an engineer, a navigator, a geographer, an explorer, and a writer. For all that work he had unconsciously prepared himself in college.

Shortly after graduation he began work as surveyor, having headquarters at Fryeburg, a quiet Maine village near the White Mountain region. Any one who saw the young civil engineer mapping hills and mountains would not have prophesied for him a world-famous career. They saw a man setting out apparently for a humdrum life, in which he would accomplish little and win small reward. They could not see, nor could he, that he was training himself for work that lay ahead.

Two years after graduation from college Robert Peary, having gained field experience, wished for more important work than that in Fryeburg. In 1879, when he was twenty-three years old, he entered the Coast and Geodetic Survey of the United States Government and was employed in making charts. October 26, 1881, he entered the United States Navy as civil engineer. In that humble way he began a momentous career.

Now the man began to develop the executive ability by which he finally made his life a triumph. At Key West, Florida, where a pier was to be built, contractors said conditions were unfavorable, the region unhealthful, the amount of money allotted for the work utterly insufficient, and therefore they were unwilling to undertake the construction.

The young engineer looked over the problem, made up his mind that he could solve it, and set to work. In spite of an attack of yellow fever, he built the pier, and not only built it within the sum allotted, but at a saving of thirty thousand dollars! By that remarkable work he led authorities to look upon him with respect.

For many years people had wished for a canal across the isthmus either at Nicaragua or Panama. Finally the United States authorities were planning to construct one at Nicaragua. There they sent young Peary on the surveying party as assistant engineer. At Nicaragua, for the first time in his life, Robert E. Peary saw really exhausting service. There, in tropical heat and jungles, in the midst of malaria and yellow fever, and in the company of numbers of more or less unruly men, the young man from the quiet New England hills worked for four years.

Robert E. Peary was twenty-eight when he began work in the intense heat. As he sweltered in the jungles and along the steaming swamps he must have thought more than once of cool regions to the north. He did not know that most of his later life he would pass in the coldest regions of the earth. Few people, today, realize that Admiral Peary spent four years of his life in the tropics, doing much the same kind of work after all, that he did in the polar regions.

In 1887, because of excellent work, he became engineer in charge of the Nicaragua Ship Canal surveys. As such he supervised the surveying of jungle land and the finding of the best ways to construct a canal, work that was arduous and exacting. Being of an inventive turn of mind Engineer Peary studied the problem of locks, with the result that he devised a rolling lock gate that had great strength and that men could manage easily.

Robert E. Peary lived a romantic and interesting life at Nicaragua from 1884 to 1888, but because of his greater work in polar exploration he led people to forget it. At Nicaragua he learned much about human nature; he was there as a commander of men, and he had to exercise both authority and tact. It was in the tropics, oddly enough, that the polar explorer gained skill in leadership.

Then, strange as it is, Peary actually began work as a polar explorer during the time when he was employed in the tropics. As a boy he had read of Elisha Kane's polar explora-

ROBERT EDWIN PEARY

tions, and in the story he felt the fascination of the ice. A long time afterward he came upon a report of ice conditions in the interior of Greenland. To one working in the heat of Nicaragua what could be more fascinating than the cold of Greenland! Promptly, he secured a six months' leave of absence, and in 1886, when he was thirty years old, sailed for the first time to the far north. He followed not only a desire to get away from tropical heat, but also a boyhood ambition.

The explorer sailed to Greenland, and there went back one hundred miles on the great inland ice cap east of Disco Bay. He reached only latitude 70° North, a long distance from the Pole, but, nevertheless, deep in the arctic regions. There he first became acquainted with conditions of arctic life, and first felt, in all fact, the fascination of the north. To Peary the fascination became overmastering. From 1886 onward it shaped and molded his life.

In six months' time the voyager was back again in Nicaragua, carrying on work as engineer in charge of surveys. He must have felt the change keenly, and have longed more than ever for the clean coolness of the north. The best that he could do, however, was to perform his daily work, and hope for means to achieve his ambition of once again venturing into the far north.

A long line of brave men had tried to map various parts of the north. John Davis in 1588 had sailed up Davis' Strait to latitude 72° 12′ North; Henry Hudson, in 1607, had gone along the west coast of Spitzbergen, and had reached 80° 23′ North; Sir John Franklin, in 1846, had gone in arctic America to latitude 70° 26′ North, and had there died; and in 1880, George W. De Long, on the ill-fated *Jeannette,* had met death in Siberia.

Around the Pole, for leagues upon leagues, lay absolutely unknown expanses, possibly of ice, possibly of land. Romancers had pictured strange scenes. Some had made it a land of tropic luxuriance; others had told of a vast opening that led within the shell of the earth. Almost every one thought of the Pole as a place of utterly unbearable cold. Geographers and scientists longed for information. That information Robert E. Peary resolved to give them.

First, the enthusiast interested the Academy of Natural Sciences of Philadelphia, with the result that he won support, and in 1891 again sailed for Greenland as chief of an arctic expedition.

In the year and a quarter that he was gone he achieved great resuts, for he discovered that Greenland, the interior of which is a plateau elevated from 5000 to 8000 feet, is an island. More than that, beyond Greenland he found new land that he named Melville Land, and other land that he called Heilprin Land, in honor of Angelo Heilprin, the first president of the Geographical Society of Philadelphia. At the same time he made a thorough scientific study of Eskimauan life.

On this journey Peary went to latitude 81° 37′ North, and made a sledge journey of 1300 miles. At once he sprang into fame as a polar explorer. The American Geographical Society gave him the Cullom Medal; the Royal Geographical Society of London gave him the Patron's Medal; and the Royal Scottish Geographical Society of Edinburgh likewise awarded him a medal.

On this first great expedition there went with him, as far as winter quarters, his devoted wife, Josephine Diebitsch Peary, whom he had married in 1888, three years before, the first white woman who ever experienced the hardships of exploration in the extreme north.

No sooner had the intrepid explorer returned to the United States, in 1892, than he began to plan for a new venture. He determined to go again to the arctic, and to go farther north than any other man had ever gone. He found it by no means easy to obtain funds for the new expedition, but with the utmost energy he set to work to earn the money. In ninety-six days he gave no less than 168 public lectures, many days lecturing twice in succession.

Although the work of lecturing called for continuous travel

in the United States, the energetic and determined man gave himself no rest. He engaged a stenographer to whom he dictated every day, preparing a book concerning his previous experiences in the Arctic regions. Mrs. Peary, always as energetic as her husband, likewise wrote a book concerning her own life in the remote north. At the same time Peary put his arctic ship on exhibition. By all these means, and by the addition of the promise of articles for the New York *Sun,* for which he received in advance $2,000, the persistent explorer raised sufficient funds for the voyage.

In 1893, more determined than ever, he sailed again for the north. On this expedition Peary met with an accident that came near to stopping his work then and forbidding it for all time in the future. A heavy floe of ice hit the rudder of his vessel, making the wheel whirl so rapidly that it broke Peary's leg. Very skilfully indeed the surgeon who had accompanied the expedition set the broken leg, strapped it on a board, and gave the patient such excellent care that he was able not only to continue work during this expedition, but also to endure the great hardships incident to his later long dash to the Pole. The surgeon who did such signal service was Dr. Frederick Cook, who, a few years later, all but took from Admiral Peary the honors of being the first man at the Pole.

On this journey also, the intrepid explorer, while again suffering great hardships, again achieved great results. He reached latitude 81° 47′ North, and discovered three immense meteorites, one of them weighing ninety tons, the largest ever found; and made a thorough investigation of the life and habits of a tribe of Eskimos who lived in these most remote regions.

On the same journey he might have lost his life if it had not been for the energy of his wife, who brought a relief expedition to find him. In the privations of arctic life, trouble had arisen and many of Peary's men had left him. Of two men who remained faithful, one was Matt Hanson, a negro who had accompanied him on his journey in 1887.

The relief expedition arrived at a time of great need. On the expedition Peary had searched in vain for a cache of pemmican and alcohol on which he had relied. He ate raw meat, and finally killed and ate sled dogs, being reduced finally to but one dog. That dog, like his master, had so nearly starved that for days after reaching camp again, where food was plentiful it continually buried supplies of food in the snow around the camp, doing its best to make caches for future need.

Peary endured hardships enough, in his various early Arctic expeditions, to deter any ordinary man from making further attempts to reach the Pole. On the long journey to Fort Conger for instance he froze his toes so that he could not walk. With the temperature 60° to 70° below zero, he rode over rough ice for 250 miles, strapped to his sled and suffering pain all the way. On his arrival at the ship, which was frozen fast in the ice, he suffered the amputation of seven of his toes, making walking thereafter always difficult. A year later, nevertheless, in 1896 and 1897, he went to the far north and brought back the great meteorites that he had discovered.

In 1898, still determined to reach the Pole, he sailed under the auspices of the Peary Arctic Club of New York. On this voyage he went to the northernmost point so far reached in the western hemisphere, to latitude 84° 17′ North. He named the most northern land in the world, a cold and icy cape in the northern part of the Greeland Archipelago, Cape Morris Jessup, after Morris K. Jessup, president of the American Museum of Natural History in New York, a retired banker active in promoting good work.

After this expedition, which occupied nearly four years, Peary spent nearly three years in preparation for still another venture. He had not yet reached the Pole, but he had a dogged persistence that would not let him admit defeat. In 1905 the explorer sailed in a vessel called the *Roosevelt*, a boat built especially to withstand tremendous strains incident to enclosure in ice, the first boat ever built in the United

States especially for Arctic exploration. On this great expedition Peary went farther north than any human being had ever gone before, reaching latitude 87° 6′ North.

In 1908 Admiral Peary was fifty-two years of age. He had been weakened by many hardships. He had suffered from a broken leg. He had but three toes to aid him in walking. He had reached an age when he could not so safely meet hardship and exposure. But he had won the highest honors ever given to any arctic explorer. He had made himself notable as a writer and lecturer, and he might have retired now to enjoy his honors. Instead, he was more determined than ever to win his way to the North Pole.

In July, 1908, Peary, dauntless as ever, sailed on his eighth Arctic expedition! On his little vessel, the *Roosevelt*, he sailed to Kane Basin, to Robeson Channel, and to Cape Sheridan. There, remote from human settlements, he lived for five months in the dreary darkness of the arctic winter, the mysterious aurora borealis waving above him. In February, 1909, he set out for Cape Columbia.

With mathematical precision the experienced explorer had worked out every detail of what he proposed to do. He knew that this must be his last supreme attempt. He could make no more.

In August, 1908, when he left Etah, he had with him twenty-two Eskimo men, seventeen Eskimo women, ten of their children and two hundred and forty-six dogs. When he left the *Roosevelt* he started with sixty-six men, one hundred and forty dogs, and twenty-three sledges. As the marches continued he reduced the numbers, first to twenty-four men, then to twenty, then to nine, then to five, with corresponding reductions in the numbers of sledges and dogs. Through his years of effort he had learned that he could reach the pole only by making the most careful plans and by following tested methods of support.

Near the 88th parallel, 130 miles from the Pole, with the ever-faithful Matt Hanson, the negro, four Eskimos, five sledges, and forty dogs, the great explorer set out on his last effort. In five days of terrific struggle against over-whelming odds, he fought his way over the ice. On April 6, 1909, exactly one month before his fifty-third birthday, Robert E. Peary stood triumphant at the North Pole!

There he raised and cheered the United States flag, and there he remained for thirty hours. He deposited various records, and then went ten miles beyond the Pole in one direction, and eight miles beyond to the right of that. He was determined that there should be no question that he had reached the North Pole itself.

On his journey from Cape Columbia to the Pole he made twenty-seven marches. On his return journey, lightened by happiness, he made only sixteen marches. When he arrived again at Cape Columbia he and his men appeared worn to shadows, so gaunt were they with fatigue. Even the sturdy Eskimos, accustomed to cold and exertion, appeared haggard.

On this last journey Peary established the fact that land does not reach so far north as the Pole. He also made observations of the polar tides and of various other phenomena, and settled forever the question about general conditions at the North Pole.

He had already written *Northward Over the Great Ice*, and *Nearest the Pole*. Now he wrote his great book, *The North Pole*.

The Congress of the United States, by special act, publicly thanked the explorer for the honor he had brought to the United States. The United States naval authorities promoted him to the rank of rear admiral in the United States Navy. Geographical societies in the United States, England, France, Germany, Switzerland, Austria, Hungary, Scotland, Italy, and Belgium awarded him honors. Everywhere people in all lands hailed Robert E. Peary as the hero who had done what people had thought impossible.

Admiral Peary's wife and his daughter must have shared in his triumph with deep emotion. The one had aided him to obtain funds for the expeditions; had made several jour-neys to the extreme north; had spent an arctic winter at latitude 78° 42′ North; and had hoped and endured all things. The other, born in the arctic regions, farther north than any white child in the world had ever before been born, had been named Marie Ahnighito Peary and nicknamed "the snow baby."

After his return to the United States, the distinguished explorer continued to lecture and to write. He became greatly interested in the navigation of the air, for which he saw a great future. In particular, he recommended that the United States establish an airplane patrol of its coasts, as a means of national defense.

Tall, smiling, amiable and companionable, he naturally made many friends. And interested as he was in all worthy causes, he appeared before the public on many occasions. In the ten years of his life after his return from the North Pole he could enjoy the satisfaction of his great achievement. He died, in Washington, D. C., February 20, 1920, at the age of sixty-four.

XIII

JOHN JOSEPH PERSHING

GENERAL OF THE UNITED STATES ARMY

AN advertisement caught his eye as he turned the pages of the newspaper. He looked more intently and read:

"On July 15 there will be a competitive examination for the appointment of a cadet at the United States Military Academy at West Point. All honest, strong, God-fearing boys of this district may take part.

J. H. BURROUGHS."

An examination! He had always stood high in his classes; he had no fear of any examination; at once he made up his mind that he would enter the contest, and that he would win.

The youth took the examination and passed it over the heads of seventeen other students who were perhaps equally desirous of entering West Point. The newspaper was the Laclede *Lancet*. The young man was John Joseph Pershing, destined one day to command the armies of the United States. Thus a boy's chance reading of an advertisement in a newspaper affected the history of his own country and of the world.

As a pupil in the local schools in Missouri, John J. Pershing earned a creditable record. When he surpassed other candidates, all of whom had prepared well for the examination for admission to West Point, he did so because he had been even more faithful than they, and had laid a solid foundation in the essentials.

Having won the appointment to the Military Academy, he

JOHN JOSEPH PERSHING

had every wish to succeed there. In order to prepare himself thoroughly for new work he went to Highland Military Academy in New York, where he made more definite preparation for West Point. In July, 1882, fully prepared in every way, John J. Pershing, then at the age of twenty-one, entered West Point as a "plebe." The personal ability, thoroughness, patience, and determination that appeared later in Pershing the general, appeared at this time in Pershing the youth.

General Pershing had the fortune to lead the armies of the United States in a war that deeply concerned the fate of Alsace, from that very part of Europe from which his own ancestors had come. When the Pershing family lived there they spelled the name "Pfirsching." They were hard-working, plain-living, honorable people. Finally, in order to better his fortunes, one of them had gone to live in America. That person, Daniel Pershing, went to Indiana County, Pennsylvania, where he lived energetically and won respect. His grandson, John F. Pershing, moved with the current of western settlement to Tennessee and finally to Missouri.

John F. Pershing, who became the father of the future general, had much of the adventurous spirit, and enjoyed the hard work of helping in building up the country to which his grandfather had come. He was as energetic as he was original and able. Setting out as member of a railroad construction crew, he displayed unusual ability as leader, and in course of time accumulated a large amount of money. From being foreman of a section of the Hannibal and St. Joe Railroad he became proprietor of a general store, and then the well-paid representative of a city business. In his own community he became a leader and the head of various local enterprises. On the Chicago Board of Trade he made at least two fortunes. In other words, he was a man who stood out above his fellows in whatever walk of life he found himself.

John Joseph Pershing was one of nine children. He inherited his father's ability and his father's power of leadership. He grew into a tall, lithe, straight young man, with keen, dark eyes, and a set, determined face. In 1880, two years before he entered West Point, John Pershing had already won the degree of bachelor of arts at the Kirksville, Missouri, Normal School. For a short time he worked as a teacher. One may imagine that though he was young and inexperienced, he maintained discipline and led his students to do good work.

In 1886, after the usual four years' course, the cadet was graduated from West Point. His commission as second lieutenant in the United States Army was signed by President Grover Cleveland, and he was at once assigned to the Sixth Cavalry. In this way, with well-founded preparation, John J. Pershing entered on active work as a soldier.

Most people fail to see the greatness of the opportunities that lie around them. Thus other officers than Second Lieutenant Pershing had orders to fulfil, but he, at least, always carried out every assignment to the full.

In 1886, the year in which he had been given his commission, he was ordered, while in the Indian region, to convey a pack train quickly across a difficult country. The young officer, so recently graduated from West Point, did his work so well that General Miles himself complimented him on the fact that he had marched a troop of cavalry, with its accompanying pack train, one hundred and forty miles in forty-six hours, and had brought in every animal in excellent condition. Young and inexperienced as he was, he had paid strictest attention to every detail. He had more than met the requirements of his first important task. Nevertheless, Second Lieutenant Pershing must many times have thought his opportunities few, and the likelihood of promotion not great. For over six years he served as second lieutenant in various army posts, and for the most part lived without great event.

At that time the Apaches were on the war path in New Mexico and Arizona. To the hard campaign against these most warlike Indians the newly commissioned officer was sent. The work was arduous in the extreme, and full of the element of danger. The hot, rough desert regions were, for the most part, utterly uninhabited, and the Indians, fully familiar with the country, were alert to every opportunity. In such a school the future general of all the forces of the United States gained his first experiences in war.

Three years later, in 1889, on another occasion, the lieutenant met an event in a manner in which he showed tact as well as the spirit of a soldier. A body of Zuñi Indians, so a messenger said, was attacking a band of white men, little better than border bandits, it is true, but white men nevertheless who appealed for help. Second Lieutenant Pershing, with a body of soldiers, hurried to the rescue. Where others in his position might have relied upon theatrical attack and thus have led to a bloody encounter, he made his way to the place where the frontiersmen stood at bay. There he parleyed with the Indian leaders to such good effect that without firing a single shot, and without offense to the Indians, he rescued all the white men. For this remarkable feat that prophesied well for his future, he was "highly recommended for discretion."

In 1890 the newly fledged Indian fighter took part in campaigns against the Sioux in Dakota. There he served again against savages who prided themselves on courage and skill in fighting. Instead of the hot deserts of New Mexico and Arizona he now had the dreary reaches of Dakota and the intense cold of the northern winter. In a certain sense he himself became a kind of Indian warrior, for until August, 1891, he commanded a body of Indian scouts.

Lieutenant Pershing, during the campaigns against the Sioux, was present as a subordinate officer at what is known as the Wounded Knee Creek Massacre. At that time the United States forces, firing upon a body of Indians largely composed of squaws and children, killed a great number of perfectly innocent people. Those familiar with the circumstances at once condemned an act that reflected no credit upon the United States. For that massacre, Lieutenant Pershing, although he was present, was in no way culpable, nor was it within his province to make reflections upon the acts of his superior officers.

In his years of Indian fighting in the Southwest and the Northwest, Lieutenant Pershing saw hard, active, dangerous service. In those years, also, he saw much that he must have thought abhorrent. Whatever may be said concerning other officers, Lieutenant Pershing did not lose the respect of the Indians whom he fought, nor of those with whom he associated. As a leader of Sioux scouts, as well as of Apaches, Lieutenant Pershing held the loyalty and devotion of savage warriors.

In 1886 he had aided in capturing a number of the bravest warriors of that most able Indian leader, Geronimo, the Apache, who had long defied the power of the United States. In 1916, thirty years later, General Pershing relied upon fourteen of those very Apaches, who certainly remembered how he had helped to capture them and to defeat their great leader, to serve under him as scouts in the pursuit of the Mexican bandit, Francisco Villa.

Later, on October 20, 1892, Second Lieutenant Pershing became First Lieutenant Pershing, assigned to the famous Tenth Cavalry. In this position he served six years.

After five years of exciting life in campaigning against warring Indians, Lieutenant Pershing enjoyed several years of scholastic peace. From 1891 to 1895 he served as military instructor in the University of Nebraska. While there he took advantage of the opportunity to study in the law school, and in 1893 was given the degree of LL.B. From 1897 to 1898 he taught military tactics in the United States Military Academy at West Point, having been assigned to that work because of his ability and excellent record.

From the quiet of scholastic life he was called to arms by the declaration of war against Spain.

In the war with Spain, in which every officer found opportunity to show the material of which he was made, Lieutenant Pershing did so well that on August 18, 1898, he became major and chief ordnance officer of volunteers. He was present at San Juan and at Santiago de Cuba, and displayed on both occasions the characteristics of a true soldier. He showed himself able to master both men and events; to pay careful attention to detail in a time of such confusion that some were likely to lose control entirely; able to work without rest; and also able to meet the enemy's fire without flinching. In fact, Major Pershing showed himself in so many ways a superior soldier that he twice won recommendation "For personal gallantry, untiring energy, and faithfulness."

At various times and in various ways during his early work as a soldier, John J. Pershing showed that he had abilities that forced higher officials to notice him, and that gave promise of achievement in the future, should he find his opportunity.

At the conclusion of the war with Spain, Major Pershing, on May 12, 1899, took honorable leave from the volunteer service. But, about three weeks later, June 6, 1899, he became Assistant Adjutant General. In the work of that office he served as efficiently as on the field of battle.

As one of the most important results of the war with Spain, the Philippine Islands came into the possession of the United States. For centuries those unhappy places had been in unrest. Many of the islands, inhabited by savages who had little respect for white authority, were in a state of constant warfare.

When the United States had to send able officers and sufficient forces to bring the islands to a condition of peace, the authorities sent the experienced soldier, Pershing, among others, as Assistant Adjutant General of the Department of Mindanao, in which capacity he served until June 30, 1901, when he again retired honorably from the volunteer service. He then became Captain of the 1st United States Cavalry. In August, 1901, he was transferred to the 15th Cavalry.

The Moros of central Mindanao being especially active in fighting the United States, Captain Pershing, from October, 1902, until June, 1903, took command of military operations against them, finding them an enemy even more dangerous than the Indians of the United States. Of his service in time of battle General Baldwin, a veteran of the Civil War, said, "Captain Pershing is the coolest man under fire I ever saw in my life."

In his work in the Philippines, Captain Pershing gave him-self heart and soul to what he did. He learned the difficult Moro language, and thus was able to talk with the natives and to learn much of value concerning their ways of thought, their wishes and their needs. From the earnestness of his work, Captain Pershing seemed to expect to spend the rest of his life in the Philippine Islands.

From 1903 to 1906 Captain Pershing served on the General Staff, where his ability and experience proved of great value. In 1905 he again saw new lands, new people, and new methods of war. He went to Japan as military attaché at Tokyo. At that time, Japan having engaged in a great struggle with Russia, Captain Pershing accompanied General Kuroki in military operations in Manchuria, seeing six months of arduous campaigning on a scale greater than he had ever seen before. For almost two years he remained with the Japanese in Japan and in Manchuria.

In the Philippines the hard-working soldier had mastered the Moro language. In Japan he learned Japanese! Wherever he went he carried with him the habits of the student, not for the mere sake of learning, but as a means of increasing efficiency in his work as an officer.

President Roosevelt, with his admiration of strong personal characteristics, looked upon Captain Pershing with the utmost favor. In 1903, in a message to Congress, the President complimented Captain Pershing by name. In 1906, three years later, President Roosevelt most characteristically swept aside all precedent concerning seniority, and promoted Captain Pershing over the heads of eight hundred and sixty-two other officers to the rank of brigadier general. While such a startling promotion naturally awoke much hostile criticism and cries of "favoritism," no one ever criticized Captain Pershing either as a soldier or an officer. Every one recognized his faithfulness to duty, his ability as a commander, and his gallantry in action.

In December, 1906, General Pershing, going to further duties in the Philippine Islands, commanded the Department of Mindanao, and served as governor of Moro Province.

Long before this, in 1899, while in Cuba, he had organized the Bureau of Insular Affairs, and had been chief of that bureau. He had proved that he had executive and administrative ability of an unusually high type. In his new work ne displayed great skill in dealing with the natives, showing that he could be both tactful and forceful.

When it became necessary to put down the warlike Moros with a firm hand, Pershing commanded military operations against them. He determined to strike, and to strike hard. On June 12, 1913, in the battle of Bagsag, he utterly defeated the Moro power, and brought about peaceful conditions that had not existed in that part of the Philippine Islands for centuries.

From war in the tropics, General Pershing returned to the quiet life at the Presidio in California, as commander of the Eighth Brigade.

In 1915, conditions in Mexico were such that they threatened the peace of the United States. The retirement of the strong old Mexican President, Porfirio Diaz, in 1911, and his death in Paris in July, 1915, had plunged Mexico into a state of civil war.

Following orders to take command, in the event of military action, General Pershing went to El Paso. While he looked for a suitable place of residence to which to bring his wife and family he met the greatest sorrow of his life, an event sufficient to unnerve even the strongest. The building at the Presidio in which his family lived burned to the ground. His wife and three daughters were hemmed in by flames and burned to death. With the memory of that event wringing his heart, General Pershing was obliged at once to give all his attention to the difficult work of patroling the El Paso border, and, in a few months, to command United States troops sent into Mexico against Villa.

The pursuit of Villa, begun in March, 1916, was a strange and dramatic episode in the history of the United States Army. Francisco Villa, a bandit and revolutionary rather than the commander of well organized forces, had a thousand means of escape and concealment, so that to capture him was well nigh impossible. Rather to awe the disorderly forces of Mexico than to capture the bandit, the authorities at Washington determined upon ordering the spectacular invasion of a neighboring country.

Although General Pershing did not capture Villa, he led a great number of men across a desert land, made rapid marches, maintained a high degree of efficiency in every part of his force, and showed himself such a capable leader that he won favorable attention from the entire country. People saw that in General Pershing they had a leader who, like U. S. Grant, was silent, grim, determined, and efficient. On September 25, 1916, General Pershing was promoted to the rank of major general in the United States Army.

It was a time when the United States needed a man of experience and of power. On Sunday, June 28, 1914, at Sarajevo in Bosnia a fanatic had fired a shot that had plunged all Europe into war. Everywhere in the world conditions were disturbed, and it seemed certain that the United States would be drawn into the great struggle. While the men of the United States hoped for peace, at the same time they wished, if the United States must enter the war, to have a leader able to meet the new and unusual conditions of modern warfare.

In 1917, when Major General Frederick Funston died, General Pershing took command of all United States forces along the Mexican border. By the turn of events, in spite of the fact that he had shrunk from publicity, he had become the leading American military figure. In April, 1917, unable longer to keep from the whirlpool that drew into itself so many nations, the United States declared a state of war with Germany; and in December, with Austria-Hungary. In June of the same year the country sent its first troops to join in the conflict.

The nation prepared with such activity that it at once registered 11,000,000 men, and in 1918, at the time of the Armistice, had under arms in the United States, according to War Department reports, 1,634,499 soldiers; and in Europe, according to General Pershing's own report, 2,071,463.

Early in June, 1917, General Pershing, appointed to the command of the American Expeditionary Force, reached France. In October of that year he temporarily became a full general of the United States Army.

He must have known that the world looked upon him with unusual interest; and must have realized that the people of Europe were inclined to laugh at the suggestion that men of the United States, unused to military life, and after very slight training, could make good soldiers. He must have felt some perplexity in commanding more than two million men in a foreign land, under strange conditions, in the new horrors of the most gigantic struggle in which the world had ever engaged.

Whatever he felt, he remained silent, determined and grim, going about his work with a sure calmness that showed that he felt himself as able as any one else to meet the great emergencies.

General Pershing believed thoroughly in discipline, not a half-way discipline, nor a discipline for its own sake, but a discipline that paid attention to every detail in order to gain efficiency. Through discipline he expected his men to develop a spirit that would lift them above every personal consideration.

Like the "Little Corporal" of the Napoleonic legends, General Pershing appeared everywhere, up and down the lines, at the seacoast where new American forces were disembarking, at the training grounds, on the battle front, in the hospitals, in the quarters of the men, in the mud of the trenches, in the cooking tents, seeing everything, correcting every in-

fringement of the rigid discipline of military life, and everywhere leading officers and men alike to see that the United
States force must be like a huge machine that would work
with precision, exactly as directed.

The General himself set an example of the military type,
for he always looked and acted the soldier. In spite of mud
and rain and the hurry of his life, he kept his uniform clean,
his boots polished, and his whole appearance as if he were
just going upon parade. Likewise, he set an example of
courage.

"You can't go into that trench," said a French officer
when General Pershing turned to enter a just-captured German trench.

If the General did not go, he could not observe new conditions on which to base new orders. Into the trench he
went.

General Pershing also had the stubborn quality that one
expects in a great soldier.

"You will unite your soldiers with our armies, and they
will fight under our orders," so, in effect, said the British,
the French and the Belgians. "Your men need our discipline and the war-wisdom of Europe."

"The soldiers of the United States will fight as an independent American army, and under their own command,"
so, in effect, said General Pershing. "They can fight as
well as the men of Europe, and they have officers who are
just as good as yours."

He had his way. Instead of sending United States soldiers
to join Allied armies, he built up an American army that
showed the people of Europe what it could do.

At the time of the Armistice the French and the British,
who had at first distrusted the ability of the American soldier to hold front-line trenches, saw General Pershing's army
holding more line than the British, and almost as much as
the French.

Where, for centuries, Europe had seen license in war, General Pershing gave strict orders to keep the individual qual-

ity of the American soldier at a standard of which the American people would approve. For example, in December, 1917, he prohibited the use of alcoholic drinks, with the exception of light wine and beer. In all ways he maintained in his soldiers a standard of life new in European warfare.

With the vast forces at his command, with the machine-like discipline that he built up, with the spirit that he developed, General Pershing made himself one of the deciding factors of the war. He himself planned the American operations at the Marne, at St. Mihiel and at the Meuse-Argonne. As a result, at the time of the Armistice he had before him an open road to the Rhine.

After Belleau Wood, in which the American troops, under French high command, did great deeds, General Pétain wrote to General Pershing:

"The last battles, where the magnificent qualities of courage and military virtue of your troops were demonstrated in so brilliant a manner, are a sure guarantee of the future. The day is not far off when the great American army will play the decisive rôle to which history calls this army on the battlefields of Europe."

Nevertheless, in spite of his insistence upon the building up of an American army, directed by American officers, General Pershing by no means withheld aid from the Allied forces, when they greatly needed it. In March, 1918, when the fortunes of the Allies were not at their brightest, he placed the entire American force then in France, at the service of Marshal Foch.

Seeing the desperate condition into which the Allies had fallen, at that time, the British general Haig had said: "With our backs to the walls, and believing in the justice of our cause, each one of must fight on to the end."

General Foch sent the American First Division to hold the German advance, to protect Amiens, and especially the railroads that supplied the British Army. The American First

Division did more than hold the Germans from breaking through the line; they captured Cantigny, a strongly fortified village situated on elevated ground. From a front a mile and a half long, General Pershing's soldiers, in two irregular lines, leaped from their trenches, moved forward for a mile, and captured the place. From the point of view of the World War as a whole, their capture of Cantigny was a local event, but the work of General Pershing's soldiers on that occasion threw a light upon the future; for it showed that he had trained men who could fight and who could win.

In June, 1918, the American marines, fighting at Belleau Wood, conducted themselves so brilliantly that the French general Degoutte commanded that the wood should be called, forever after, in all official papers, "The Wood of the Marine Brigade." In that struggle the Americans lost 7,870 men, but they commanded the attention of several German divisions.

In the great movement called the Aisne-Marne, General Pershing's men again fought under French high command, but this time they appeared in such numbers that they surpassed all previous records of American forces engaged in battle, for no less than 200,000 American soldiers took part in the great series of battles, losing 45,000 men, but utterly overcoming German resistance. General Pershing first had drilled his great forces; and then had tested their valor by placing them under General Foch and watching their conduct at Cantigny, Belleau Wood and the Aisne-Marne, and now, seeing that his men had won the respect of all Europe, he demanded that they be permitted to fight as an American army and under American high command.

On September 12, 1918, the day before his fifty-eighth birthday, having assumed full command of the First American Army, General Pershing attacked and took the St. Mihiel salient, defended by nine German divisions. In twenty-seven hours of desperate fighting he took a position that the Germans had held for four years. Thus, on his birthday, he rejoiced in having won the most profitable twenty-seven hours of the entire war, for he had liberated more than one hundred and fifty square miles of territory.

In his final report he said: "At the cost of only 7,000 casualties, mostly light, we have taken 16,000 prisoners, 443 guns, a great quantity of material, released the inhabitants of many villages from enemy domination, and established our lines in a position to threaten Metz."

In September, 1918, General Pershing ordered a great advance between the Meuse and the Argonne, employing 700,000 men. When the British and the French learned exactly what he intended, they said, in effect: "The German lines are so strong, and the region is so utterly destroyed, that your attack cannot succeed. Save your strength for some other attempt."

General Pershing, his grim face set more grimly than ever, ordered the advance. He knew the machine that he had built up by his iron discipline, and the spirit that he had developed. From September 26 until November 1 he continued advancing and fighting, advancing twenty miles and using up forty-seven German divisions. He lost 117,000 men but he captured 26,000 prisoners, 847 cannon, and 3,000 machine guns, and led immediately to the Armistice on November 11, on which day the Americans were still advancing, and had just fought into the possession of Sedan. In his report of his conduct of all these great operations on a scale colossal as compared with all previous American military movements, General Pershing used less than one hundred pages. Like Grant, he was a man of few words.

Upon his return to the United States, after the withdrawal of his great armies, he remained as he had been before, silent, unobtrusive, and self-possessed, seeking no favors because of what he had done.

In 1919 he received permanent rank as general, an office held before by only four persons: George Washington, Ulysses S. Grant, William T. Sherman, and Philip Sheridan. In

1921, General Pershing became Chief of Staff, and continued until his retirement to use his great ability in the service of the United States.

The chance reader of an advertisement had made himself one of the world's greatest soldiers.

XIV

THEODORE WILLIAM RICHARDS

CHEMIST

HIDDEN away in a laboratory at Harvard University, a man of medium height bends over a complicated series of glass tubes. He looks intently at what is going on within those gleaming tubes, bent into such a maze of curious forms. He does not notice that you approach. At first he does not hear you speak. He is interested solely in his apparatus. He bends over it fascinated. That man is Theodore William Richards, professor of chemistry in Harvard University; in 1914, by vote of the Swedish Academy of Sciences, winner of the Nobel Prize in chemistry.

In all probability, aside from students of science, few general readers know the name of Professor Richards. The world often concerns itself with sensational figures of the moment, and for a time at least, neglects people of real importance. It lets an Æsop whose fables may inspire the centuries live as a slave; a John Bunyan whose allegory may give spiritual comfort to many generations write unnoticed in a jail and die without public honor; it tears an Antoine Lavoisier from his laboratory and sends him to the guillotine; it permits a William T. G. Morton to save humanity from pain and an Edward Jenner to save it from disease without giving great reward.

Too often, in daily newspapers, the general reader gives attention to shadowy figures of a day, to people whose lives are for the moment and not for the years. The person who reads nothing but the daily paper is likely to know more about athletes and politicians and those who by sensational acts astonish or outrage the public, than about men who strive to benefit mankind or to add to the sum of human knowledge.

''Who is he?'' such a person asks when he hears the name of Professor Richards. ''When was his name in the papers?''

The scientist, however, knows the name, and knows also that when the athletes and the politicians, the fleeting actors of sensational deeds have long been totally forgotten, new investigators will still build upon the work that the man accomplished.

Professor Theodore W. Richards is an investigator in atomic chemistry, a man who has made the most painstaking studies of atomic weights. In the Wolcott-Gibbs Memorial Laboratory of Harvard University, a laboratory of which he is the head, he has conducted experiments that call for delicacy and patience far beyond the ordinary.

Professor Richards is director of one of the best equipped chemical laboratories in the world. With the aid of his assistants, drawn from many lands, he investigates all that concerns inorganic and physical chemistry.

In that laboratory, single problems alone often call for weeks, months and even years of effort, frequently without leading to the results desired. The work of investigation depends so largely upon the purity of substances employed, freedom from interference from outside influences and absolute accuracy in every part of the work, that the investigator pauses constantly to check and to re-check, and at every turn to question everything. Professor Richards, by necessity, is one of the most accurate men in the United States.

Perhaps the great chemist inherited that love of accuracy from his father, William Trost Richards, who was an artist, a distinguished marine painter, whose works appear in many galleries; or from his mother, who was an author. At any rate, both parents were persons of culture and accomplishment. Both, strangely enough, contrasted with Professor Richards' career, turned to the romantic side of life more

Photo from Wolcott Gibbs Memorial Laboratory, Cambridge, Mass.

THEODORE WILLIAM RICHARDS

than to the practical or the scientific. Both, however, one must note, keenly observed nature as well as people, and both made studies of what they saw, and, whether in painting or writing, both tried to make accurate reports. That the inheritance was good is proved both by the great work that Theodore Richards did in chemistry, and also by the work that his brother, Herbert Richards, did in botany, for both sons, instead of following romance, turned to science. The same strong inheritance shows itself in the work of Theodore Richards' sister, Anna Richards, who accomplished much in figure and landscape painting.

Theodore William Richards was born in Germantown, Pennsylvania, January 31, 1868. In 1914, when he won the Nobel Prize, he was forty-six. Long before he gained world-wide fame by winning a Nobel Prize, he had made himself one of the most distinguished of scientific investigators, and had won other awards of great importance.

When he was graduated from Haverford College in 1885, with the degree of bachelor of science, he was only seventeen years old. Even as a boy he had learned the art of study and had begun to cultivate habits of accuracy that later made him successful in his life work. In the first place he had lived in a home where he saw and read many books, and where every influence led him toward study. In the second place, being by nature interested in science, from the very first he gave most attention to scientific studies. Fortunately for him, while a student at Haverford he came under the instruction of men who had real love for their work, and who were therefore able to inspire him with the desire to pursue scientific studies still further.

After graduation from Haverford, therefore, Theodore Richards entered Harvard University, the institution with which he was to be connected for many years to come, and to which he was to bring honor both at home and abroad. As the private soldier entered the army of Napoleon, so Theodore Richards entered Harvard, carrying hidden in his knapsack a marshal's baton.

In the University, Theodore Richards continued to study in the same quiet and conscientious manner that had characterized him at Haverford. Within a year, by 1886, he won the degree of bachelor of arts, and within three years of advanced graduate study, the further degrees of master of arts, and doctor of philosophy. In all this work, naturally, he gave most earnest attention to chemistry, a subject in which he felt increasing fascination as the years went on.

From the very first this natural chemist displayed unusual interest and ability in laboratory work. He had the patience to spend many hours, if necessary, in preparation for experiments, and the ability to accomplish results beyond the average. Like Sherlock Holmes, he had powers of induction and deduction that enabled him to advance directly to results. From his first student days Theodore Richards found in chemistry the pleasure that others find in idle amusement. Because from his work he gained so much pleasure he devoted himself eagerly to it and advanced rapidly.

"Find that work," said a philosopher, "to which you can give your whole heart, even if you starve your body, and you will gain happiness."

Most of those who achieve great success in life, care far more for their work, whether painting pictures, carving statues, composing music, erecting beautiful buildings, writing works of literature, or exploring unvisited regions of the earth, than they do for any advantageous result other than the joy of working. He who works for pay, gets pay alone, and with it weariness and discontent; he who works for love, gains joy that money cannot buy.

Because Theodore Richards had shown himself especially interested in chemistry, and especially able, the department of chemistry at Harvard asked him to remain in the institution as a teacher. For two years, therefore, from 1889 to 1891, the young chemist worked as an assistant in chemistry at Harvard, aiding Professor Joseph P. Cook, one of the leading American chemists and an investigator of high rank. He was willing, even eager, to begin at the bottom of the ladder, because by so doing he had the freedom and the opportunity to carry his own studies still further, and to continue to experiment along his own lines.

But he did not slight his duties. Those in charge of his work noted with pleasure the way in which he performed his allotted share of the daily tasks, and prophesied for him an honorable future. But even they could not foresee what rank in chemistry the young scholar would attain.

In 1891 Theodore Richards became instructor in chemistry at Harvard, and continued in that position for three years, until 1894. In those years he served his apprenticeship, and developed the spirit of a master. He did his work so successfully that in 1894 he became assistant professor, a position in which he must have taken due pride.

Thus far, Professor Richards had followed the well-worn track that leads from elementary and high school through college and university to a professorship. As yet he had done little that was especially remarkable beyond the work of scores of other young men following much the same course. Others of his early associates stopped at various points in the upward march, or continued with him, toward professorships. In one way, however, he was making himself notable beyond most of the others, and that was by giving ever-increasing attention to accuracy.

The young chemist refused to jump at conclusions. He refused to accept statements unless he could see them proved by experiment or by demonstration. He questioned and tested at every turn. Because he led others to do that also, he became a most valuable aid in encouraging laboratory work of a high character. That regard for accuracy which from the very first made him somewhat different from his early associates, increased as time went on, becoming more and more the basis of all his work in research.

At the German Universities of Göttingen, Munich, Leipsic, and the Dresden Technical School, where he went to study further, he came into touch with great German scientists, from whom he learned new patience and new care. He found those leaders in chemistry men willing to devote infinite pains to solving chemical problems. He saw also that by their methods they had raised Germany to first rank as a land of scientific study and progress.

Professor Richards thoroughly learned the German methods. He adopted those methods, added to them the inventive skill and the originality characteristic of Americans, and then aided materially, in his later work, in raising the standard of American scientific study. So well, in fact, did he succeed that in 1907 he went to Germany as a most welcome visiting professor and there taught in the University of Berlin. Before that time, however, in 1902, he had become research associate in the Carnegie Institute at Washington. That work he has carried on ever since, in connection with his principal work as director of the laboratory at Harvard. In 1908 he gave the Lowell Lectures in Boston, thus associating himself with a long line of distinguished men who gave lectures on the most important topics relating to human progress.

The Prussian Government gave Professor Richards the signal honor of inviting him to become full professor of inorganic chemistry in the University of Göttingen, an important university founded in 1734, suggesting that he do no other work than carry on original research, and direct the most advanced students. Germany, ever jealous of the reputation of her own scientists, never did greater honor to a citizen of the United States than then, in thus asking an American chemist to come to Germany and direct advanced students.

Since Harvard could not afford to let so valuable a man go, the authorities at once made Professor Richards full professor at Harvard, giving him the same unlimited opportunities to carry on research work that he would have had if he had gone to Germany to work and teach.

Two graduates of Harvard, Dr. Morris Loeb and his brother, James Loeb, gave twenty-five thousand dollars each toward building a specially equipped laboratory for Harvard University. Dr. Alexander Forbes and various others gave fifty thousand dollars more toward the proposed chemical laboratory. Thus in 1913 there came into being the celebrated Wolcott Gibbs Memorial Laboratory of Harvard, a laboratory so well constructed and so completely equipped for advanced chemical research that there are in the United States no others that equal it, and only two or three that offer equal opportunities in the entire world.

The celebrated Davy-Faraday Laboratory in London, England, named for two of the greatest of English scientists, Sir Humphrey Davy and Michael Faraday, and the Van't Hoff Laboratory in Utrecht, Holland, named for the great Dutch chemist, Jacobus van't Hoff, give as great opportunities for original work. So also does the Hofmann Haus in Berlin, the home of the Berlin Chemical Society, named for August von Hofmann, a German chemist, and the founder of the *Deutsche Chemische Gesellschaft* (German Chemical Society). Except for those great laboratories, Professor Richards has at his command a place for investigation wholly unsurpassed.

The Wolcott Gibbs Memorial Laboratory, of which Professor Richards has charge, was named after Wolcott Gibbs, Rumford Professor of Chemistry at Harvard from 1863 to 1887, a great analytical and inorganic chemist, a most inspiring teacher, an investigator who kept up his work and his enthusiasm to old age, and a writer of influential books on chemistry. This great laboratory is devoted entirely to research work, being not at all an ordinary college laboratory for the instruction of undergraduates, but one only for the use of scholars. Those who work there are all trained investigators, seeking not to learn what some one else has found out but to discover entirely new truths in chemistry. There are few such places in the world, and certainly no others in the United States.

Professor Richards directs and guides research in the Wolcott Gibbs Memorial Laboratory. He works as slowly as he pleases, or as long as he pleases over a single problem. Sometimes he spends months merely in preparation for work

He may repeat experiments a thousand times, testing every point. He works under no other instructions than the one most glorious instruction: "Find the truth." In a certain sense, he has achieved the Nirvana of the scholar.

In that laboratory for the discovering of truth about matter, all differences of race and nationality drop away, and the leader and his workers become merely human beings striving to solve the puzzles of nature. At one time, there worked together under Professor Richards' direction, four Canadians, an Icelander, a Dane, a Japanese, several Germans, and various Americans of varying origins, twenty-four workers in all, and every one of them actively employed in aiding in original research of the most advanced type.

In his work with others, Professor Richards shows himself a great laboratory leader. He is kindly, sympathetic and inspiring, willing to go to great lengths to help others. He is somewhat reticent himself except when he talks upon chemical subjects. Then his eyes take on new light. He wastes no words, but speaks directly to the point. Though comparatively slight in figure, he is capable of carrying on most exhausting work, due, no doubt, to his never-ceasing enthusiasm.

The research in which Professor Richards has been principally interested concerns the fundamental properties of chemical elements. In others words, in his research he goes to the very soul of matter. He deals in particular with the atom. He re-determined the atomic weights of the various elements, and studied the relation of those weights one to another. He experiments with the densities, the compressibilities and the behavior of atoms. He aims, in fact, to find some answer to the greatest questions that chemists have raised: "How are the elements related? How and why do they differ? What does this mean for chemistry?"

In his experimental work this investigator aims not to find new ways of using power, or to make new and useful products, but simply to find hitherto unknown facts. Men who come after him may make use of the truth that he discovers. That is their task; his is to lead the way.

In an address that Professor Richards gave concerning the work of the Wolcott Gibbs Memorial Laboratory, he said that he aimed in his work to "deal with mysteries of nature which are among the most fundamental of all those presented to the physical chemist, for the nature of the chemical elements underlies all the mechanism upon which life depends."

The savage had around him all the potentialities that could turn his flaming camp fire into a producer of steam and electric power, the round log on which he sat into the thousand wheels of a factory, the wood and mineral about him into a flying machine capable of carrying him over the maze of his forests and lakes. In those potentialities he saw nothing. He understood too little about nature. Endless ages had to pass, while people lived little better than animal lives. Then thousands of years had to pass while men slowly studied the secrets of matter. They saw a log float and sat upon it; they hollowed it, and sat in it. They used weapons of wood; then of stone; then of soft copper; then of bronze; then of steel. With infinite slowness men learned facts about nature. Gradually they learned to use their knowledge.

Today, in the minute region of the atom, scientists may be unveiling the power of the future. Whether people realize it or not, the behavior of chemical elements, the nature of atoms, that seem so remote from ordinary interests, are all-important. Just as there was always the possibility of electric power that men were slow to find, so there may be the possibility of tremendous atomic power, that men some day will find. Such work as Professor Richards carries on will do much to lead the way to the future.

In the distant past, men made scientific discoveries largely because of accident. When men did make discoveries they found it difficult to make known what they had learned, because they had insufficient means of spreading information. Every man who investigated at all lived to himself like a hermit in a cave, while all around him were ignorant or fanatical people all too ready to persecute him for a wizard.

Today, men like Professor Richards devote their lives to attempting to discover new scientific truth. When they succeed they speak in a universal language, for at once they send the results of their work to every civilized land in the world. Today, great scholars, instead of working separately, work together. In science, as in mathematics, there are no differences between races, few barriers of language, and no hostility of creeds. Since two and two make four in every possible language, no radical nationalist ever insists that in his country two and two make three, or five. Scientists meet on a common basis, eagerly uniting in the search for new facts of existence.

Professor Richards, in his work, makes use of people of any nationality, so long as they have the ability to aid him. The results of his work he makes known to scientists in every part of the world, just as they make known their results to him, and to others of their fellow scientists. Perhaps, in all history, there was never a nobler fellowship than this fellowship of men bound to search, like the knights of Arthur, not for a mysterious Holy Grail, but for truth, ever elusive, always beautiful, and always awe-inspiring.

Aided by his corps of competent assistants, Professor Richards studied the atomic weights of various elements. Many he found were not known accurately, and these he corrected, a work of absolute importance to the accurate study of chemistry in any of its aspects. For, without a knowledge of the exact atomic weights of oxygen and hydrogen, one cannot even know just how much of each there is in water. He entirely revised the atomic weights of oxygen, copper, barium, strontium, calcium, zinc, magnesium, iron, nickel, cobalt, uranium, cæsium, sodium, chlorine, potassium, nitrogen, silver, sulphur, carbon, lithium, radioactive lead, gallium, and aluminum.

To revise the atomic weight of any one of the elements named above would have been a feat. To revise such a large number was a remarkably great accomplishment. Naturally, so exact and scholarly a task required long and patient work. In order to determine the atomic weights of the various elements Professor Richards had to procure ideally pure substances with which to work. Since the elements whose atomic weights he studied do not occur generally in nature in pure forms, the investigator had to devise methods to obtain pure substances with which to experiment. In other words, in order to carry on the very experiments that he thought most important, he had to make a long series of preliminary preparations that called for a use of time that those not accustomed to the patience of science might think too great. Sometimes, for example, Professor Richards worked for an entire year in an effort to find one substance absolutely pure. In order to do that he had to put aside the main work that he had in mind, and devote himself to other details. If he had lacked patience he would have lost the day.

In his work with weights Professor Richards had to use a balance that outside causes could not disturb. He had to regulate even the very temperature of the balance, lest the effect, even of slight and distant heat, such slight heat, for example, as the heat of the body of the person making the experiment, should change the results. He had to make special balances, place them in specially protected places, and check every possible source of interference.

While the ordinary person is content, of course, with approximate accuracy in weight, Professor Richards had to have absolute accuracy, humanly speaking, for absolute accuracy to be sure is figurative, absolute accuracy to the very minutest measure being practically impossible. Nevertheless, humanly speaking, he had to have absolute accuracy. He weighed to one one-hundredth of a milligram, or in ordinary terms, about one three-millionth of an ounce! It is difficult to conceive of accuracy like that! Such accuracy is so near to the perfect that it almost ceases to be human accuracy at all, and becomes something so unusual as to be worthy of the name "miraculous."

In order to carry on his work Professor Richards constructed much original apparatus, making much of it from glass, of which he is a remarkably expert blower.

For fifteen years he worked, checking and re-checking, guarding, devising, planning, working with astonishingly minute bodies and astonishingly minute forces. By the end of that time he had given to the world more information about atomic weights than had all the most learned scientists who had lived in the preceding hundred years!

Such a triumph of scholarship is one in which Americans may well take pride. Since the breaking of international records in athletics is heralded in every newspaper, here was the breaking of an international record that might well have been proclaimed in very large type headings. Science, however, does not seek to break records. Science is careless alike of records and of fame. The scientist has for his one purpose the discovery of truth.

Professor Richards carried on all his painstaking, delicate experiments in connection with atomic weights, not in the hope of doing better work than the preceding scientists had done, and thus of gaining credit for himself, but merely in the hope of finding the actual truth about atomic weights, and therefore about the elements.

By learning exactly what the weights are, how they are related to one another, and whether they remain the same under all possible conditions, he might find answers to some of the great questions about the nature of matter.

He asked a thousand questions whose answers he tried to find. Thus he investigated the effects of heat, chemical thermodynamics, or heat capacities, in their relation to energy, the thermodynamics of amalgams, surface tensions, and other physiochemical problems. The scientist, instead of having a simple problem, had one that continually expanded and led to new problems. In the atom, apparently, in a world far beyond the microscope, nature has hidden her inmost secrets, all the mysteries of physical and chemical force, perhaps all the mysteries of life and thought itself.

Professor Richards, with his delicate balances and his patient experiments, invaded the mysterious arcanum and questioned the inner nature of matter.

"What is an atom?" he asked. "How much space does it occupy? What is its relative position in space?"

Because the investigator was a genius, gifted with unusual skill in precision, he found the answers to some of the questions he asked, and gave those answers to the world.

Professor Richards is now the highest authority on atomic weights. Because of his new investigations, and the advance that they gave to chemical and physical studies throughout the world, he was awarded the Nobel Prize, as well as many other notable honors. Through the qualities of patience and of accuracy he made himself one of the world's great chemists.

Honors of various kinds came to the scholar in return for his long hours of investigation in the laboratory. The American Chemical Society, in 1914, made him its president, and the National Research Council, in 1916, was glad to include him as a member. Honorary degrees came to him from Yale, Haverford, Pittsburgh, Clark, Harvard, Pennsylvania and Princeton, in the United States; from the Royal Bohemian University of Prague; and from the universities of Berlin, in Germany; of Oxford, Cambridge, and Manchester, in England, and of Christiania, in Sweden.

In 1910 Professor Richards became the Davy medalist of the Royal Society of London; in 1912 the William Gibbs medalist of the American Chemical Society; in 1914 the winner of the Nobel Prize in chemistry; in 1916 the Franklin medalist of the Franklin Institute; in 1922 the Le Blanc medalist of Paris.

Nevertheless, if he himself were asked what was the greatest of all the rewards that he won, he would answer, "The pleasure of the work."

XV

THEODORE ROOSEVELT

PRESIDENT OF THE UNITED STATES

A MAN leaping a horse over a high fence; a Rough Rider leading a charge up a bullet-swept hill; an explorer lying fever-stricken in a canoe on a tropical river; a diplomat standing with the Kaiser as the troops march by; a vigorous public speaker leaning forward in his earnestness and shaking his fist at his audience; a student of history bending over the writing of books, these are the pictures that flash into mind when one hears the name Theodore Roosevelt.

Essentially a hard-working, hard-fighting, hard-hitting man, Theodore Roosevelt threw himself with his whole heart and with all his powers into every work or every cause that interested him. From the time of his birth in 1858 until his death in 1918, in his sixtieth year, he lived every minute to the full.

Because he lived so completely, so full-heartedly, so earnestly, he made himself great in every phase of his life. He succeeded in many different ways, in any one of which he might have made himself remembered. He succeeded so greatly in all ways that he established his fame, not alone as one of the most remarkable men of modern times, but as one of the most remarkable men of many centuries.

Throughout his life, merely as an individual and not as an officeholder, by means of his way of living, through personal contact, public addresses, contributions to periodicals, and the general influence of his strong personality, he did more than almost any other man of his times to mold public opinion.

At all times Theodore Roosevelt was a person whom people loved to watch, because he was always peculiarly individual and peculiarly interesting. He made more ''copy'' for periodical writers than did any other person of his generation.

As an important public official, the holder of many great offices, this high-minded citizen worked with such intense devotion to duty, and such supreme determination to carry out the full purposes of any office that he held, that he gave new power and new honor to that office. He held every public office, whatever it was, as a public trust, throwing himself into the work of serving the people with a zest that made him a power beyond the ordinary. If he moved from office to office, to the Presidency itself, he did so because he showed efficiency rather than because he sought power.

As a soldier this many-sided man did remarkable service for his country. While he made himself one of the most picturesque of military figures, he served with self-sacrificing energy and genuine heroism. He made his regiment of ''Rough Riders'' not only a regiment that held the attention of the country, but also a regiment that moved with dauntless spirit. He knew and loved his men as so many brothers and willingly braved the anger of superiors by insisting upon regard for his soldiers' health and the maintenance of their efficiency.

At first in the war with Spain, subordinating himself to another whom he looked upon as more experienced in military affairs, he ended by making himself a well-loved leader, typical of American dash and enterprise.

Always an interested observer, he traveled more widely than most men, making his way into the heart of Africa, and exploring unknown regions in South America. He adapted himself to circumstances, enjoyed to the utmost all that goes with life in the wilderness, took his full share of hardships, and at the same time carried with him numerous beloved books, and continued to work as an energetic writer.

He did not travel as a chance observer, but as a scientist, and he added materially to the world's knowledge of animal life and to its information concerning geography.

As a diplomatist this student of history and world affairs influenced the civilized world. He molded opinion in Europe, affected the affairs of the British Empire in Egypt, gave suggestions at the Guildhall in London for the management of the British Empire, advised with the Kaiser of Germany, and by a bold stroke made it possible for the United States to construct the Panama Canal. By that work, which he looked upon as the greatest of his life, he materially changed the trade paths of the world, entirely altered conditions in South America, and gave the United States increased power. He exerted so great an influence toward international peace that in 1906 he won the Nobel Peace Prize.

As an author, this lover of books wrote a shelf full of important works, some of them histories of standard value; others books of intimate biography; still others books of natural history, travel experiences, and literary comment; essays in political economy and broad-minded comment on public affairs; delightful personal essays, and books of collected addresses. He did not make his books noteworthy by substance alone but by his style as well, for he wrote as he lived, with energy and power. Having great natural phrase-making power, he coined new expressions, not fleeting phrases, but vital combinations that have remained in use.

As President of the United States, Theodore Roosevelt made himself the most notable of all peace-time Presidents. While in office he affected every current of American public life; showed himself broad-minded, liberal, and tolerant; defied conventions; insisted upon honesty, manhood and public service, regardless of race or creed; and led the great body of American people as no other President ever did. Theodore Roosevelt, without doubt, was the most thoroughly all-around man who ever wielded great public influence in the United States, a man whom one might try to copy in a hundred different ways but whom no one might hope to imitate in all. He was unique, a forceful, and potent personality, a stimulus toward all that is best in American life.

Since concerning such a man anecdote must be common, hundreds of stories tell of Theodore Roosevelt's exploits in various fields of activity, showing him as the active and familiar companion of thousands of men who represented various types of social life, pugilist as well as scholar. Every man whom he met told anecdotes about him, and every anecdote redounded to the credit of the virile, energetic leader. Cartoonists took Theodore Roosevelt as their particular subject, picturing him as energetic, tireless, forceful, and commanding, even when they ridiculed him. While like all great and powerful men who are doers rather than observers and commenters, he had enemies, one might gather together all that those enemies said against him without finding any grave and deep-seated fault in the man.

Theodore Roosevelt, like all men, had faults, but he had them as the results of the virtues that made him great, rather than as the results of selfish or antagonistic tendencies. He was called impetuous, but because of his impetuosity he accomplished what he undertook. He loved a fight and held his end up well. He used what is often called undignified invective, but he maintained principles that met every one's approval. He cared little for convention and precedent, but thereby he promoted manliness, efficiency, and tolerance. He was unwise in venturing into the big game regions of central Africa, and the jungles of unexplored tropical regions of South America, but by that lack of wisdom he gained some of the keenest pleasure in his life. He may even have played a somewhat Machiavellian part in leading to the secession of Panama from Colombia and the subsequent treaty between the United States and the newly-formed republic with regard to the Canal Zone, but by so doing he led to the construction of the Panama Canal, to the entire change of health conditions in Panama, and to the vast benefit of the world.

On the whole, Theodore Roosevelt made of himself, in the

opinion of thousands of his fellow countrymen, an ideal American. Always intensely patriotic, he believed sincerely in the United States, and in the principles on which the United States was founded. He had the typical American dash; the characteristic carelessness concerning routine, ceremony and convention; and the inherited democratic spirit that leads Americans to look at manhood rather than name, social rank or wealth. He was himself a college graduate and scholar, but he associated intimately with men who were not scholars. Born to wealth and a long-honored family name, he had no pride in any artificial standards.

The first of Theodore Roosevelt's ancestors to live in America came from Holland in 1649. Like so many other substantial Dutch settlers, the Roosevelts prospered in the new world. They accumulated money and gained influence. In 1700, and in three succeeding generations, ancestors of Theodore Roosevelt were New York aldermen. Others were Members of Congress, State Assemblymen, State Senators, and one was a Justice of the Supreme Court of New York. Still others of the family were leading merchants and public benefactors, as the Roosevelt Hospital indicates. Hard-working, thrifty, determined, characteristics that they gave to their descendant, they all aided in making the new country.

Theodore Roosevelt's father, for whom the future President was named, Theodore R. Roosevelt, was born in 1831. As a glass importer he made a fortune. As a public-minded citizen he led to the formation of the Union League Club. As one who wished to help the unfortunate he founded the Orthopedic Hospital. This active man of affairs sent his son to Harvard, enabled him to enjoy experiences upon a ranch in the West, and gave him the means to enter more fully into life than he could otherwise have done.

Theodore Roosevelt who was to be the twenty-sixth President of the United States, was born in the four-story house at 28 East 20th Street, in New York City, October 27, 1858.

His mother, Martha Bullock Roosevelt, was a member

Photo by Clinedinst.

THEODORE ROOSEVELT

of a prominent Georgia family, her grandfather, in 1776, having been the first governor of Georgia. She was descended from sturdy Scotch-Irish, French Huguenot, and Palatine German ancestors. Thus from both the father's and the mother's side Theodore Roosevelt came from old, influential American stock. He had a more notable inheritance than almost any other man who became President.

From the first, Theodore Roosevelt was manly and active, but as a boy he was far from strong. Naturally bright, he learned to read while still in skirts. He studied in Professor McMullin's Academy, not far from Madison Square, and also, because of his poor health, with governesses and tutors at home. When he was nine years old his parents took him to Europe, where he visited Rome and Paris, and saw, without much permanent gain, such other places as Naples, Mt. Vesuvius, and the highlands of Scotland. At thirteen he again accompanied his parents on a foreign tour, this time visiting Egypt and going up the Nile to Luxor. Although only a boy he had such strong scientific tastes that he made a really valuable collection of birds of the Nile region, a collection now in the Smithsonian Institute in Washington, D. C., certainly a remarkable collection for a boy to make. On the same journey he traveled much on the Continent, and spent a winter in Dresden.

Having prepared for college in Cutler's Private School, New York City, he entered Harvard in 1876, his heart set on continuing his work with birds, and becoming a naturalist. Throughout his boyhood he had spent much time at his father's country home at Oyster Bay, Long Island, where he rode horseback, swam, and walked, and led a most vigorous life. At Harvard, therefore, he threw himself into college life, entering into all college activities, becoming champion lightweight boxer of the university, and an editor of the *Harvard Advocate*. In his studies he gave most attention to philosophy, history, and political science. So great was the young student's interest in history that he began to write, while still a college student, his now famous book, *Naval Operations of the War between Great Britain and the United States, 1812-1815.*

After his graduation in 1880, with the degree of bachelor of arts, he went again to Europe, where he went on a walking trip in Germany, and climbed mountains in Switzerland, observing political conditions everywhere he went.

On his twenty-second birthday, October 27, 1880, the year of his graduation, he had married Alice Hathaway Lee, daughter of George Cabot Lee. It was while on his wedding trip that he climbed the Matterhorn, for which feat, as well as for climbing the Jungfrau, he became a member of the London Alpine Club.

Once again in the United States he studied law in the Columbia Law School, as well as in the office of his uncle, Robert B. Roosevelt. Without completing his legal studies, he plunged at once into a political career. He had high hopes, high ideals, and a determination to do something useful in life.

Two years after his graduation from Harvard, when he was only twenty-four years old, he won an election to the New York State Assembly; later he won two succeeding elections, and became at once so prominent a leader that he was candidate for the position of speaker.

In 1884, at the conclusion of his term in the Legislature, he became delegate to the Republican National Convention. Young as he was, he made a powerful speech at the convention, and impressed his party.

Bishop William T. Manning, in speaking of Theodore Roosevelt after his death, said, "His whole life was one of devotion to his country." It is indeed a fact that from the time of his graduation from Harvard until the day of his death, Theodore Roosevelt kept before him the ideal of doing service for the land in which he lived.

On February 14, 1884, less than four years after his wedding day, the rising leader grieved for the death of the bride of his boyhood. Disheartened by that and other sorrows, he left his political work for nearly two years and lived in the seclusion of a western ranch. Nearly three years later, in London, England, he married Edith Kermit Carow, daughter of Charles Carow, of New York. She was his faithful companion throughout the rest of his life.

It is difficult to think of the strong, athletic, horseback-riding, adventurous Theodore Roosevelt as ever anything else except strong and sturdy. Nevertheless, as a boy he had suffered much from asthma, and had been slight and far from strong. He met this condition as he met everything else in life, by fighting. He took regular exercises that he planned himself to meet his needs. He lived much in the open air, resolved to make himself as strong as any one else.

It was partly because of his sorrow, partly because of reasons of health, and partly because of his natural love of "roughing it," that he spent about two years, from 1884 to 1886, on a ranch that he bought near Medora on the Little Missouri River, in North Dakota. There, in a primitive, cowboy community, he dressed, lived, worked and acted like a cowboy. He rode hard-mouthed, riotous horses, took part in the rough life of the ranch, and defied all who moved against law and order. When Montana thieves took some of his property, Theodore Roosevelt, with two companions, sprang upon horseback and rode after them. For two days the pursuers followed the trail across desolate country. When one of Roosevelt's associates fell, broke his arm, and could not continue the pursuit, Roosevelt sent the remaining man back with the one who had broken his arm. Then he himself, alone, went on after the thieves. Although those were rough days, and that was a rough region, where men carried revolvers that they were quick to use, Roosevelt forgot all that, in his determination to catch and punish the thieves. He followed until he found their camp, crept upon them alone, surprised them, held them covered with his pistol, and brought them back as prisoners. He was "clear grit" through and through.

His associates on the ranch learned in a very short time

that the rich young man who had so recently come from an eastern college was no weakling, either in strength or spirit, but a man as ready to do and dare as they were. In his rough life on the ranch the new frontiersman did not forget scholarly interests. He observed in detail all the picturesqueness of cowboy life, made accurate notes, and from them and memory, later on, wrote various books about ranch life. In 1886, when he was twenty-seven, he published *Hunting Trips of a Ranchman;* in 1888, *Ranch Life and the Hunting Trail;* in 1893, *The Wilderness Hunter.*

From his experiences in the West, Theodore Roosevelt gained interest in the men of early days who had gone into the region as pioneers. He read all that he could find concerning the experiences of those adventurers. From such interests and such reading he wrote in 1886, *Thomas Hart Benton,* a biography, and a volume in the American Statesmen Series, and between 1889 and 1896 his remarkable work *The Winning of the West,* a history that stands today as 'he standard work, an authority on the subject.

Thus, within a few years after his graduation from Harvard, Theodore Roosevelt had put his impress upon political life, had had many romantic, dashing experiences in rough frontier events, and had made himself an author of high rank. In the glory of his later life people forget the wonder of his early achievements.

In 1886, at the age of twenty-eight, the student-rancher-author returned to New York City, where he became candidate for the office of mayor. He did not win the election, but he made a strenuous campaign, and won a greater percent of votes than any other Republican candidate for Mayor of New York had received up to that time. More than that, he announced that he stood for honesty in public service, and made himself a noted public figure.

From 1889 until 1895 he served actively as a United States Civil Service Commissioner, working with all his customary energy for the purifying of public life, and doing more than almost any one else had done for the promotion of Civil Service examinations as a basis for Government service.

During these years he closely observed men in public life, and continued to study American history. In 1882, in his history of the War of 1812, he had proved his ability to find and use historical material and judgment, and had shown power of expression not at all common in young men of twenty-four. In 1887 he published *Gouverneur Morris,* another volume in the American Statesmen Series. In 1891 he brought out another history, *New York City;* in 1897, *American Ideals and other essays.*

This man of many parts went before the American people as a remarkable figure in public life, at once a man of action and a scholar; a politician and a profound student of history; a practical executive and an idealistic author. He interested people profoundly and held their attention.

From 1895 until 1897 this well-balanced idealist served as president of the Police Board of the City of New York, such a police commissioner as the city had never had before. He went everywhere, and saw everything, at all hours of the day and night. He made every delinquent police officer in the city fear the appearance of his characteristic eye-glasses and gleaming teeth. In the two years of his work he brought about such notable reforms in the police department of the city of New York, showed such courage in performing his duty, and worked so tirelessly, that he made himself the best known New York City official, as well as a prominent national figure.

In 1897, at the invitation of President McKinley, he became Assistant Secretary of the Navy, and did strenuous work in building up the United States naval power. In 1898, when war was declared against Spain, he resigned his honorable position. A fighter in every fiber of his being, an intense patriot, and proud of the history of his country, he could not remain safe at an official desk while others fought.

Now he remembered the rough, hard-riding men with whom he had worked and fought in his ranch days in the

Dakotas. He knew they were men of iron, "men with their boots on," who would fight to the last breath. With Surgeon Leonard Wood, a man who, though a surgeon, had fought with Indians, he organized the First Cavalry, a regiment popularly called "Roosevelt's Rough Riders." The men of the regiment he himself chose, not alone from ranchmen but from all ranks of hard-riding, hard-hitting men with fighting spirit. He formed a regiment more picturesque than the "Red Devils" of the Civil War, an organization that made the greatest impression upon the public mind. Believing that he himself lacked the military training requisite to command the regiment, the patriot organizer assumed the position of lieutenant-colonel under his experienced friend, Leonard Wood, as colonel. In the heat of Cuba the regiment took part in sharp fights, fully living up to its name as a fighting regiment.

For his gallantry at the battle of Las Guasimas, and on the promotion of Colonel Wood to brigadier general, Lieutenant Colonel Roosevelt was promoted to the rank of colonel of the regiment. As commander of the regiment Colonel Roosevelt led his men in the charge up San Juan Hill.

Accounts of this, and pictures of Roosevelt and his men, filled the papers of the United States, making him at once a great national hero. Backed by his remarkable record in official life, by his upholding of high civic ideals, and now by his voluntary and most courageous service in battle, Theodore Roosevelt commanded a following such as few Americans ever had. From thousands of people came the demand that he be given high public office.

In 1898, when the citizen-soldier was mustered out of military service, he was triumphantly elected governor of the State of New York. In the two years in which he held the office he carried on independent, active, aggressive work in support of causes that he believed good and important. He went hither and yon in the state, personally inspecting and observing everything, making numerous speeches, meeting thousands of people, and coming closer to the heart of the common people than had any previous governor of the state.

Political leaders, annoyed by Governor Roosevelt's constant insistence on political honesty, took advantage of the demand that he be nominated for the Presidency. Thinking that they could avert his political progress, and at the same time remove him from the State of New York, they brought about his nomination for the Vice-Presidency.

To the surprise of many, Governor Roosevelt accepted the nomination, and apparently put aside his opportunities in order to gain the higher office. In 1901, six months after he had asumed office as Vice-President of the United States, the assassination of President McKinley made him President.

Shocked and grieved as the people of the nation were, they saw in Theodore Roosevelt a man for the times. They admired the habitual boldness with which he acted. While sometimes they feared his impetuosity, they always found him a man of caution. They admired his powers as a statesman and rejoiced in his frank manhood as an individual. The man of destiny awoke such enthusiasm that in 1904 he was nominated for the Presidency, and was swept into office by the largest popular majority ever given to a candidate up to that time.

In his Presidency, the White House became more than ever a center of interest. Everything that the President did was unusual, or individual, or picturesque, and yet everything that he did was in strict accord with American traditions, the interests of good government, and the carrying out of established laws.

While holding the office of President, Theodore Roosevelt did not forget his interests as a man. He took part in long rides that fatigued even experienced cavalry officers; he leaped his horse over high fences; he entertained all sorts and conditions of men, without regard to prejudice or custom; he boxed with friends, and even with pugilists, losing the sight of one eye in a friendly bout, without complaint and even without making his loss known to the public; he romped with his children; hurrahed at the sight of old ranch or army comrades; and went once more on rough hunting expeditions.

At the same time, while his ebullient spirits led him to

the roughest sport, he continued to read and to study, to
carry on all the varied activities of his strenuous life, and
to perform his work as President in a way that made him
a power in the world.

When he was governor of New York he had published his
book, *The Rough Riders.* Then, even while occupied with
the exhausting duties of the Presidency he published various
books: *Oliver Cromwell,* the life of a man whose spirit he
admired; *The Strenuous Life,* in which he set forward his
belief in living intensely; and *The Deer Family,* a book that
won high praise as a valuable contribution to natural history.

John Burroughs, the nature lover, said of Theodore Roosevelt: "He was a naturalist on the broadest grounds."

While President, Theodore Roosevelt also published *Outdoor Pastimes of an American Hunter, American Ideals,* and
Good Hunting, and found time to bring out an eight volume
collection of his works. That is a remarkable output for one
who took part in so many activities, and who had to meet the
many demands made upon him as President of the United
States.

During his administration, President Roosevelt took the
bold step of recognizing the newly formed Republic of
Panama, and thus of leading to the immediate construction
of the Panama Canal. He spoke so emphatically in favor
of international peace, and did so much to bring about peace
between Russia and Japan, that in 1910, he was awarded the
Nobel Peace Prize. He continued to uphold honesty in public office, established the Department of Commerce and Labor,
affected the relations of government and great industries, led
to the idea of conservation of resources, urged national defense, and prompted Civil Service reform.

At the conclusion of what was practically his second term
as President, many wished Mr. Roosevelt to serve again, but
in deference to American traditions he declined to accept
the nomination.

Relieved from the trammels of public office, Colonel Roosevelt fulfilled a desire that he had long had, and at once

plunged into the heart of equatorial Africa on a hunting trip for big game. The story of his African adventures he told in *African Game Trails*. On his return from Africa the ex-President visited Egypt and Europe. Everywhere he was received like a king, and made addresses that changed the current of history. When he returned to America he met in New York a popular reception that equaled those given to Roman leaders returning in triumph from great wars. He found himself more than ever the idol of the people.

For a short time he devoted himself to writing, producing besides his *African Game Trails, True Americanism, African and European Addresses, The New Nationalism, Realizable Ideals, The Conservation of Womanhood and Childhood, History as Literature and Other Essays*, and *Theodore Roosevelt, an Autobiography*. When he had retired to private life he had accepted an invitation to become contributing editor of the *Outlook*, and from 1909 to 1914 he wrote regularly for that publication.

In 1910 he went to London as Special Ambassador of the United States to attend the funeral of King Edward VII.

In 1912 he accepted the nomination of the Progressive Party for the Presidency and won 4,000,000 votes, Woodrow Wilson, with 6,000,000 votes being elected; the Republican nominee, President William H. Taft, receiving fewer votes than did Colonel Roosevelt.

In 1913 Roosevelt traveled in South America, where he gave numerous addresses, and where his desire to take further part in exploration was stimulated.

In 1914 Colonel Roosevelt led an exploring party into untraveled jungles of Brazil, traced a river, afterward called *Rio Teodoro*, for six hundred miles, studied and investigated every condition in the jungle, and, with the exception of the time when he lay sick with fever in the bottom of a canoe, continued to write industriously. On this expedition he endured such hardships that he undoubtedly shortened his life.

As a result of this most strenuous journey of his life he

wrote *Through the Brazilian Wilderness.* In the same year, 1914, he brought out, in two volumes, his notable work, *Life Histories of African Game Animals.*

The year of the beginning of the World War found Colonel Roosevelt in Spain and England.

In the retirement of private life he longed for power to carry out his beliefs. With pen and voice he set forward principles that he thought all-important. When the United States declared war he immediately offered to raise an entire army division and to go to the front with it, an offer that President Wilson declined. Unable to go himself, he sent his four sons.

His son Kermit served with motor machine guns in Mesopotamia, and later with the 7th Field Artillery of the United States Army, winning the British Military Cross, and the Montenegrin Cross. His son Theodore served in the 1st Division of the American Expeditionary Force, took part in various battles, received honorable wounds, and was given the Distinguished Service Cross of the United States, and the Legion of Honor and *Croix de Guerre* of France. His son Quentin met death in battle as an aviator of the 400th Aero Squadron, A. E. F., and his son Archie became a captain and likewise served most gallantly in France, suffering wounds in battle.

At all times during his life, Theodore Roosevelt coined and freely used many vigorous expressions which have become idiomatic phrases, such as "the square deal," "the big stick," "weasel words," "pussyfooter," "the Ananias club," "public malefactors of great wealth," "hyphenated Americans," "race suicide," and "fifty-fifty loyalty." Because of his freedom in using such expressions and his activity in defending his reputation or his assertions, many thought him too pugnacious.

In his last years this most remarkable of men wrote *A Booklover's Holidays in the Open, Fear God and Take Your Own Part, Foes of Our Own Household, National Strength and International Duty,* and numerous articles for periodicals.

In his home at Oyster Bay, Long Island, he remained to the last a picturesque figure, riding horseback daily, taking part in local affairs and maintaining a delightful family court to which came important people from all over the world. To the surprise and grief of the people of the United States, at a time when he seemed likely to become again a triumphant candidate for the Presidency, a sickness that resulted from his exposures in South America proved fatal. The great man died January 7, 1919.

Thus passed from the stage of American life one of the most individual, able, and influential persons who ever lived in the United States. Throughout life he had followed his own saying: ''We must spend and be spent in the endless battle for right against wrong.''

XVI

ELIHU ROOT

Winner of the Nobel Peace Prize

A DIGNIFIED man speaking before an assembly of dignified men, that is the picture of Elihu Root that men will longest remember. His career shows what remarkable influence a single man may have in the councils of nations.

Elihu Root is great as a lawyer and great as a statesman; he is greater still as a man who accomplished much for international peace.

Without representing pacifism he upheld arbitration; without minimizing the dignity and the rights of individual nations he set forward the reasonableness of submitting differences to some form of judicial decision. He did what few men in the history of the world have been able to do for the cause of good feeling between governments.

Elihu Root was awarded the Nobel Peace Prize in 1912, in particular for bringing peace in Cuba and the Philippine Islands, and a better understanding between the United States and Japan. He might well have been awarded that prize in other years; for 1912 did not mark the beginning nor the end of his work for peace. For many years, on many notable occasions, he has spoken earnestly for his great cause.

Of his belief in arbitration the *Boston Transcript* said: "He did not believe that the golden age could be brought into existence by treaty or statute, but he was confident that the age of iron might be softened by nations agreeing to try arbitration, not as the last resort but as the first."

Himself a lawyer of the highest ability, Elihu Root had faith in the necessity of courts, and equal faith in the ability of courts to advance human interests. While he did not think it possible to bring the world entirely to peace, he did think it possible to lead nations to become more reasonable. Being that kind of idealist who bases his idealism on the conditions of practical life, Elihu Root became a man of severely practical nature, and not at all an empty dreamer. On many occasions this matter-of-fact idealist made definite, practical proposals, as plain, as substantial, as lacking in romantic glow as the laws that regulate daily affairs, and yet beautiful with the light of peace. He combines in his nature the visionary and the pragmatist. Not fervid with hopes that cannot be realized, he made himself a man of realities. While some have called him hard and cold, without the warmth of prophetic vision, he is at heart a man of fire.

Of Elihu Root's ability such a keen judge of men as Theodore Roosevelt said: "He is the ablest man in public life; the wisest man I ever knew." The New York *World* said: "He is one of the few living statesmen of the first intellectual rank."

This genuine statesman was born in Clinton, New York, February 15, 1845. His father, Oren Root, had been principal of the academy at Seneca Falls, New York. When the boy was five years old the father became professor of mathematics and astronomy in Hamilton College. There he taught for many years, making himself one of the most influential teachers in any eastern college.

Professor Root's pupils nicknamed him "Cube Root," and so when his son, Elihu, at the age of fifteen, entered Hamilton, they called the boy "Square Root." As might have been expected, the professor's son devoted himself to study, especially mathematics, in which he took first prize. When he was graduated in 1864 he was valedictorian of his class.

Having made himself an earnest student while in college, he continued to study in after years. Perhaps because he gave so much attention to mathematics he developed the sensible, practical, straightforward type of character.

In the year after his graduation, when he was a boy of twenty, Elihu Root taught for a time in Rome Academy. Wishing to become a lawyer rather than a teacher, he studied in New York University, and in 1867, being then twenty-two years old, gained the degree of bachelor of law.

In teaching at Hamilton, Professor Oren Root had made a host of powerful friends. Thinking of his son's welfare, he said, ''Elihu, I'm going to give you letters of introduction to some rich men I know. They'll help you just as much as I would.''

To the old gentleman's surprise and pleasure, Elihu answered: "Please don't. I don't want any letters of introduction. I want to make my own career. I propose to make friends without family pull. I want to find out whether I am a man or a mouse.''

Since any young man who starts life in that way is certain to win some degree of success, Elihu Root succeeded in standing on his own feet. He began at the bottom of the ladder, making his work give him friends and produce influence that enabled him to rise in his profession. In addition to having much natural energy and ability, he was a young man of culture. He was especially able to think straight. Aways unwilling to jump at conclusions, he insisted upon precedent, authority, evidence, and good reasoning. For a young man he made a reputation very quickly.

Within three years from the time when Elihu Root had gained his degree of bachelor of law he had a good law practice. Within less than ten years he had become a corporation lawyer, expert in complex matters, commanding a practice that itself commanded respect. All this he had brought about through hard work and his own ability. He had paddled his own canoe.

As the years went on, Elihu Root made himself still more notable in legal work. In 1883, when he was thirty-eight years old, he accepted an appointment from President Arthur, as United States District Attorney for the southern district of New York. Then for two years he served in that important office, giving to it his best efforts. At the conclusion of his term he retired to private life, resuming his own great practice. At that time he became an important public figure but by no means the great figure that he became later.

In 1894 he was delegate at large to the New York Constitutional Convention, and served as chairman of the judiciary committee. He had gained the reputation of being one of the ablest and best informed lawyers in the city of New York.

In 1899, when he was fifty-four years old, he accepted President McKinley's invitation to become Secretary of War. In order to accept the position, in which he served from 1899 to 1904, he left a law practice that brought him annually many thousands of dollars, and accepted a comparatively small salary.

Elihu Root had found his work in life, had made himself proficient in it, had become a veteran, and although well over middle age, was at the beginning of his really great work, his effort toward world peace.

As Secretary of War, although he re-organized the United States Army, and established the General Staff, he showed himself more inclined toward peace than toward war, and had met many difficult situations with tact. In particular he had brought about better conditions in Cuba and in the Philippine Islands.

The conclusion of the war with Spain having left problems that threatened grave disorders, Secretary Root, instead of relying upon force, preferred to rely upon reason. Since in all his preceding work in life he had made it his practice to go to the bottom of every affair, and to act upon facts and not upon impulse nor desires, he wished to know all the truth connected with disorder in Cuba and the Philippines. When he had gained possession of the facts he would know how to act. Therefore he sent a commission to study the natives, to find the differences between them, and to lay before him, as Secretary of War, all the basic facts, together with recommendations for procedure.

Having learned the conditions, he outlined the organic law

both of Cuba and of the Philippine Islands, including constitution, judicial code, and system of laws, a work so important and so far-reaching that people still speak of it as one of the great services done by an American in the interests of a foreign people.

In order to learn conditions in South America, a continent that the opening of the Panama Canal was to bring into close touch with the United States, Secretary Root himself made a tour of the most important countries.

In 1903, as member of the Alaska Boundary Tribunal, a body that took up one of the most serious questions between nations, Mr. Root gave himself untiringly to the work, again demanding to know all the facts in the case before he expressed an opinion.

In 1905, President Roosevelt, impressed with the great lawyer's remarkable ability, invited him to become Secretary of State. As Secretary of State, Elihu Root likewise profoundly affected international relations. Having the noble conception of an international court of arbitration, he worked unceasingly for the establishment of such an institution.

During his period of service as Secretary of State, Elihu Root negotiated no less than twenty-four general arbitration treaties with sister nations, a record such as no previous Secretary of State had ever made. For almost the first time in history a high official of a powerful government led in practical proposals to bring about peace on earth. The Secretary of State did this without proposing peace at any cost. He presented no proposals that might lead to a sacrifice of national dignity, even by the smallest and weakest of nations. In his idealism he remained sensible and practical, and kept within the bounds of actual conditions.

High-minded though idealists may be, they are often dangerous because they refuse to see the world as it is. On the other hand, hard-headed and practical men sometimes hinder progress because they place emphasis too often on aims that are low. The hopes of the world hang on men who combine idealism and practical reality, for while such men hitch their

ELIHU ROOT

wagons to stars they remember that they drive on earthly roads.

In his work as Secretary of State, Elihu Root won the admiration of the world because he not only planned for the future but also adapted his plans to the present.

In one of his speeches Mr. Root said, "What happens today or tomorrow is of little consequence. The tendencies of a nation are all that count."

The Secretary of State had no thought that he could change the world of his day. He believed that he could lead people toward the reasonableness of judicial procedure. He looked far into the future, seeing a world guided by law and a sense of justice. Toward that world of the future he hoped to direct the steps of the present. His method was to stimulate the wish to give fair dealing to every nation. In all his work as Secretary of State, Elihu Root made it evident that he wished the United States to think, not of money or power, not of commercial expansion or increased territory, but of justice to all men. He was one of many Americans who led the United States to assume an ideal position in world affairs such as no other nation ever before held.

Such men as Elihu Root, and such principles as those that he upheld, led the United States, in various years and under different great leaders, to say to the people of Cuba: "We do not wish to take possession of your island; we do not desire to profit at your expense; we wish only to see you happy and prosperous, living under the reign of equal and just laws."

Such leaders led the United States to devote to the good of the people of China the great sum China paid as indemnity for damages inflicted in the Boxer Rebellion.

Such leaders and such principles led to the established conviction that the aim of the United States in the Philippine Islands should be the good of the Philippine people, including their ultimate independence. Principles of that sort are far indeed from theatrical, militaristic imperialism that disregards the rights of weak nations. The spirit that Elihu

Root helped to strengthen is the spirit of fellow-feeling, sympathy and helpfulness.

In a notable speech at Rio de Janeiro in Brazil, Secretary Root, as representative of the people of the United States, said: "We wish for no victories but those of peace, for no territory except our own; for no sovereignty except the sovereignty over ourselves. We deem the independence and equal rights of the smallest and weakest member of the family of nations entitled to as much respect as those of the greatest empire."

When the leaders of all nations come to hold such views, the people of the world will be closer to living in that age of gold of which poets have sung. The student of history, studying the centuries, sees one long series of wars of conquest and aggrandizement. He sees leaders openly proclaiming selfish ends. He sees the destruction of great cities, the ruin of fertile lands, the untold misery of millions of people, because men in age after age have believed in power rather than justice.

Such a book as Gibbon's *Decline and Fall of the Roman Empire* emphasizes all too strongly the belief that human selfishness causes human misery. In the centuries of which Gibbon wrote, no one had respect for weak nations. And in the centuries since the fall of Constantinople, the world-conquerors, whether represented by a few men like those who followed Pizarro to the conquest of Peru, or by many like the hosts that followed Napoleon to the conquest of Europe, would have laughed at any one who upheld the beliefs that Elihu Root set forward in his speech at Rio de Janeiro. In contrast with the past such a speech appears in its proper light, and shows that some, at least, of the leaders of today differ as materially from the leaders of the past as white differs from black, as human sympathy and sense of justice differs from brute selfishness.

From the romantic point of view, the life of Elihu Root shows no such series of remarkable episodes as the life of Charles XII of Sweden, Napoleon Bonaparte of France, or

Frederick the Great of Prussia, but his influence upon the world for good excels the influence of any one of the more romantic figures. Without being a pacifist Elihu Root believed in bringing the world to peace. Without believing that he could destroy war, he believed that he could do something to lessen the number of wars. As he had slight faith in the work of the soldier, so, too, although himself a diplomatist, he had slight faith in the work of the diplomat, in which he saw craft, trickery, deceit, and subtle dealing. He preferred to rely upon courts, upon open discussions, upon the full presentation of facts, and upon a wish to give justice rather than to gain national advantage. As he said: "What we need for further development of arbitration is the substitution of judicial action for diplomatic action." He aimed, in fact, to promote among nations a kind of orderly procedure, an understanding of needs and rights, and a reliance upon international tribunals for the giving of equal justice.

To the ideals for which he stood Elihu Root was at all times ready to give most unselfishly of time and strength. He had already sacrificed much of the income of his great law practice in order to assume public office at all. Although some attacked him as supremely selfish, calling him cold and self-centered because he did not permit himself to be swept away by emotion or empty idealism, he gave himself wholeheartedly to the cause of world peace.

When Elihu Root prepared a brief in support of the interests of the United States in the Newfoundland Fisheries Dispute, a matter in which he represented the United States before the Hague Tribunal, he spent many months in work, making the most exhaustive studies, going to the very heart of the matter, and sifting every particle of evidence. He spent eight days in presenting his final argument. He had worked with the utmost earnestness, and had used experience and ability of the first rank, but all for good will, without receiving any payment whatever from the United States.

In 1910, Elihu Root was counsel for the United States in the North Atlantic Fisheries Arbitration Case. In that year too, he became member of the Permanent Court of Arbitration at the Hague, as well as president of the Carnegie Endowment for International Peace. He had become one of the most notable figures in the world, standing emphatically for peace and justice.

When one realizes that respect for legal procedure and for court decisions lies at the very base of civilization, he realizes something of the great work accomplished by this man who led nations to respect that which most deeply affects individuals.

In 1913 Mr. Root served as president of the Hague Tribunal of Arbitration between Great Britain, France, Spain and Portugal concerning church property. Here, in a matter that involved much delicacy, and that contained the germs of much trouble for the future, Mr. Root assumed a commanding influence over nations.

From being an unknown young lawyer, entering upon life in New York and desirous chiefly of relying upon himself, he had become one who influenced the destinies of nations, not through fear and the sword, but through justice and the courts.

In 1917 he visited Russia as special ambassador of the United States, and addressed the Russian Duma.

In 1921 Elihu Root was a member of a commission of international jurists called together to consider plans of great importance to the world's peace, the Council of the League of Nations having invited the governments of the civilized nations to send their most representative lawyers to formulate plans for a permanent court of international justice.

Mr. Root took prominent part in the discussions. For many years he had given his most earnest attention to the problem of international peace, and he, preëminently, was the man to give wise, constructive advice. As a result of the deliberations the Commission reported plans that led to the establishment, in 1921, of the new permanent Court of International Justice, one more effort made by the world's most thoughtful leaders to establish the rule of law among nations.

In November, 1921, he again represented the United States as commissioner plenipotentiary at the important International Conference on the Limitation of Armaments.

That conference, which met in Washington, D.C., brought about an agreement by which the most powerful nations, through good will alone, made solemn agreement to limit their armaments in accordance with conditions that in no way weakened their relative standing. Perhaps, of all movements that ever took place in favor of peace, that was the most immediately practical, for it bore instant fruit.

The astonished citizens of various lands saw great governments, instead of increasing the load of taxes for the multiplication of battleships and further development of military power, actually destroying battleships for which they had paid millions of dollars, and at the same time willingly reducing the size of armies. Such a beating of swords into plowshares the world had never before looked upon! Elihu Root must have felt an infinite satisfaction after his years of effort toward peace, to see, at last, such a step. When he had first begun to speak in favor of international peace no one would have prophesied that such a plan as the limitation of armament would ever be adopted by great nations.

The world had long cried, "Peace, peace!" when there was no peace. It had needed leaders who would be as resolute for peace as other leaders had been for war. Most of all, it had needed men who could see that peace, as well as war, has its practical side, and that it cannot be gained through mere wishing.

In 1925, when the Locarno agreements made peace in Europe practically certain for years to come, Mr. Root, then at the age of eighty, again saw, through the progress of years, the high fulfilment of his hopes. He said: "That series of agreements is the proof of returning sanity to the European world; proof that what no orators could bring about, what no essayists, no editorial writers, no discussions, could accomplish, the logic of events has gradually effected."

In political life in the United States, Elihu Root always

played an important part that brought him many enemies, but even they admitted that he was one of the most brilliant men in public life.

The fact-demanding lawyer had made his mind in so many ways "a cold hard logic engine" that he seldom fell into mistakes. From his boyhood, with his mathematical mind, he had insisted upon accuracy. The worst with which his enemies can charge him is that he was cold and forbidding. They failed to see under his insistence upon reality the spirit of an idealist.

In many ways Mr. Root is an old-fashioned gentleman. He is a man of dignity, who always dresses in formal manner. In his nature he has almost nothing of the romantic rough-rider. He is courteous in the coldly formal manner of days less free and easy than our own. Of course he lacks the magnetic power of those who permit emotion to sweep them into hysteria. Likewise he is too much a man of fact to become anything of a demagogue, and too much an idealist to become a leader who would willingly deceive.

Those who hope to find him other than a straight-thinking, practical-minded man of affairs, express disappointment. Some of his enemies made bitter attacks upon him. They saw honors come to him, high representative offices, membership in important international committees, a high place in the councils of his party, college degrees, and public praise. They accused him of having selfishly worked for empty honors, things of the moment soon forgotten by all. To all attacks Mr. Root returned no answer. Even under abuse he maintains dignity.

In one of the most severe attacks the one who spoke against him admitted, "He is thorough, incessant, steady." What better praise could any public leader have? He had not trimmed his sail to meet every varying wind of doctrine, but he had kept a steady course. No one ever accused Elihu Root of insincerity, of light-minded seeking of pleasure, or of weakness of intellect.

Deeply sincere in all that he ever said and did, he commands respect. Serious in his attitude toward life, he lives with a dignity that might well be imitated. Willing to study every problem until he masters it, he has made himself one whom people heed.

Particularly in political life he attacked all forms of invisible government and every kind of trickery. He attacked machine government as well as corrupt leaders. A citizen of the United States, the most democratic nation in the world, he believes sincerely in democracy, having faith that popular government is the only government that can long conserve the rights of people.

At the same time, while he believes in the opinion and the vote of the people, he does not believe in giving to them the very rod and sceptre of government. While he believes that the expression of the people should be final he feels sure that the men who carry out that expression should be representatives for the people, experts in their work.

"Men in the mass," he said, "can frequently determine better than any individual what ought to be accomplished, but the more difficult thing of determining how to accomplish it is usually beyond their ken."

As a politician Mr. Root so won the respect of his party that he was made chairman of the New York Republican State Conventions of 1908, 1910, 1913, 1914, 1916, 1920, and 1922. He was president of the New York State Constitutional Convention in 1915. In 1904 he was temporary chairman of the Republican National Convention, and in 1912 temporary and permanent chairman. Such positions show how active he was in political life and how much he won the admiration of his associates.

In private life, Elihu Root did active work for many good causes. He was chairman of the board of trustees of the Carnegie Institute of Washington, D. C., trustee of the New York Public Library, president of the Union League Club, the Century Club, and of other important bodies, president of the American Bar Association, member of many important committees, chairman of the United States Government War

Saving Investment Society, and active worker for a hundred other good purposes. It is remarkable that a man so interested as he was in great affairs could find time to express interest in so many others of less importance.

Although Elihu Root never aspired to authorship, he wrote some half dozen books that command respect, the titles showing the interests of the man and indicating something of his hopes. In 1907 he published *The Citizen's Part in Government;* in 1913, *Experiments in Government and the Essentials of the Constitution;* in 1916, *Addresses on Government and Citizenship,* and *The Military and Colonial Policy of the United States;* and in 1917, *Latin America and the United States; Russia and the United States;* and *Miscellaneous Addresses.*

In his writing he is clear, direct and forceful, writing without affectation, and aiming at forcible expression of thought rather than at charm of style. In all that he writes he shows his sympathy, his admiration of that which is good, and his practical idealism.

Mr. Root became doctor of political science of the University of Leyden; member of the faculty of political and administrative science of the University of San Marcos, Lima, Peru, the oldest university in the Americas; doctor, *honoris causa,* of the University of Paris; doctor of laws of the University of Buenos Aires; and the holder of high honorary degrees from some fourteen American colleges and universities.

In 1909 he became United States Senator from the State of New York, and served in that high position until 1915.

Since his graduation from Hamilton College in 1864 the son of the old college professor has remained deeply attached to his college. He is a member of its board of trustees, has attended its commencement exercises regularly, has given addresses at the opening of the college years, and in a thousand ways expressed his love for Hamilton. Those who accuse Mr. Root of coldness of nature certainly cannot know the warmth of his affection for Hamilton College.

Perhaps his own words speak best both for his love for the college, and of his aims in life.

"There is a plain old house in the hills of Oneida overlooking the valley of the Mohawk, where truth and honor dwelt in my youth. When I go back, as I am about to go, to spend my declining years, I mean to go with a feeling that I can say I have not failed to speak and to act in accordance with the lessons I learned there from the God of my fathers."

XVII

JOHN SINGER SARGENT

ARTIST

A WOMAN who had the soul of an artist and the heart of a mother taught her small son how to draw and how to paint in water color. Because she herself loved to paint in water color, and likewise loved to teach her boy, she found great happiness. Out of her two great loves she stimulated the skill and the ambition of her son, John Singer Sargent, who became one of the greatest of modern painters.

At first Mary Newbold Sargent had merely found amusement in teaching her boy how to draw, and then, later, how to work with colors. When she saw how eagerly he looked ahead to the hours for drawing and painting, how closely he noticed and reproduced every detail, how wonderfully well he succeeded past the skill of most boys, she felt an interest that grew into ambition, both for herself and for her son.

At that time, the Sargent family lived in Florence, Italy, the very home of art. Not far from their residence they saw palaces and galleries filled with works of great painters. Wherever they went, they met people who talked of art and artists. They lived, as it were, in a city of pictures, the place of all places to awaken high ambitions to follow in the footsteps of great masters.

Nevertheless, John Singer Sargent's father was not an artist, although he appreciated art. He was a physician who for ten years had been surgeon in a Philadelphia hospital. He traced his descent from people who had been pioneers, soldiers in the American Revolution, and Indian fighters;

strong, active outdoor men who had had neither time nor taste for art.

From that realistic paternal strain, Sargent the painter gained almost as much as he did from his artistic inheritance from the mother. However much he lived in the world of beauty, John Singer Sargent never left the world of reality. He saw people as they are. He remained hard-working, practical, and so much a man of ordinary life that he looked more like a banker than an artist. As his father, the physician, had looked at people and diagnosed their physical selves, so the artist son looked at people and diagnosed their inner lives. Sometimes he was almost cruel, so some critics said, in putting upon his canvas that which he saw. However that may be, he at least painted life exactly as he saw it.

Most of his life Sargent painted portraits. Then, perhaps because the spirit of his mother rose supreme, he became a great symbolic painter, and one of the greatest of modern mural artists. When he died, April 15, 1925, at the age of sixty-nine, he had won greater fame than do most artists. Everywhere he had been acclaimed a master during his lifetime.

Today Sargent's paintings hang in the Uffizi Gallery of Florence; in the Luxembourg at Paris; in the Tate Gallery in London; in the National Gallery and the Corcoran Gallery in Washington; in the Metropolitan Museum of Art in New York; in the Public Library of Boston; the Art Institute of Chicago; The Brooklyn Museum in Brooklyn; the Boston Museum, and in many other places.

Reproductions of pictures by him appear in books that have had great circulation. Some of his paintings, like the famous painting of Hosea, have become so popular that copies of them hang on the walls of many American homes.

Some said that Sargent had no imagination, that he lacked sympathy, that he failed to show deep insight. Such critics had to acknowledge the great popularity of some of Sargent's work. Those who wondered why Sargent painted certain pictures often found themselves obliged to admire them.

Although John Singer Sargent was an artist, he never lived in the proverbial garret. Since his family was rich enough to reside abroad, he lived, as a young man, in a delightful way in the American colony in Florence. At no time in his life did he have to struggle for recognition. As a mere boy he succeeded easily. When he was only a young man he had already gained a high reputation. When he had grown to maturity he had won great sums of money for his work. At no time did he feel either the sting of poverty or the hard necessity of work. He painted because he loved to paint; he worked because he had his heart in what he did.

From the very first the artist was cosmopolitan. Although his parents came from old American stock, he himself was born in Florence, Italy, January 12, 1856. Oddly enough, he learned German before he learned English. He spoke Italian, French, and Spanish with ease. At times he made his home in Italy, in France, and in England. He traveled in various parts of Europe, including Spain, and in Syria, Morocco, and Egypt, as well as in other parts of Northern Africa.

At various times this foreign-born American visited the United States, but generally, because of art associations, he preferred to make his home elsewhere. In spite of his cosmopolitanism, Sargent remained at heart an American. When Queen Victoria invited him to become an English subject he said he was an American and that he would always remain an American. Although he worked for many years in England, painting portraits of the nobility, he placed his greatest work in the United States, on the walls of the Boston Public Library.

As a boy John Sargent had the good fortune to gain a thorough classical education before he turned entirely to art. Because he made himself a scholar before he made himself an artist, he gained power to paint mural pictures that made people wonder at his erudition. He had gained a foundation on which he could build great conceptions. In fact, John Singer Sargent made himself a many-sided man.

He loved music almost as much as he loved painting, and at one time in his life even thought seriously of devoting himself entirely to music. His work likewise showed many-sidedness. He made himself a most versatile painter, confining himself to no one type of work. Thus he painted children, landscapes, animals, bits of foreign cities, and interiors, besides his portraits. As well as working in oils, he painted delicate water colors, eighty-three of which hang in the Brooklyn Museum. When many people thought he would restrict himself to realistic portraits, he painted his symbolic mural sequence, "Judaism and Christianity."

In addition to being a painter and a musician, Sargent was a reader of books. In early life, when he had begun to read, he had formed habits that he continued. From wide reading he gained his scholarship in history and his sympathy with the spirit of the past.

By the time John Sargent was eighteen he had finished his ordinary school education, in Italy and in Germany, and had made a most enthusiastic beginning in painting. Ever since his childhood, when he had learned from his mother the beginnings of his art, he had made pictures. These he had put away carefully, no doubt, little thinking how great an artist he was to become.

Like all who have the artistic sense, the young painter was extremely sensitive. He loved his work but he hesitated to show it to people. One day when a man who knew a great deal about art, visited his home, John Sargent, then only a boy, shyly showed the more skilful man the work that he had done. Perhaps because of the praise he then won, the boy determined to go on with his painting. That spirit of shyness Sargent always retained. He did not live a hermit existence, nor was he morose, but he always kept much to himself. Thus he lived alone, walked alone, and worked alone. He had few intimates; he avoided such convivial circles as those in which Sir Joshua Reynolds delighted.

Although the distinguished painter had no distrust of his work, he hesitated to put it before people. He first had to have it perfect. Once he rubbed out a picture of a head and painted it over thirty or forty times before he felt satisfied with it. When he had worked every day for seven months on the scaffolding in the Boston Public Library, and had completed his work, he still wished for some months more in which to make it better.

Some who call Sargent an impressionist, speak of his quick brush, of his instant appeal, of the ease with which he worked. They fail to notice that while he produced a great amount of work, he showed patience almost beyond belief.

As a boy John Sargent showed painstaking qualities even more notably than after he became a man. In his early drawings he gave minute care even to the slightest line, making his drawings precise in the extreme, and aiming at absolute perfection. As a man, however, he cultivated a quick power that made people forget that he had gained his skill by first working with utmost precision. From the Academy of Fine Arts in Florence the boy went, at nineteen, to Paris. There he showed his work to the great artist, Carolus Duran, who examined it, and then said, in a somewhat uncomplimentary tone, "Well, well! You'll have much to unlearn!" and then, secretly glad at heart, took him as a pupil.

Carolus Duran belonged to the so-called "direct" school of painters. He believed in realism. Instead of aiming at poetry of effect he aimed at truth to life. He believed that one should first see clearly and then work skilfully. With such beliefs young Sargent found himself most sympathetic, and so he became an apt pupil who gave dignity to the studio in which he worked. Even as a pupil, he did such good work that his associates looked upon him as one not of common clay.

For one of his first portraits the young painter made a picture of his beloved master, Carolus Duran, a mature, masterly work that he exhibited in the Paris Salon of 1877, the year in which he became twenty-one. That he should have been able, at so early an age, to paint such a portrait is indeed remarkable, for it seemed as if he had avoided the usual period of apprenticeship, and had gone at once before the world as a master.

Two years later, in 1879, Sargent set out to see something of the world. Being young and romantic, he turned toward a land of which he had dreamed, the land of Spain, with its mountains, its muleteers, and its romance. There he enjoyed picturesque sights, ancient Moorish ruins, and all the color and charm of a land that has produced many great painters. In particular he gave attention to the work of Velasquez, whom he put before himself as an ideal. The traveler lived for a time in Madrid, and there learned much concerning the character of Spanish life. In those seemingly idle, carefree days he went about with the understanding eyes of an artist, observing all that went on around him. In many ways he lived as close to the heart of Spain as did Washington Irving.

When the young painter returned to his studio in Paris, he exhibited pictures of Spanish dancers. So well had he caught the languorous charm of Spain that he made an immediate success. In a much later picture that he painted in New York, he portrayed Carmencita, a Spanish dancer famous at the time. In that painting, which now hangs in the gallery of the Luxembourg, the lover of Spain caught something of the Spanish fire. According to the picture, Carmencita has just entered to begin her dance. She holds her head erect in a kind of challenge. By her expression, her pose, her golden yellow costume, one might almost say by her very breathing, she fascinates.

In another painting that Sargent likewise produced at a later date, the artist showed a different side of life, drawn from his memories of Spain. In that picture, "Padre Sebastiano," instead of the fire of the dancer's spirit, and the suggestion of music, dance and merriment, he shows opposite qualities. Padre Sebastiano sits writing. Surrounded by a multitude of things, he has no thought for anything that is present. His deep eyes look into the regions of inspiration. In that picture Sargent, by subtle suggestion, reveals an inner nature, as marked as in the picture of Carmencita. But how different!

Some critics say that Sargent failed to give to his pictures any subtle quality; that he painted the exterior only; that he made no revelation of inner depths; that he failed to lead those who look at his paintings to go beyond his canvas. Can such critics look at his "Carmencita" and "Padre Sebastiano" and feel no sense of compelling power?

All who travel in Spain must think of the Moors when they see the ruins of their ancient walls, or the existing beauty of the marvelous buildings that they erected in Seville, in Granada, and in Cordova. Sargent grew interested in them, and wished to see something of Moorish life. Therefore he crossed the Strait of Gibraltar and visited Morocco. In that wild country he found a charm that appealed deeply to his artistic sense. With his sister, who like himself was an artist, the romantic realist went on frequent trips to the lands along the Mediterranean. Because of his close associations with his sister who, following her mother, worked only with water colors, Sargent developed an ability in the use of water colors that he might otherwise have failed to discover. Through his foreign trips, therefore, he gained material for his work, and developed a medium through which to express himself in a new way.

At various times the artist traveled in Spain, in Morocco, in Italy, and in Egypt and Palestine. From such journeys, in which he sketched wherever he went, he felt an effect that can hardly be estimated. He traveled not as an ordinary sight-seeing tourist, but as one who saw beauty of form, color, and effect wherever he went. If he had never made any use whatever of the material that he observed, he still would have gained rich and helpful impressions.

Sargent has been called a lonely man, perhaps because he never married and because he cultivated few strong friendships. He preferred to live by himself and to work without companions. He did, however, maintain a close association with his sister that reminds one somewhat of the association between Charles and Mary Lamb, or of that between William and Dorothy Wordsworth.

On his return from his first Spanish travels the painter opened a studio in Paris, where he remained until 1884, when he was twenty-eight. Then he left Paris and moved to London, where he continued to reside for the remainder of his life.

Perhaps he did not wish to continue in Paris and rival the work of his master, Carolus Duran. Perhaps he felt the sting of criticism, for his work had aroused much discussion, some praising it for brilliant qualities; others finding fault with its lack of finish. Since Sargent at this time made no attempt to produce smooth, finished surfaces, preferring to produce his effects quickly, and to let brush work remain as brush work, he may have felt angered. At any rate, whatever the reason, he left Paris and became a permanent resident of London.

Sargent curiously interwove his own career with that of Henry James, the novelist. Three years after the painter removed from Paris to London he won a medal of the second class for his picture called "Portrait of a Young Lady." Henry James saw the picture and admired it. He liked the painting so much that he wrote about it and made it famous. Both men were Americans who made their homes in London. Both succeeded remarkably: one in the art of painting, the other in the art of writing. Both were realists; both drew pictures of human beings; both made searching analyses of character. Between the two there was a kind of spiritual kinship. In 1914, many years after Henry James' first appreciation of his art, Sargent exhibited a portrait of the author.

It was in 1876, when Sargent was only twenty, that he first visited the United States. In 1887, 1889, 1895, and in many other years, he visited the land that he felt was his own, even though he lived elsewhere. In the United States on many occasions he exhibited his works. To the people of the United

States he was always most generous, so that it is no accident that so many of Sargent's paintings now hang in American galleries.

In 1890 he had first established his fame with the great body of the American people by painting for the Boston Public Library his celebrated "Frieze of the Prophets." The picture of "Hosea," one of that series, became immediately popular, so that copies were reproduced by the thousands, and the name of Sargent came upon every lip.

In spite of that, Sargent never gained popularity with the great body of common people. For many years he devoted himself to subjects that did not appeal to popular taste, especially that of the United States. If, in the end, he won success in the eyes of many of the people of the United States, he did so because he had versatility and surpassing greatness as a painter. As for the quality of his work, he himself looked upon a large part of it as failing to represent the best of which he was capable.

Sargent made a great series of masterful portraits, painting pictures of many of the leading people of his time. He won so much success in this type of work that he led people to forget that he had painted in many other fields. The great artist had a way of catching an ordinary attitude, a way of holding the hands or of resting the arm, or a habitual expression, that made his pictures most realistic. He saw the inner personality of the person whose portrait he painted, and then painted exactly what he saw.

Whatever the public thought of his work, some of his sitters, at least, expressed frank disappointment. They had wished him to paint them as they wished to be, not as they actually were. They called him hard, bitter, and satirical, when they might have called him true to life.

Sargent's picture of "Madame Gatreau," for example, a picture now in the Metropolitan Museum of Art in New York, a notable profile of a famous beauty, called forth a great deal of comment, both hostile and friendly. Many people, familiar with Sargent's portraits, say that he could not paint a satisfactory picture of a beautiful woman. They looked for the angel, and found that he painted a woman of earth.

Nevertheless, he did paint portraits of beautiful women. His picture of "The Countess of Warwick and Her Son," shows a statuesque figure, flowing robes, a beautiful face, and indicates pride of rank and name. His picture of Ellen Terry as Lady Macbeth is particularly effective, her long tawny hair hanging in braids over her shoulders as she lifts the crown to her head, her attitude and expression speaking of queenliness and resolution. That picture sold first for $6,000, and later for $15,000, prices, paid during the lifetime of the painter, that speak much for the worth of the work. After his death some of his pictures sold for $30,000, and one, "San Vigilio: a Boat with Golden Sail," for $35,000. His entire collection sold for about $1,000,000! These are the prices paid for old masters.

In group pictures of women, Sargent likewise won success, although here again he met criticism for grouping and arrangement.

His picture of Lady Elcho, Mrs. Tennant, and Mrs. Adeane, "The Three Graces," charmingly combines the ideal and the human. His group picture of the Misses Hunter, unusual in arrangement, is especially interesting.

If Sargent did not gain high success in his delineation of beautiful women, he certainly did succeed in painting pictures of elderly women. His portrait of Mrs. Marquand, for example, is altogether appealing. In the picture, the woman, whose years are evident, sits at ease, her hand resting quietly on the arm of the chair, her head held slightly to one side, a smile on her countenance. She thinks of other days, or listens, unresistingly, to something that is being said. She shows the sweetness and charm of age.

Whatever may be said of Sargent's pictures of women, his portraits of men are remarkably strong. In the great master's painting, "Coventry Patmore," the author of *The Angel in the House,* smiles as if about to speak. In another, Lord

Ribblesdale, in hunting clothes, stands as if about to enter the sport of the chase.

In a way, the keen-sighted portrait painter caught his subjects off their guard and thus saw them at moments when they were most their real selves. Because of this he put on canvas, not the fleeting impression of a moment, but the genuine personality of the individual.

In his numerous visits to the United States the world-famous artist painted many pictures of distinguished Americans. Thus he made notable portraits of President Roosevelt, President Wilson, John D. Rockefeller, and General Leonard Wood. President Roosevelt he caught at a characteristic moment, that of speaking before the public, and showed distinctly the challenge, the manly dignity, the strength, and the forcefulness of that virile American.

"Sargent had too unsympathetic a heart to paint children well," say some of his critics. "Children must have annoyed him."

Certainly the painter produced no remarkable series of child portraits. Still, he was too great an artist, too varied in range, not to paint notable pictures of children.

The most attractive of his child portraits is that of "Miss Beatrice Goelet," a picture that shows the very simplicity of childhood, the open-eyed wonder and the appealing sweetness. The little girl, in a long dress, stands wonderingly, beside her a cage in which there is a parrot, suggesting the world of her amusements rather than the world of work.

Another child picture the artist called "Carnation, Lily, Lily, Rose," a title that led Sargent's famous contemporary, James McNeil Whistler, to re-name it "Darnation Silly, Silly Pose," although Whistler thought more of his play on words than he did of criticism. The picture, unique, effective, and charming, shows two little girls in a garden, lighting Japanese lanterns. The colors of the flowers, the delicate, softly-fading tints of the Japanese lanterns illuminated faintly by freshly-lit candles, together with the air of happiness and peace that the picture suggests, make this piece of Sargent's art, even if it may not be called a child portrait, at least a remarkable painting of child life.

Sargent painted a dog picture that might well be called a portrait. "Pointy" he called it. The dog sits alert, interested, and watchful. His bright eyes fairly twinkle, as if he questioned the artist who painted his picture. Any one who has seen a dog wait for some word from his master, must at once feel sympathetic toward this picture, which Sargent certainly painted with real interest.

A picture that is surely a portrait but that bears no name, is called "Italian with a Rope." That is a vivid picture, something that caught the eye of the artist in one of his Italian rambles. The Italian, laughing, rakish, stands with his hand on a rope, as if about to ring a chime of bells in some campanile. The man who could paint a picture like that had hearty zest in life. He was a lover both of men and of romance.

In his many experiences in foreign lands, Sargent found a wealth of material for painting. Like the artist in Washington Irving's *Sketch Book* who rambled from place to place, sketching, not famous buildings nor busy streets, but merely picturesque places that caught his fancy, so Sargent rambled and sketched, making no effort to paint scenes upon which every one looks. He left it to men who might follow Joseph M. W. Turner, to portray the charm of familiar scenes in Venice, to others to picture the ruins of the Forum at Rome, or the shattered beauty on the Acropolis at Athens. He remained content to paint scenes that interested him, scenes that others might pass without noticing, but whose beauty he reproduced on canvas.

One such picture shows boats lying at rest in a harbor, a simple, homely scene, full of suggestion. Another shows two girls fishing, their faces intent on what they do, the light falling on the water and making it a place of fairyland, the ripple of the country stream almost making itself audible. Sargent not only felt interest in the warmth and color of the Mediterranean but he also particularly enjoyed traveling in mountain lands. In the Tyrol, which he found especially interesting, he painted various pictures.

Notable among these is one called "Mountain Sheepfold in the Tyrol." There are the cattle, the quaint houses of the Tyrolese people, and back of them the mountains like huge walls.

Another picture he called "Trout Stream in the Tyrol," a picture of a mountain stream dashing down the steep slopes.

"Albanian Olive Gatherers," "A Glacier Stream," "A Garden ai Corfu," and "Vespers," are still other pictures of similar type.

Another entirely different type of foreign picture is "A Venetian Interior," a painting that has much ornate detail. It shows a spacious room in which four people sit in talk, two of them old and two young, the couples sitting far apart. The room is such a one as few travelers ever enter, suggesting the rich quality of the old world and its older ways.

John Singer Sargent, in fact, was one of the most versatile of modern painters. He had many interests, and he possessed ability to accomplish many types of work. He led a most active, energetic life, delighted in his work, and kept himself employed in it. He was entirely happy in his success.

"Few artists in the history of the world," said Hamilton Minchin, who was personally acquainted with Sargent, "can have had so brilliant a career. Success came to him early and never left him."

For many years the noted artist devoted himself principally to painting portraits. He found recreation in foreign travel, and in turning from time to time to painting pictures that differed widely from the work for which he gained the most praise and most money. The painting of portraits he did not look upon as work for which he wished most to be remembered. "I have long been sick and tired of portrait painting!" he said.

In 1890 he won fame for his "Frieze of the Prophets" in the Boston Public Library, a type of work that he now made the basis of still greater fame. During a period that spread over nearly thirty years he worked on a great symbolic mural series, "Judaism and Christianity," also for the walls of the Boston Public Library. The first series, which he completed in 1895, he called "Judaic Development"; the second series, completed in 1903, he called "The Dogma of the Redemption"; the third series, completed in 1916, he called "The Theme of the Madonna." With reverence, with scholarship, with good judgment and with great skill, he made a series of symbolic pictures that form his lasting memorial. In them, instead of hard reality, or the suspicion of cynical views of human life, the observer sees fancy, poetry, sympathy, and beauty.

The nobility of his symbolic "Madonna of the Sorrows"; the divine motherhood of his "Ancilla Domini"; the symbolic mystery of all the pictures in the mural series, show Sargent as a great symbolic artist.

In 1919, during the World War, the famous painter exhibited at the Royal Academy in London a picture called "Gassed," that shows how deeply the sensitive man felt the horror of war, and with what sympathy the artist looked upon the soldier.

John Singer Sargent came to his fame remarkably early in life, but he developed immeasurably, a fact far more to his credit than his early brilliance.

"The most spirited, dashing and brilliant of portrait painters," one critic called him. "The greatest of our portrait painters since Stuart," said another. "A supreme stylist," said a third.

To all this one might add, "One of the most able, most fortunate, and most successful men of modern times."

XVIII

HENRY VAN DYKE

AUTHOR

"Wouldst view what Nature's portraiture is like?
The Dame herself hath sat to this Van Dyke."

In such complimentary words did Edmund C. Stedman, an American literary critic, speak of the work of Henry van Dyke, a man who so loves nature that he leads others to love it also.

Henry van Dyke does not write essays of nature observation of the kind that John Burroughs wrote, nor does he make any attempt to be minute or scientific in his writing. Instead, he records impressions, expresses admirations, and shows himself so thoroughly in love with the outdoor world that he leads his readers to share his enthusiasm.

In one of his poems this outdoor author wrote:

"To Thee I turn, to Thee I make my prayer,
God of the open air."

More than almost any other writer of the present day Henry van Dyke has led people to a noble or reverent enjoyment of the beauties of nature, for if, with William Wordsworth, he can say that he went

"By the sides
Of the deep rivers, and the lonely streams,
Wherever Nature led,"

with Wordsworth he can also say:

> "I have felt
> A presence that disturbs me with the joy
> Of elevated thoughts."

Still, Henry van Dyke is not one who merely stands and meditates. He is active, energetic and virile, one who tramps the forest trails, whips the trout brooks, climbs wooded mountains, and takes virtual possession of all the outdoor world.

"Who owns the mountains?" he asks in one of his essays, and then answers his own question by saying that they who enjoy them really own the mountains. In that sense of ownership Henry van Dyke has large landed properties. He owns forests, lakes, mountains, and little rivers without number. He is richer than those who own what "Ik Marvel" called "castles and great estates in Spain." He has an ownership even more real, having spent many days and nights in the open, in vigorous, hearty outdoor life, for he is a most enthusiastic disciple of Izaak Walton, and could name half the fishing brooks of the country.

But Henry van Dyke has made this love of nature, and its after effect of leading other people to enjoy the outdoor world, by-products, as it were, of his busy life. By vocation he is a preacher and teacher; by avocation he is a writer of essays, stories and poems; by natural instinct he is a lover of the open air.

"For real company and friendship," he says in one of his essays, "there is nothing outside the animal kingdom that is comparable to a river."

There are few such writers. Many who love nature try to teach us something about it, to lecture when we would simply sit and dream. Still others use nature as mere background against which they show dramatic events of human or animal life, in the tragedy or comedy of which we forget the delight of quiet.

Henry van Dyke is more like Robert Louis Stevenson than

like these writers. He takes us with him on excursions into quiet places; is human, companionable and interesting; and through his words makes us realize the charm of what lies in the open air. Then, too, Henry van Dyke is much more than a mere nature-lover who writes enthusiastically about nature. As one of his critic friends, in speaking of him, said, he is "a poet-critic-essayist-novelist-educator-lecturer-fisherman-pulpiteer."

This literary worker has led a busy life and achieved success in many fields. Although at different times he has emphasized, more or less, as circumstances brought it about, the pulpiteer, the essayist, or the educator, he has, as a matter of fact, always combined all the fields of work. He still deserves every part of the name the critic friend gave him, and even more, for he is a man of varied gifts, of active life, and of great accomplishments.

The fisherman-essayist is too much a lover of life to be content in any one limited field of work or to devote himself heart and soul to following up any one chance success in the hope of gaining more of popularity. He is one of the happiest of men, because he always does what he likes to do and because he finds the things he likes to do well worth the doing.

"I would rather receive a little money," he says, "for doing work that is congenial and that comes naturally, than a great deal of money for doing something that is demanded by literary fashion, or undertaken for the sake of the price it will bring."

Certainly this companionable author has found the doing of what is congenial an easy pathway to success. In the United States, people look upon him as one of the most popular of authors. In Germany people read his *First Christmas Tree* under the title of *Der Erste Weihnachtsbaum;* in France people read his *Broken Soldier* under the title of *Le Soldat Épuisé;* in Holland they read his *Blue Flower* in the book called *Die Blaume Bloem.* In Sweden, Holland, Spain, France, Germany, and even in far-away Japan and China, people read, in their native languages, translations of his *Other Wise*

Man, a story so excellent that it became a world classic in the lifetime of its author.

Something extremely appealing to common humanity gives Henry van Dyke's books wide circulation. A spirit of gentle companionship; a charming way of expressing faith, longings, hopes, and joys of common humanity; and a genuine sincerity, do for his books what style alone could not do. As in Robert Louis Stevenson's writing, the personality of the man appeals to us, for of all our modern writers, Henry van Dyke is most pleasingly personal.

This popular writer came to his work by good inheritance, first from his Dutch ancestors who came from Holland to America in 1652, a full two hundred years before 1852, the year when Henry van Dyke was born; and secondly and immediately, from his father, Rev. Dr. Henry J. van Dyke, a noted preacher and public leader of the generation before.

Henry van Dyke's father was more than an educated man; he was a companionable person, and a lover of nature. Likewise, he loved to go fishing. When his son was old enough he took the boy into the woods with him, where he taught the youngster how to find pleasure along the streams and under the trees. He showed his son, through actual living in the open, that life and comradeship close to the heart of nature will open new worlds of beauty and wonder.

Strange as it may seem to some, Henry van Dyke was not a country boy, but a city boy. He was born in Germantown, Pennsylvania, a suburb of Philadelphia, where his father held a pastorate. In Brooklyn, New York, where the family moved when he was a child, Henry van Dyke spent his boyhood and gained his first school training. Perhaps the very fact that the boy grew up in city surroundings led him to have a more wondering love of the country. To him the city streets were familiar; the country represented the far-away, and the romantic.

The son of a father who was so great a lover of the outdoor world and of fishing could hardly escape gaining an equal love for nature. In *A Boy and a Rod,* Henry van Dyke tells something of his early experiences along the brooks, and says that he always had especial fondness for those passages in the Bible that speak of some of the Apostles as fishermen.

In his first schooldays in Brooklyn Henry van Dyke began to write; for even then the wish to express his admirations was as much part of his nature as were his enthusiasms. At sixteen, the boy, having become a graduate of Brooklyn Polytechnic Institute, set off at once for Princeton University, hoping to follow in his father's footsteps, to become a preacher, and to continue, for relaxation, to find his way to country streams. All those ambitions, happily for him, he fulfilled. As his father, for thirty-eight years, was pastor of the Second Presbyterian Church of Brooklyn, and in 1876 moderator of the general assembly, so Henry van Dyke, for eighteen years, was pastor of the Brick Presbyterian Church of New York City, and in 1902-03 moderator of the general assembly.

Then he went further, and surpassed his father, for through his books he became an inspirer of people of many lands. More than that, he entered into public life, and as ambassador to the Netherlands and Luxemburg, played a prominent part in the early events of the World War. He had gained, and the world had gained, because he had cultivated early ambitions to follow in his father's footsteps.

At Princeton, from which Henry van Dyke was graduated in the class of 1873, the young man succeeded especially in writing and in speaking. He wrote for college periodicals, won prizes for essay writing and became senior class day speaker. He was at that time an enthusiastic collegian, and he has remained one ever since.

From the time when he first entered Princton at the age of sixteen, Henry van Dyke has maintained some form of connection with the university, as student, as loyal alumnus, or as much-loved professor of English literature.

This earnest man, who devoted a great part of his life to the ministry, is by nature a teacher, that is, so ardent a lover of books and of right living that he cannot help but commu-

nicate his enthusiasms to others. He does not think of preaching, or of teaching in the class room, as a means of gaining
a livelihood, but as a passion, an enjoyment, as keen as his
love for free life in the hills and along the streams.

When the young man left Princeton in 1873, he taught
school for a year in Brooklyn. With all the interest and zeal
of youth, and fresh from the university class rooms, he believed in study and scholarship. With it all, he had the fire
of a great love for literature. He had already practiced
writing and speaking, and had won honors. In that first
year of his teaching he made a strong impression upon his
fortunate students. Twenty-seven years later, in 1900, Henry
van Dyke again became, by profession, a teacher. In that
year he became professor of English literature in Princeton
University, where he remained for many years.

In the meantime, between 1873 and 1900, he had not ceased
to be a teacher. In spite of all his attention to theological
studies and to church work, he had continued to find enjoyment in reading good books, in which, as those know who
read his magazine articles concerning great masters of literature, he found pleasure, refreshment, and a sense of personal
companionship with great souls. He read, not for the mere
love of learning, for he is not at all the dry-as-dust type of
scholar, interested most in facts and dates, sources and variations of manuscripts and editions, but for love of human
companionship. In books this bibliophile found living per-
sonalities, rather than the words of men who had lived, died,
and passed away forever. Therefore he read with a sympathy, understanding, and sense of fellowship that led him
to interpret clearly because he loved deeply. Since he sincerely enjoyed books he could not keep from talking and
writing about the ones that interested him most.

While a college student he read Tennyson's poems with especially appreciative sympathy, finding in them an almost
reverent care in expression, a weighing of every word and
syllable, and a combination of word-music and thought that
marks a great master in poetry. More than that, he found

in Tennyson a love of the ideal, and a belief in the conquering power of righteousness. Then, too, in the *Idylls of the King* particularly, he found much use of allegory.

As every reader of Henry van Dyke knows, he himself reveals a spirit much akin to that of Tennyson. Henry van Dyke is meticulous in his use of English, writing prose that has artistic power as well as strength of thought; and verse that is similar in some respects. He directs all his writing toward the ideal, leading toward higher joys and never toward baser pleasures. He, too, delights in allegory, of which he has made the most effective use of any modern prose writer. His most popular story, *The Other Wise Man,* is a parable, a species of allegory. In addition to that story, Henry van Dyke has written much that is symbolic and allegorical.

The young student's enthusiasm for Tennyson continued after he left Princeton. He developed his thoughts, put them on paper, and finally, at the age of thirty-seven, in 1889, brought out his critical book, *The Poetry of Tennyson.* No better commentary on the work of Tennyson has yet appeared, the exposition of *The Idylls of the King* being particularly happy. That book, without question, is Henry van Dyke's greatest contribution to scholarship, a work that has brought thousands to closer acquaintance with the spirit of Tennyson.

Lord Tennyson himself, a man not given to commenting on what critics said, wrote Henry van Dyke a kindly letter in which he said that the Princeton scholar had found in his poetry all that the poet had tried to express. Three years after the publication of that book of interpretative criticism Henry van Dyke visited Lord Tennyson in his English home. He found the great Poet Laureate most friendly, though an extremely old man, who ordinarily held himself aloof from strangers.

After this year of teaching in Brooklyn, Henry van Dyke entered the Princeton Theological Seminary. There he studied theology, but he was unable to keep his hand from making books. He edited the *Princeton Book,* contributed to other Princeton publications, and made himself a local name as writer. He was graduated in 1877. In the following year he went to Germany, where he studied in the University of Berlin. On his return in 1879 he was ordained a Presbyterian minister.

For twenty-two years the scholar engaged in the active work of the ministry, but he continued his reading, his writing and lecturing, and his country excursions. Instead of confining his teaching to the pulpit he found a greater audience than he could reach with his voice alone.

In the first four years of his ministry, the literary, country-loving preacher was pastor of the United Congregational Church of Newport, Rhode Island, in those four years showing such unusual gifts, and such attractive personality, that he was asked to come to the Brick Presbyterian Church at Fifth Avenue and 37th Street, New York City. There he preached and worked from 1883 until 1900.

As a preacher Dr. van Dyke showed breadth of interest, tolerance, and open-mindedness that attracted attention, and he worked with a devotion not limited to his own church. For these reasons he made himself one of the great preachers of New York City.

His first book, *The Reality of Religion,* published in 1884, when he was thirty-two, grew out of his studies in the seminary, and his work in the ministry. His second book, *The Story of the Psalms,* published three years later, united his love of religion and his love of literature. After those first books Dr. van Dyke wrote many others on religious subjects. As a matter of fact, in the broad sense of the word, he made all his books religious, because all make for sympathy with men, companionship with nature, and a reverent view of life. He wrote some books, however, that are more technically religious, such being *Sermons to Young Men,* 1893; *The Christ Child in Art,* 1894; *The Gospel for an Age of Doubt,* 1896; *The Gospel for a World of Sin,* 1899; and *The Poetry of the Psalms,* 1900.

Too often, people familiar with Dr. van Dyke's more popular work overlook the fact that he has written so much that strictly represents the work of the minister.

From the time when Henry van Dyke published his *Poetry of Tennyson,* in 1889, he became a prominent figure in the literary world. Before that time, however, he had written his work on *The National Sin of Literary Piracy,* having for one of his virtues a fearlessness in expressing his own opinion, whether in literature, in church discussions, or in such work as he performed when United States Minister to the Netherlands and Luxemburg.

In 1895 the man who so enjoyed his vacation fishing experiences, published his first really popular book, *Little Rivers,* a book of essays about country and forest excursions. In that book, which deals with quiet ways, with brooks that laugh their way from the mountains, and with wide landscapes, the nature lover wrote with a charm that is still fresh. As a result, he made the book a modern classic, a fit companion for all who love the outdoors.

In one of his poems Dr. van Dyke expresses his delight in a country brook:

> "Only an idle little stream,
>   Whose amber waters softly gleam,
>   Where I may wade through woodland shade,
>   And cast the fly, and loaf, and dream."

That spirit he expressed in all its richness in *Little Rivers.* From the time of the publication of that book he gained recognition as an essayist whose work will live.

Only a year later, in 1896, he published his famous story, *The Other Wise Man,* a story that had a more phenomenal success than almost any other American short story ever written. *The Other Wise Man* was read and re-read. It was brought out in a variety of editions, made into a school text book, and translated into many languages. From the day of its publication until the present time, the story has continued to

appeal to an ever-widening circle of readers, partly because
it tells, in fascinating allegorical form, a story of altruism,
and partly because it is the work of a true writer who gave
polish and finish to his work. With daring originality it adds
to the three Wise Men of the Bible story a fourth who, because of a series of delays brought about by constant readi-
ness to aid his fellow men, never reached his goal, but who,
in his dying moments, saw the vision of Him whom he sought.

Following the example set by Charles Dickens, Dr. van
Dyke wrote a long series of Christmas stories, writing with
rare charm, and with a born story-teller's power. In those
stories, which include *The First Christmas Tree*, 1897; *The
Lost Word*, 1898; *The Toiling of Felix*, 1900; and *The Mansion*, 1911, he emphasized "peace on earth, good will to men."

Through stories of various kinds Dr. van Dyke became one
of the best loved of American short story writers. From time
to time he gathered together in book form the stories that he
had first contributed to magazines, such books including *The
Blue Flower, The Unknown Quantity,* and *The Ruling
Passion.*

Dr. van Dyke writes with notable artistic finish, making
some of his stories vigorous out-of-door narratives, suggested
by his experiences in the wilderness; some, allegories or modern parables; some, as the title, *The Unknown Quantity*, suggests, stories that deal with forces beyond those ordinarily
recognized. Although he is a prolific writer he has never
chosen to cast any story into the form of the novel, perhaps
because he cares too little for mere realism, and still less for
mere romance. He is never the idle teller of an idle tale.
Without question he has peculiar mastery of the familiar essay
and the idealistic short story.

In addition to the books mentioned, this interested writer
has written at least one notable book of travel, *Out of Doors
in the Holy Land*, 1908; a series of literary essays, *Companionable Books*, 1922; and many books of poems; for he is a
poet as well as an essayist and story writer.

The titles of Henry van Dyke's works show his phrase-making ability. *Companionable Books* reveals at once the spirit the author wished to arouse in his readers. *A Quaint Comrade by Quiet Streams* tells the best that can be said about Izaak Walton. *An Adventurer in a Velvet Jacket* aptly applies to Robert Louis Stevenson.

Since in all his prose work Dr. van Dyke showed the quality of a poet, he naturally turned to verse as well as to prose. In 1897 he published *The Builders, and Other Poems;* in 1904, *Music, and Other Poems;* in 1909, *The White Bees, and Other Poems;* and still more volumes of verse. As might be expected, he delights in metre and rhyme, rather than free verse, but he uses a great variety of poetic forms. In his poetry he excels when he writes of love of the outdoors, or love of country. He writes poetry that has those delicate and idealistic qualities that his prose would lead one to expect.

In 1908 Dr. van Dyke became American lecturer at the University of Paris. Because in himself he combined the scholar, the educator, the man of letters, and the genial patriot, he was a most fitting ambassador from the new world of letters.

In 1913, just a year before the beginning of the World War, President Wilson, with whom Dr. van Dyke had been associated at Princeton University, appointed him United States minister to the Netherlands and Luxemburg. At that time there was no hint of war, and no thought that the position would be anything except the usual position of honor and of dignified responsibility. No one foresaw the series of events that were to make the office one of the principal points of interest to the United States. Dr. van Dyke, always proud of his descent from the hard-working, energetic, intelligent people of Holland, pleasantly anticipated his work in the land from which his ancestors had come.

The new minister had been at his post but a short time when the sudden beginning of the World War threw Europe into consternation. American tourists, who had been in various places on the continent, hurried to Holland as a place of safety. In a moment they saw their plans for business or pleasure overturned; their bank facilities taken from them; and their steamship tickets for the return voyage to the United States made worthless. At once they appealed to representatives of the government of the United States, wherever they could find them. To Dr. van Dyke, as minister to the Netherlands and Luxemburg, there came an unusually large number of these panic-stricken refugees. Dr. van Dyke, comparatively inexperienced as he was in such matters, so conducted himself that he won the applause of his country. He worked night and day, making provision for his unfortunate fellow countrymen. At the same time he strongly upheld the rights of American citizens, and defied military demands. Although he had never before had to meet a situation of that kind, he met the complicated conditions with the skill of a trained diplomat and the insistence of a patriot.

On one occasion when his waiting rooms were crowded with Americans whose excitement led them to forget self-respect, he appeared at the door and asked simply, "Are there any Americans here?"

There came a hush of surprise, for every one knew that all in the room were Americans.

"Yes," they cried, "we are all Americans."

"Oh," said the American minister to whom they were appealing, "I thought Americans always gave women the first place."

Those who crowded before the door fell back. They felt the rebuke and regained self-control.

Until 1917 Dr. van Dyke stayed at his post, maintaining the rights of all Americans who appealed to him; refusing to sanction unjust demands; organizing work for relief, and keeping in constant communication with Washington.

When he resigned the position that so unexpectedly had become an outpost in time of war instead of a position of honor in time of peace, he returned to the United States. Unable to remain quietly at home when his country was at war, he became chaplain in the Naval Reserve service, holding the rank of lieutenant commander. At the same time, with voice and pen, he sturdily upheld the principles for which the United States had entered the war. At the conclusion of war service he returned to the calm of his home at "Avalon" in Princeton.

The house in which he lives, to which he gave a name suggested by Tennyson's *Idylls of the King,* is itself romantic, an old colonial mansion erected five years before the beginning of the American Revolution. It has a hospitable entrance hall, delightful rooms, and in particular a library large enough to satisfy the most ardent book lover. Prominent in that room of books is a picture of Tennyson, the master-poet. Around the house are lawns and trees, suggestive of the woodland. It is indeed "Avalon, the isle of the blest." There among his books Dr. van Dyke continues to read and to write. From there he goes to give lectures or to preach occasional sermons. "In my opinion," he says, "the best way to learn to write good English is to read good English." To that one may add what he himself has illustrated; the best way to write books that people will love is to read books that people already love.

The visitor will find Henry van Dyke curled up in the comfortable chimney corner, reading with all a boy's first interest, his mind perhaps adventuring with John Ridd into the valley of the Doones, or going with the hero of *The Cloister and the Hearth* from one stirring event to another, or following the fortunes of the learned Hypatia in ancient Egypt. At another time the visitor may find the booklover reading favorite passages from Browning, or Shakespeare, or his beloved Tennyson; or else writing patiently and slowly, with a pen, as he writes all his books, some new work of his own.

When Dr. van Dyke spoke at the University of Paris on "The Spirit of America," he said that the American is characterized by the instinct of self-reliance, a love of fair play, an energetic will, a desire for order, and an ambition for self-development. All these truly American characteristics Henry van Dyke illustrates emphatically in his own life.

XIX

WOODROW WILSON

President of the United States

An enthusiastic crowd of friends and supporters swept to the residence of the newly elected governor to express joy in his victory. They cheered tumultuously when the man, who had never before held public office, stepped forward to speak. To their surprise they heard words that had in them nothing of personal triumph, nothing of egotism. "I do not feel exuberant or cheerful. . . . I feel more like kneeling down and praying for strength to do what is expected of me." In these words Woodrow Wilson expressed the seriousness of purpose characteristic of him at all periods of his career.

When he became Governor of New Jersey he was fifty-four years of age. He had made an honorable record as student, teacher, author, and as president of a great university. He had studied history and government as few men study those subjects; had written and spoken on great public questions; and had made himself a power in shaping public thought, but he had not, up to that time, held any political office whatever. He was new and untried, his work as a statesman lying entirely before him.

Fourteen years later Woodrow Wilson died. In the few years between his election as governor of New Jersey and his death at the age of sixty-eight he had become the most commanding figure in the entire world. He had led the United States through a great war that had called into being an army of four million men, and he had shaped the destinies of Europe. He had set forward an idealism that many looked upon as the hope of the world. He had suffered keenly, seen many of his hopes blasted, and through it all, he had kept the same spirit of serious devotion to duty that he had expressed when elected to his first office.

In his boyhood home in Augusta, Georgia, Woodrow Wilson gained much of the spirit that moved him through life. Long before he himself had been able to read he had enjoyed hearing his father, Joseph Ruggles Wilson, a lover of books, read aloud. That father, keenly appreciative of the best in literature, emphasized words and phrases of unusual beauty or power, re-read favorite passages, and commented on what he read. He made his evening reading a regular part of the family life. He influenced his son far more than he ever knew. Joseph Ruggles Wilson was a scholar. In 1844 he had been valedictorian of his class at Jefferson College. After graduation from the school of theology at Princeton he had combined teaching and preaching. In the one field he became a college professor who strongly influenced his classes; in the other he became a much-loved pastor.

His father, Woodrow Wilson's grandfather, was likewise a lover of the printed word. He had come from Ulster, in Ireland, in 1807, and had married an Irish girl whom he had met on the voyage to America. At first he had been a printer, but he had been ambitious and had become an editor.

From his father, the professor of rhetoric, the public speaker and the lover of books, and from his grandfather, the editor, Woodrow Wilson must have inherited the tendencies that led him to become a master of English. From his Irish ancestry he inherited a genial smile, and a love of humor that made him a teller of anecdote.

Woodrow Wilson's mother, Janet Woodrow Wilson, influenced him still more toward learning and seriousness of purpose. From her father, a Presbyterian minister who had come from Carlisle in England as a missionary to Canada, she had learned to love books. In her life she fulfilled the old conception of plain living and high thinking. She wished her son to go into life with ideals, and a determination to carry them into effect.

Three days after Christmas, 1856, Woodrow Wilson was born in Staunton, Virginia, where his father was pastor. In later years he felt pride in the fact that he was born a Virginian, and that he was the eighth from that state to become President of the United States. While Woodrow Wilson was still a child, his father's work as a minister led the family to move from Virginia to Augusta, Georgia, where Woodrow Wilson spent much of his childhood.

In those days the boy who was destined to grow into manhood and become President of the United States, did not go by the name of Woodrow, but of Thomas, for he had been named "Thomas Woodrow Wilson" after his mother's father, the missionary, the Rev. Dr. Thomas Woodrow. The small boy found some of those years in Augusta almost as anxious for him as they were for his parents. From the time when he was five years old until he was nine he heard the fife and drum, saw soldiers, and child as he was, felt something of the bitterness and terror of war. In those years, which made so deep an impression upon him, he saw and felt enough to learn, with all his heart, to hate war.

Then, after the Civil War, when Woodrow Wilson was fourteen, the family moved again, this time to South Carolina. There he went to an academy where he prepared for college. In 1873, when he was seventeen years old, he entered Davidson College in North Carolina. Boylike, and moved by high spirit, he set out to do everything, playing baseball on the college team, taking active part in meetings of a literary society, and at the same time studying with conscientious effort. Never at any time in his life strong and hearty, he broke down, and went home sick and discouraged.

The youth knew that all his people had been educated, and that they had lived to hold influential positions. Because with such an ancestry he could not give up, he continued to read and study at home. In 1875, when he was nineteen and largely self-prepared, he entered Princeton University. There, in a sense, he really began his career.

While a student at Princeton, in 1879, at the age of twenty-three, Woodrow Wilson wrote his first important political paper, an essay entitled *Cabinet Government in the United States*. In that essay, a remarkable paper for one so young, Wilson showed deep interest in problems of government. More than that, he showed that he had studied widely, and gained a clear understanding of complex problems. Although only a college student he wrote an essay sufficiently good to find publication in the *International Review* and to be prophetic of his own career.

At Princeton, Woodrow Wilson did not spend strength unwisely, but he did continue his interest in athletics and in other college activities, making himself a leader. Unable to take part in athletic contests he became one of five directors of the Princeton Football Association. He wrote for the literary magazine, and became the managing editor of the *Princetonian*.

In his studies, during the four years of his college course, he maintained an average of 90.3 per cent. Perhaps it was only natural that he should do best in those lines of work that had most interested his people, that is, in literature, history, philosophy, ethics, and political science. Neither then nor later in life was he interested in pure science.

In fact, Woodrow Wilson never gained faith in science as a factor making for human happiness. In a public address made when he was president of Princeton University he said:

"I am much mistaken if the scientific spirit of the age is not doing us a disservice, working in us a certain great degeneracy. Science has bred in us a spirit of experiment and a contempt for the past. It has made us credulous of quick improvement, hopeful of discovering panaceas, confident of success in every new thing. . . . It has given us agnosticism in the realm of philosophy, scientific anarchism in the field of politics. . . . It may be suspected of having enhanced our passions, by making wealth so quick to come, so fickle to stay."

Photo from Kadel & Herbert, N. Y.

WOODROW WILSON

Instead of turning toward the ministry, as might have been expected of one with such an ancestry, Woodrow Wilson turned first to the study of law, not because he wished to become a pleader at court, but because he felt a real interest in the making of law, and in studying the legislative side of government with understanding. In order to fulfil his aims he entered the law school of the University of Virginia, in 1879, the year of his graduation from Princeton. There the law student did much to develop his skill as a public speaker. He had been gifted by nature with remarkable phrase-making ability and a voice that had strong appealing character. He succeeded well, for at the law school he won the gold medal of the Jeffersonian Society for power as a public speaker. While a student in the law school he further cultivated his voice by singing, and became a member of the college glee club. At the same time he continued to write for college periodicals.

In spite of physical weakness Woodrow Wilson had a dynamic quality that led him at all times to take an interested part in the life of the world around him, whether that world was the world of the college, the law school, the state, the nation, or the wide world of civilization. He was at all times in life a thinker, an idealist, and a man who wished to communicate his ideas to those about him.

In the law school, this hard-working student met the fate that he had met before; he broke down in health and had to abandon his courses. In 1880, at the age of twenty-four, the young man returned to his home, discouraged and wondering what he could do to continue the career he had planned.

All his life Woodrow Wilson struggled against physical weakness. In spite of so great a handicap, he accomplished an immense amount of work in study, in writing, and in educational and public life. He wielded a great influence, and finally bore upon his shoulders the heavy responsibilities and anxieties of his country's part in the World War. In the face of all that, he lived to the age of sixty-eight, a fact that speaks volumes for his unconquerable spirit. He had will power that helped him to succeed in spite of everything.

Driven from the law school by ill health he continued his legal studies at home, as well as he could, and with such good effect that in 1882, two years after he had had to leave the school, he went to Atlanta to practise law.

Probably he never had much desire to become a practising lawyer. He felt interest in the fundamental spirit of law rather than in legal work. He had studied history with keen interest in the development of civilization, in the growth of government, and in the expanding power of democracy. In Atlanta, while he practised law, he continued scholarly studies, probably at the cost of losing clients. Certainly he won no notable place as a lawyer. Any one might have prophesied that this desultory lawyer would soon do as he did, that is, leave his law office and devote himself entirely to the study of history and government.

In 1883 the student went to Johns Hopkins University, one of the most scholarly institutions in the United States, where he continued the work in which he had been so long interested. In the following year he became a fellow of the university. A year later, while still a student in Johns Hopkins University, he taught history in Bryn Mawr College. Now, apparently, Woodrow Wilson had found his work in life, the teaching of history and government.

As a student he had made an exceptional record. In 1886 he won the degree of doctor of philosophy, his thesis *Congressional Government: A Study in American Politics* being a painstaking study of American government. Instead of writing the customary type of thesis that the authorities might read, accept, and place upon the shelf to be forgotten, he wrote a thesis that became a classic in political literature. If Woodrow Wilson had never become President of the United States, or even governor of New Jersey, his thesis, written when he was only twenty-nine years old, would have been almost as highly valued as it is today. It is a thoughtful, original treatise concerning American government.

It is remarkable how definitely and how unconsciously Woodrow Wilson prepared himself for the great work that was to be his in later life. So far as he knew, so far even as his ambitions pointed, he was preparing himself merely to teach, whether in the class room or through the pen. He could not know that actually he was preparing himself to lead the American people through perplexities of a kind that had not presented themselves to any other President of the United States up to his time.

In 1886 Dr. Wilson became professor of history and political economy in Wesleyan College in Middletown, Connecticut. He was thirty-two years old, serious in his college work, still intensely devoted to study, still writing articles on his favorite subjects, and always keenly observant of the political life of the United States.

At no time in life did Woodrow Wilson shut himself in the seclusion of his study. When he was a student he interested himself in college activities; when he was a professor he interested himself in public conditions related to his studies in history and in government. As a teacher he made his class room a practical training ground for helpful American citizenship.

It is still possible to learn exactly what Professor Wilson taught to his classes at Wesleyan, for one has only to turn to his book, *The State: Elements of Historical and Practical Politics.* That book Professor Wilson published in 1889, a year after he had gone to teach in Wesleyan. As a matter of fact, he had prepared the skeleton of the book as a basis for class room work. In it he revised and expanded talks that he gave to his classes. He wrote the book as the result of careful preparation for daily teaching, and of consequent class discussions with students.

The earnest professor must have made those hours in his class room fruitful for his students, for instead of following a cut and dried method of teaching, he brought together new and original results of study. Thinking clearly, logically and strongly himself, he taught his students to think in the same way.

Later he wrote a book called *The State,* a work that long has been an authoritative exposition of government, a text that thousands of students in many colleges have studied, not because Woodrow Wilson wrote it, but because the book is unique in its strength.

Professor Wilson's teaching, books, personal influence, and the value of the numerous articles that he wrote, gave him a great reputation, and led in 1890 to his appointment as professor of jurisprudence and political economy in Princeton University. For twelve years, perhaps the happiest years of his life, the scholar taught at Princeton. He could think of his father's long and honorable career, and feel that he himself had also succeeded. Then, too, he had the pleasure of knowing that his father watched his success and rejoiced in it, for Joseph Ruggles Wilson lived to the good age of eighty-one, and before his death saw his son become president of the great university of Princeton. In his years of teaching at Princeton, Woodrow Wilson, in the full maturity of manhood, continued the work he loved. He taught his classes with the same inspiration as at Wesleyan, gave many public addresses, and wrote numerous magazine articles and books that became so popular that they brought him large financial returns. He received scholastic honors and became increasingly a man to whom people showed high respect.

In the quiet of his study he created books that he touched with the spirit of scholarship, and made beautiful through masterful phraseology.

In 1893 he published *Division and Re-Union,* 1829-1889, a close study in United States history, and *An Old Master, and Other Political Essays;* in 1896, *Mere Literature and Other Essays,* and *George Washington,* a fascinating, realistic biography. In addition to these books he contributed numerous articles to such standard periodicals as the *Atlantic*

Monthly and *Harper's Magazine.* In 1901 this now popular author began to publish in *Harper's Magazine,* as a serial that ran for a year and a half, *A History of the American People,* a work afterwards published in five volumes, the most popular book that he ever wrote.

If Woodrow Wilson had died in 1902, at the age of forty-six, he would have been remembered as a scholarly, influential man, as one who had achieved great public success, and as an American author of remarkable ability. He would have left books that would have been read and studied for years, and that would have been mines of quotations. The many who admire Woodrow Wilson's scholarly work must regret that his fourteen years of political life so obscured the brilliance of his work as a teacher, as a public speaker, and as an author. No matter how much one approves the work that Woodrow Wilson did in his years of holding political office, he cannot help believing that in his years of scholastic success in Princeton, Woodrow Wilson found his greatest happiness.

As professor, Woodrow Wilson made himself well known and popular. Always interested in all that he saw around him, he expressed himself frankly in favor of high ideals in education. He believed with all his heart in study, scholarship, and the development of citizenship. In view of his own genuine scholarship, his proved ability as an educator and his wide popularity as a thoughtful writer, it was only natural that he should become, when the occasion offered, president of Princeton.

In 1902, at the request of the trustees, he assumed the presidency of the university, and thus began work as an administrative officer. For nine years he carried on the dignified duties of a university president. In those years he became less the student and the writer, and more the doer. In those nine years, also, he gained training for the higher executive offices that he was soon to hold. For almost the first time in his life, too, he met strong opposition. At all times he had decided views of his own, and did not easily yield to the opinions of others, nor trim his sails to catch the wind of popularity. When he declined to accept for Princeton a great gift that involved terms that seemed to him to dictate university procedure, he aroused against him many strong men in the faculty, and especially among the alumni. In spite of bitter opposition, he kept on his own way. In a certain sense, both at Princeton and at Washington he made his strength his weakness. At least it was injurious to his popularity. Aside from matters of university policy President Wilson continued to win popular favor. As educator, speaker, and writer, he won increasing numbers of supporters. In the first place, since he himself was so naturally studious, he believed in hard work and opposed all breaking down of scholarly traditions of the past. "There are some drill subjects," he said, "which are just as necessary as measles in order to make a man a grown-up person." As an educator he had greater faith in the humanities than in scientific studies. In his opinion, literature, philosophy, ethics, and history are of supreme importance. In other words he looked at the ideal rather than the practical. As a writer of books naturally would, he believed profoundly in the educational value of literature, saying: "In order to be national a university should have, at the center of all its training, courses of instruction in that literature which contains the ideals of the race." In addition to these markedly strong beliefs he held also that a university should be democratic. For that reason he opposed all social conditions that militated against a full democracy of life or of spirit.

As time went on, through his published works and his public addresses, the educator and author became a national figure. Since he knew so much concerning history and government, he spoke boldly for causes in which he believed. Under such circumstances, it gradually became natural that the unnatural should occur, that is, that the people of New Jersey, turning from mere politicians, should make a college professor and president governor of their state.

From 1911 to 1913 Woodrow Wilson had the honor of being

governor of New Jersey. In those years he developed still more in personal power, and more notably than ever upheld principles for which he had always stood. Thus he opposed political dishonesty, did much to improve the work of education, and laid great emphasis on democracy in government. By his stalwart insistence on such American principles he made himself an outstanding figure before the nation.

As a result, he awoke demands from all parts of the United States that he should enter the contest for the Presidency. Nevertheless, in view of much hostility to an educator as officeholder he was not swept into office. At the Baltimore convention of the Democratic party, Woodrow Wilson was not nominated until forty-six ballots had been taken. Even then he would have met defeat at the polls if it had not been for the division in the Republican party made by the formation of the Progressive party under Theodore Roosevelt. As it was, Woodrow Wilson saw his two great opponents win a million more votes than he did, although he won in the electoral college, of course, where William H. Taft, the Republican candidate, gained eight electoral votes, Theodore Roosevelt, the Progressive candidate, eighty-eight, and Woodrow Wilson, the Democratic candidate, four hundred and thirty-five.

Thus Woodrow Wilson, the student, professor, university president, and state governor, became President of the United States on March 4, 1913. He was then fifty-seven years old. On November 7, 1916, he was reëlected for a second term. On March 4, 1921, he left the White House, after eight years of the most unusual, most noble, and most self-sacrificing work that any President ever performed. Three years later, February 3, 1924, he died.

The eight years of Woodrow Wilson's Presidency were years of such importance that they dwarfed everything else in his life. They were years of anxiety and of war, years when new problems of the greatest importance for the future came before the United States, years in which the United States became a world force such as it had never been before.

In those years President Wilson conducted himself in a way that gave new dignity to the great office that he held. More than that, surpassing in that respect any other governmental head in all history, he made himself the spokesman for world democracy. At the close of the World War he laid down principles for the League of Nations, having for his great aim the ending of all war.

Those trying years would have given any President some form of opposition. The problems were so new and so great that they called forth varying suggestions for solution. The times demanded a council of the wisest men, regardless of party or position, but the circumstances demanded immediate action rather than slow development. Therefore fate threw upon Woodrow Wilson, as the occupant of the Presidential chair, the heavy burden of responsibility. As President he must act, and act at once!

In little over a year from the time when Woodrow Wilson entered upon his high duties, the United States had to send armed forces to occupy Vera Cruz in Mexico. About two months later, June 28, 1914, the assassination of Archduke Francis Ferdinand of Austria led to the outbreak of the great war in Europe that finally involved the United States. In less than another year the Germans sank the "Lusitania." The people of the United States seethed with emotion, some demanding one procedure, some another. Through all this, President Wilson kept high dignity. In troubles in Mexico he had already set forward his doctrine of patience and of general good will.

"Everything that we do must be rooted in patience," he had said. "We can afford to exercise the self-restraint of a really great nation, which realizes its own strength and scorns to misuse it."

At another time, with reference to Central and South America he had said: "The United States has nothing to seek in Central and South America except the lasting interests of the peoples of the two continents."

These same principles President Wilson applied to his

course of action in connection with the war in Europe. In spite of the sinking of the "Lusitania" and of other vessels in spite of the submarine warfare, in spite of the dangers that appeared to threaten civilization, he endeavored to maintain the neutrality of the United States. "He kept us out of war" became the slogan in the campaign for his reëlection in 1916. President Wilson made two appeals to European nations in the interests of peace but without avail. When at last he saw the warring passions so strong that the United States could no longer withhold, he entered upon the war in Europe with the zeal of a great national leader.

On April 2, 1917, the War President asked the Congress to declare a state of war with Germany. Under his influence the United States registered 11,000,000 men, raised a military force of nearly 4,000,000 men, and in a year and a half sent over 2,000,000 to fight in Europe.

Woodrow Wilson's own speeches and messages went across the world like armies. Fired with belief in "self-determination," the right of all peoples to govern themselves and full of the spirit of right and justice, they went far and wide, awakening thought, stirring old hopes, calling into being great popular forces, and representing an idealism that every one knew must ultimately win.

In January, 1918, when the long war had exhausted almost all the combatants, President Wilson proposed fourteen points as a foundation for world peace, and in October of the same year the Central Powers agreed to accept those points as a basis of peace.

Filled with enthusiasm for his great ideals, President Wilson broke all precedents by sailing for Europe in December, 1918, accompanied by four other American commissioners, to meet with the most influential men of the great nations to determine terms that should close the World War. With all the skill at his command he urged liberal conditions, and in particular the adoption of a league of nations. After some twelve weeks he made a hurried visit to the United States where he found many of the leading men of the

United States Senate strongly opposing the proposed covenant of the League of Nations. In less than two weeks he sailed again for Europe, and did not return for four months. Insistent as ever, he saw the peace treaty drawn up to include his proposal for a league of nations. In July, 1919, when he placed the treaty before the United States Senate he met immediate opposition to a plan that he looked upon as a great step forward in the development of civilization. In September of that year he appealed to the people of the United States, going on a long journey across the continent, speaking earnestly in favor of his ideas, and sparing himself no exertions for what he believed to be a great cause.

Through years of intense strain, the efforts he had expended in Europe, and the energy that he put forth in his public speaking, he had worn himself out. Shattered in health, he withdrew from his speaking tour and returned to Washington, little better than a physical wreck. There for weeks he lived in close retirement, sick and unable to carry on the greatest battle in which he had ever engaged. His opponents, by a million majority, came into control of both houses of Congress. He saw his treaty defeated. He saw the November elections bring his principles no support.

Woodrow Wilson left the White House March 4, 1921, a broken and disappointed man, but he kept alive the fire of his spirit. In his last speech, given by radio from his private home in Washington, and broadcast far and wide throughout the country in a weak, trembling voice, the man who would never give up, urged support for the League of Nations. On February 3, less than three months from that time, he died.

In one of his speeches some time before, Woodrow Wilson had said: "I would rather fail in a cause that I know some day will triumph than win in a cause that I know some day will fail."

XX

WILBUR AND ORVILLE WRIGHT

Inventors of the Airplane

Two boys, brothers, the older eleven years of age, played together in a simply furnished room. Suddenly they heard steps, and looking up, saw their father enter.

"Ah! here's something for you!" he said, and tossed a buzzing contrivance into the air.

With a whir of wings, the thing flew to the ceiling, bumped, and fell to the floor.

"What is it?" the boys cried. "It flies!" Both jumped for the toy, now lying on the carpet.

They picked up the cork-bamboo-and-paper thing, twisted its rubber bands again, and let it go.

With a rush the toy flew again to the ceiling, while the two boys shouted and the father laughed, glad to see that his sons liked the plaything he had brought them.

Who would have thought that the bringing of that toy would change the ways of men, give a new means of communication, revolutionize war, and enable explorers to sail at will over polar ice or tropic jungles?

Because Bishop Milton Wright, then a man fifty years of age, brought home that whirligig, that flying toy, and gave it to his two boys, Wilbur and Orville Wright, one eleven, the other seven, he set in motion the remarkable train of events that led his sons, in 1903, to invent the airplane.

Through their play, those two American boys changed the ways of the world for all time to come. Amused by the toy, they tried to see which could make it mount higher. Then they studied it, found out just how it worked, and made another one like it that flew just as well.

"Why not make a bigger one?" said one brother.

"Of course!" said the other.

"We can make a better one, I know!"

They did make another flying toy, and hurrahed excitedly to see it go.

"Let's make a great big one!" said one of the experimenters.

"Let's!" said the other, with equal enthusiasm.

There they met defeat. They used up all their rubber bands and tried in every way that they could think of, but beyond a certain size they could not make their toys fly. At last they put the whirligigs away and turned instead to something that they could make go just as high as they pleased—their kites.

Because they had unusual interest in kite-flying, they made better and better kites, and prided themselves on flying them higher than any other boys could fly theirs.

That play they carried on for life. Grown into manhood, for the sake of play the two brothers made a kind of box-kite, or glider, that they could fly when they held it by a string. Then they made another large enough to glide along when one of them lay on it, or rather, in it.

"Why not make a bigger one, a better one?" they said again.

They did, and made a glider in which one of them, they found, could go a considerable distance. "Why not make it go where we please?" they said. Then they soon learned how to control and guide their gliding apparatus.

"Why not make it move itself, wind or no wind?"

They made a light engine, placed it on the flying-machine, flew with safety, and made their machine go where they wished it to go.

The two Wright brothers were the first in the world to learn how to fly. They had not tried to make money. They had not tried to become famous. All that they had tried to do, when they first began their experiments, was to have a good time.

Curiously enough, perhaps, for boys, they had united their play with study. If Wilbur and Orville Wright had merely played, and had not studied as well, they would never have invented the airplane. Neither of them ever went to college; neither, in the strict sense of the word, was a scientist. Nevertheless, by nature, both were students. They wished to know the "why" and the "how."

They had studied their first flying toy, found how it worked, and made a better one. They studied their kites, found just what shapes, sizes, and kinds of kites flew best, and then flew their own kites more successfully than other boys flew theirs.

In manhood the two brothers made the most patient study of the principles on which they based their great invention. They studied and experimented slowly, with all the patience of the most highly trained scientific investigators. They read all the books they could find that in any way concerned the subject. Since there was no one who could teach them how to fly, they taught themselves. They did not invent the airplane through a lucky accident, but as a result of daring experiments combined with long, intensive, scientific study.

For centuries men had looked upon flying as impossible of attainment. In the story of Icarus, who made wings that carried him until the heat of the sun melted their wax and thus cast him into the sea, the ancient Greeks laughed at the folly of attempting flight. In the latter part of the nineteenth century such stories as "Darius Green and His Flying Machine" made people think those who tried to fly were ridiculous half-wits who would come to disaster.

In the face of all this laughter of the centuries, one of the Wright brothers, after the invention of the airplane, said, "It is easier to learn to fly than it is to learn to walk." In a period of only three years two brothers, who had been nothing more than makers and repairers of bicycles, did, for the pleasure of doing it, what people for ages had thought impossible!

First, they had to master three problems: the problem of making wings strong enough to carry men; the problem of finding a source of power that would propel wings and men through the air; and the problem of holding balance and giving desired direction while in flight. Although these were scientific problems that called for scientific answers, the two brothers who had never attended college or university solved them correctly.

In the first place, Wilbur and Orville Wright were brothers in thought and in deed. They lived, studied, and worked as one man. To that remarkable partnership in ideas and in work the world owes the airplane.

Wilbur Wright, the elder brother, was born near Millville, Indiana, April 16, 1867. Orville Wright was born in Dayton, Ohio, August 19, 1871. Their parents were educated and prosperous people. In their home they had a library of more than two thousand volumes, covering all the important fields of learning. The mother, in a time when it was not customary for girls to do so, had attended college and acquired a liberal education. She died in 1889, when the older brother was twenty-two years old; thus she did not live to see her sons become famous.

Milton Wright, the father, was a college graduate, a college professor, and at one time the head of a college. He was active, energetic, and enterprising, following in early life the hard work of a circuit-rider, going in 1857 as a missionary to Oregon, then an almost trackless wilderness, becoming editor of a religious paper, and, in 1877, bishop of the United Brethren. He lived until 1905, two years after his sons had discovered the art of flying. However, even he did not see his sons become famous.

Curiously enough, for a few years, the invention of the airplane, though one of the most astonishing, revolutionary, and useful ever devised, created scarcely a ripple in the world. For five years it remained virtually unknown. It failed to impress people who saw it or who read about it, because the people of the United States had laughed too long at the story of "Darius Green and His Flying Machine" and had seen too many attempts to fly come to grief.

Oddly enough, the two members of the Wright family who did not receive a college education accomplished the most for the world. At the local high school in Dayton, Ohio, they were faithful students, but in no way made themselves notable. Two older brothers went to college, and a sister, Katherine Wright, followed the classical course at Oberlin, but Wilbur and Orville Wright remained at home. The ones who had the least school training developed a new science!

After her student days at Oberlin, Katherine Wright, who had studied with her brothers in the Dayton High School, came back to her old school to teach. While she worked as a teacher, she did so much to help her brothers that the world owes her a debt, as it does to so many other self-sacrificing mothers and sisters. When the brothers, merely for amusement, began to experiment with gliders and the first rude airplanes and needed money to buy materials, this schoolteacher sister drew upon her small salary and sent them money with which to carry on their work. When, engaged in making their most important experiments at Kitty Hawk, North Carolina, they sent her photographs showing their "flying-machine," she showed the pictures to the principal of her school, William Werthner, and interested him in what her brothers were doing. When they wished to read from technical books written in German, she asked Mr. Werthner to make translations for them. When they went to Europe, Katherine Wright went with them. There she shared, as she well deserved to share, in the public honors given to her brothers.

When Wilbur and Orville Wright were mere boys they had become interested in printing, and established a small newspaper, and had gained for it a remarkable circulation. They wrote, printed, and delivered their own papers. Not satisfied with any press that they could buy, they made one of their own, and made it so well that it worked satisfactorily.

As a matter of fact, the whole Wright family was inventive. Bishop Wright invented a kind of typewriter, and often amused himself by making other ingenious devices. Lorin Wright, a brother, invented a hay-press.

From printing, the energetic brothers turned to the bicycle business. Both delighted in riding bicycles, and they made themselves experts, able to win races or to ride wheels in ways that most others could not imitate. Because they enjoyed mechanics, they made improvements in their own wheels, and finally set up a shop where they made and repaired wheels for others. They devised all sorts of bicycles, and best of all, they satisfied all their customers. Thoroughness marked everything they did. In making an airplane, absolute thoroughness is necessary.

They might have come to grief in their first experiments in flying if they had not trained themselves, through years of faithful work, to be painstaking. Although they were naturally ingenious, they wished to learn more about the work in which they found enjoyment. Therefore, they procured books about mechanics, and read them with the utmost interest. In order to understand such books they had to study mathematics. Actually, without intending it and without knowing it, the two gave themselves a practical education in engineering.

Although brothers and the closest of companions, Wilbur and Orville were distinct in personality. Wilbur, four years older, led in scientific study; Orville led in active experiment.

In 1896, they read of the death of Otto Lilienthal, a German inventor who had attempted to fly, had made more than two thousand glides, and had finally lost his life in one of his experiments. Deeply impressed by the event, it turned their attention toward attempts to fly. They remembered their former success in flying kites. Why not make a kite that could carry a man?

So they made a machine something like a huge box-kite,

two parallel planes that they held by a light line. They
tried flying this in a strong wind.

With this device, and with a second much like it, they made
daring experiments, for they took turns in riding on their
great kite. Thus far they depended upon wings and wind.
They learned enough to convince them that what they needed
was some kind of power that would more than equal the
power of the wind.

Disappointed in their hope of finding the power of the
wind strong enough to raise their apparatus and a passenger,
they turned to gliding. They found that they could fly their
machine and operate it for a time by pulling strings. They
hoped to start from the summit of a hill, glide through the
air, and make the glider do what they wished it to do.

These experiments they began in October, 1900, at Kitty
Hawk, North Carolina. For three years they continued their
work, but without much sign of success. They learned about
wings and balance and control, but for a long time they could
do no more than glide short distances.

In 1901, Octave Chanute, a Frenchman, who had made
more than a thousand glides and whose work they had long
admired, joined them at Kitty Hawk, discussed their problems, watched their experiments, and gave them all the aid
he could.

They had chosen for their gliding experiments, a sharp hill
called "Kill Devil Hill." There they found it exciting
enough to lie prone on their apparatus and sail off into the
air, even if they went only two or three hundred feet. If they
could fly thus a short distance, they believed that they could
find the means of going much farther.

The daring brothers did not find it easy to make their
glider do what they wished it to do. They found it acted
with the same peculiar waywardness with which a kite be-
haves, now darting this way, now that, and refusing to yield
itself to control. But they courageously laughed at their
mishaps and kept on. "What makes the machine act so?"
they asked. They must learn more about the effect of the

wind on the planes. So instead of continuing to make useless flights and take needless risk, they began to study pressures and surfaces. They made numerous experiments with wind-vanes of many shapes and sizes. The two bicycle makers worked with all the patience of men who had been trained by years of experience in scientific laboratories.

The inventors now devised rudders that they could move with the utmost ease. Then they made those rudders move in connection with the wings.

In September and October of 1902 they went at least a thousand times to the top of their hill and glided off through the air, every time gaining new control and gradually increasing the distance that they could go. Some of those flights they extended to six hundred feet, that is, to the length of almost three ordinary city blocks.

Such experimenters as Otto Lilienthal and Octave Chanute had tried to gain control of flying-machines by movements of the body, placing the weight now here, now there. They were not able to make the instantaneous mental responses and the equally instantaneous movements required. They had followed a method by which one could hardly hope to succeed.

The Wright brothers made no effort to control their machine by shifting about in it. They decided to make the machine itself aid in the work. They planned to move the wings, when necessary, so that they could catch the air in a different way, to sit almost motionless, and, with slight movements of the hands, control levers that in turn changed the inclination of the wings. They observed every motion of their glider and every effect of the wind. They learned not only how to move the wings, but two rudders that they had made, so that they could keep the machine under control for the greatest length of time.

In spite of all their care they had many adventures. Sometimes they lost control for a moment, and their machine landed them pell-mell. Sometimes they found the wind too strong, and landed upside down, most ingloriously. Wilbur Wright, who was a humorist, and his brother, who was an optimist, took all these mishaps as part of the work of the day. They knew they were not adventuring blindly, but following the results of scientific study, and they determined to succeed.

The Wrights saw that they could control their machine while it was in the air, but that gravity soon brought it down to earth. Therefore they needed a source of power that would keep the machine going. Then they thought of using propellers.

In this field they now made a thorough investigation, with the result that they learned that some of the largest steamships were failing to make use of all the power at their command. After many experiments, Wilbur and Orville Wright developed the propeller for the airplane.

Aside from its circular motion, they made the blades of their propeller so that they would strike the air, and lift, as well as pull, the machine.

Next, the two young men had to find an engine that would have force enough to operate the propeller at high speed, and, at the same time, would be light enough to be of use in a machine designed to fly through the air. If it had not been that the gasoline engine had already been invented, they would have met at this point an insuperable difficulty.

When they wrote to automobile manufacturers and asked for an eight-horse-power engine that would not weigh more than two hundred pounds, they met with a complete lack of interest. Instead of being troubled by that, they set to work and in six weeks made an engine of their own! They were determined to fly.

They had now investigated, scientifically and through practical experiment, every phase of the principles involved in flying. They were prepared to bring all their results together, and, do what men had never done before—to fly!

So little had guesswork played a part in their preparation, that they actually succeeded at once. They found that even their propeller, that they had based on mathematical calculations, gave them in work sixty-six per cent. of the power employed.

December 17, 1903, in the presence of an audience of five people, Wilbur and Orville Wright flew!

First, on December 14, they went to their newly made airplane.

"Who shall go first?"

"Toss a coin and see!"

Wilbur won the toss. With full confidence, but with a beating heart, he lay at full length on the airplane, gave the signal that all was ready, grasped all the controls, and set off. Three and one-half seconds later, he landed with a rush, deep in the sand!

Next, on December 17, three days later, Orville took his turn. He was in the air only twelve seconds, hardly enough time in which to catch his breath, but in that time his machine jumped up and down in a most alarming manner and finally plunged toward the ground, but landed in safety!

That was the first time in all history that any flying-machine had lifted itself into the air by its own power, carried a man safely at high speed, and come down to earth without a mishap and without digging into the ground. That twelve-second flight was the beginning of successful aviation!

That day at Kitty Hawk the triumphant brothers made four successful flights, the longest distance being only three-fifths of a mile, and the longest time in flight a little less than a minute!

A brief moment, but enough to prove that human flight was possible and to spur the Wrights on to make flying practical. Of their later difficulties they wrote: "With the machine moving forward, the air flying backward, the propellers turning sidewise, and nothing standing still, it seemed impossible to find a starting-point from which to trace the various simultaneous reactions."

In 1904, on Huffman Prairie, near Dayton, Ohio, the broth-

ers went on with their experiments. They had troubles
enough to discourage any one. Sometimes their engine would
not work at all; sometimes it heated too easily. The sprockets
came loose; the propeller shaft developed a flaw; and the
tubular shafts cracked. Altogether they had adventures without number—but they kept on!

In 1905, the brothers flew twenty miles in thirty-three
minutes.

In 1906, they brought their machine so fully under control that the man who operated it no longer lay down, as he
had done up to that time, but sat up in a somewhat comfortable position.

Now they made a contract to furnish to the United States
authorities a machine that would carry two men, as well
as fuel, go at the rate of forty miles an hour, and stay in
the air long enough to cover 125 miles. They had won full
success.

In 1908, Wilbur Wright went to France, where he made
successful flights and won great public honors, including the
Michelin Prize. A year later, in 1909, the man who had
been only a maker and repairer of bicycles, demonstrated before the King of Spain, the King of England, and the King
of Italy that he could fly and at all times keep perfect control of his machine. In the same year, with his brother, he
received a medal given by the Congress of the United States.

Wilbur and Orville Wright now found themselves the most
talked-of men in the world. They received honors, medals,
titles, degrees, and money in a way that might have turned
the head of almost any one. But through all this avalanche
of praise they continued simple, hard-working, and modest.
They devoted themselves just as earnestly as ever to studying
the problems of flight. In that work they continued together
until May 30, 1912, when Wilbur Wright, then at the age of
forty-five, died of typhoid fever.

Always conservative, always basing their work on proved
scientific principles, the brothers had avoided all serious accidents except one. In 1908, when Orville Wright was flying

in company with Lieutenant Selfridge, one of the propeller blades broke, and both men were dashed to the ground. Lieutenant Selfridge met his death. Orville Wright broke his leg and several ribs. Aside from that sad event, they experienced the best of fortune.

Orville Wright has continued to investigate the many problems still connected with aviation. He is now chief engineer of the Wright Aëronautical Company, and director of its laboratory at Dayton, Ohio, where he carries on his great work.

Today, airplanes fulfil many purposes, carry passengers and mail, aiding in map-making, in forest protection, in travel, in exploration, and in advertising. In a thousand ways they fulfil the purposes both of peace and of war.

Wilbur and Orville Wright, through their interest, study, patience, and skill, invented the means of control used in every airplane that flies today in any part of the world.